Confederate Cor

MW00789126

Confederate Correspondent

The Civil War Reports of Jacob Nathaniel Raymer, Fourth North Carolina

JACOB NATHANIEL RAYMER

Edited by E.B. MUNSON

McFarland & Company, Inc., Publishers
Jefferson, North Carolina, and London

LIBRARY OF CONGRESS CATALOGUING-IN-PUBLICATION DATA

Raymer, Jacob Nathaniel, 1836–1909.
Confederate correspondent : the Civil War reports of Jacob Nathaniel
   Raymer, Fourth North Carolina / Jacob Nathaniel Raymer ;
   edited by E.B. Munson.
        p.   cm.
   Includes bibliographical references and index.

   ISBN 978-0-7864-3954-6
   softcover : 50# alkaline paper ∞

      1. Raymer, Jacob Nathaniel, 1836–1909.   2. Confederate States
   of America. Army. North Carolina Infantry Regiment, 4th.
   3. United States — History — Civil War, 1861–1865 — Personal
   narratives.   4. United States — History — Civil War, 1861–1865 —
   Regimental histories.   5. United States — History — Civil War,
   1861–1865 — Campaigns.   I. Munson, E. B.   II. Title.
   E573.54th.R39   2009
   973.7'82092 — dc22   2008047186

British Library cataloguing data are available

On the cover: Jacob Nathaniel Raymer ca. 1900's (Courtesy McClain
family); North Carolina Map, 1861-1865, tracing Raymer's trip of 250
miles from Statesville to Garysburg (courtesy North Carolina Department
of Cultural Resources)

Manufactured in the United States of America

McFarland & Company, Inc., Publishers
   Box 611, Jefferson, North Carolina 28640
   www.mcfarlandpub.com

To my wife Jane
For 49 great years.

And to our sons and their families
John and Diana and granddogs Dexter and Gigi
Paul and Anne-Marie and granddaughters Megan and Sara
Will and Jessica and granddaughters Alexis, Madison, and Samantha.

And to the memory of Jacob Nathaniel Raymer
Company C, 4th Regiment North Carolina Troops.

TABLE OF CONTENTS

PREFACE AND ACKNOWLEDGMENTS

Books begin in strange and wonderful ways. This one began in 2006 as volume 3 in a series of books I am compiling of Civil War letters written by North Carolina soldiers to their hometown newspapers. Many of these newspapers that survived the conflict have been microfilmed by the North Carolina Office of Archives and History. As I worked through the newspapers from 1861 through 1865, I began to find a number of letters from the 4th Regiment North Carolina Troops and decided to focus just on that regiment. This decision was due partly to sentiment: Major-General Bryan Grimes, a colonel of the 4th, was a native of Pitt County, and his old homestead is just twenty miles away from Winterville, where I reside.

I began to find letters from a soldier in that regiment who signed his with a single name — "Nat." Soon I had over forty letters from this soldier, and I began to focus on him. Outside of the letters, however, I didn't know much about him. In *North Carolina Troops 1861–1865: A Roster*, compiled by Louis H. Manarin and Weymouth T. Jordan, Jr., I found a Jacob Nathaniel Raymer in Company C of the 4th. I felt this was Nat, because he was listed in the 4th Regimental Band, to which his letters made reference. Still, I wanted stronger evidence, and when I read Colonel E. A. Osborne's *History of the 4th Regiment*, I found it. In his acknowledgments to individuals for the help they had given him was this line: "To Mr. Nathaniel Raymer, a member of the band of the Fourth Regiment, who sent me his letters written during the war under the signature of 'Nat,' in *The Statesville American*."

I was not able to locate Nat's letters to the *Statesville American*. WorldCat, an online database of library holdings worldwide, lists only five libraries that contain microfilm copies of this newspaper, and their holdings begin

1

with the edition of November 14, 1865. If Nat did have letters published in the *American*, those letters are lost. Fortunately, however, he was also published in the *Carolina Watchman* (Salisbury, N.C.) and the *Iredell Express* (Statesville, N.C.). I found those letters at the North Carolina Office of Archives and History, which microfilmed these newspapers from the originals that are held in the libraries of the University of North Carolina at Chapel Hill, North Carolina State University, Duke University, and the Library of Congress.

What I had now was the Nat Raymer of the Civil War, but I wanted to know about him before and after the war as well. I knew that he had returned to Iredell County in 1865, gone to Arkansas in 1883–1884, and later moved to Texas. That was all. I searched online information from historical societies, census records, newspapers, and other material in these states without much success. Then by chance I happened on a website for a genealogical forum for the fifty states. Posted on the Texas website in 1999 was a query asking for information on Jacob Nathaniel Raymer. The seeker was Kathy McClain Hutto, Nat's great-great-granddaughter. That was the key that opened the door to Nat's civilian life.

My journey into the peacetime life of Jacob Nathaniel Raymer has been a rewarding experience. It was a journey made easier by the generosity of his descendants who shared their time, photographs, records, Nat's pre- and postwar writings, transcriptions of his handwriting, and oral histories of him. Other individuals also offered help along the way, and their assistance is likewise greatly appreciated.

I would especially like to thank the following members of Nat's family for sharing material that brought his civilian days to light: Edith McClain Moss, Nat's great-granddaughter; Lois McClain Carter, also Nat's great-granddaughter, who, sadly, died on February 3, 2008, as the book was nearing completion; Nancy Moss Miller, Kathy McClain Hutto, and Deborah McClain Strole, Nat's great-great-granddaughters (Nancy Moss Miller gets a special "thank you" for funding restoration of ambrotypes of Nat and other family material from which many of the photographs in this book were made); and Susan E. L. Lake, whose great-great-uncles Warren E. Bailey and James C. Tompkins married Nat's daughters, Lulu and Cora, respectively.

I am also indebted to the following individuals for their contributions: John R. M. Lawrence, Department Head, North Carolina Collection, Joyner Library, East Carolina University, for many helpful suggestions; R. Lee Hadden, historian of the 4th Regiment, for sharing a copy of his unpublished manuscript *The Bloody Fourth: The Roster of the Fourth North Carolina*

Regiment CSA, 1861–1865; Roy Winkleman, Director, Florida Center for Instructional Technology, College of Education, University of South Florida, for permission to use illustrations from the center's Civil War ClipArt file and Civil War maps; Donna E. Kelly, Administrator, Historical Publications, N.C. Office of Archives and History, Department of Cultural Resources; Connie Hammond of the Western Reserve Historical Society and Archives, Cleveland, Ohio; Linda Acrey, for checking material in Arkansas; Sherryl Miller of the Lonoke County Museum, Lonoke, Arkansas, for searching records in Little Rock for information on Nat; Andrea Avery, genealogist, for sending material about Nat in Texas; Bunny Freeman, Co-County Coordinator, Henderson County, Texas, GenWeb Project; Joel Reese, Local History Librarian, Iredell County, N.C., Public Library; Joe Link, Secretary, Statesville Masonic Lodge #27, for indentifying Nat's Masonic affiliation; and Bruce Mercer, Texas Grand Lodge Library and Museum, for identifying Nat's Texas Masonic Lodges.

Nat's letters provide a first-hand account of the lives of foot-soldiers in the ranks of the Army of Northern Virginia. Since copies of the *Carolina Watchman* and the *Iredell Express* followed the 4th Regiment on the march, Nat's fellow-soldiers read what he wrote. To preserve the integrity of his writing, I transcribed the letters as they were originally published. A careful reader will note inconsistencies in Nat's spelling, especially in geographical names. For example, Culpeper and Culpepper were used interchangeably; Spotsylvania was sometimes Spottsylvania; and the Shenandoah River became Shenendoah. Minié ball was usually "minnie" ball. Nat spelled it that way, as did other writers, including his friends James Columbus Steele and William Gorman, whose material I quote. Other spellings that strike us as strange today might have been common during the Civil War period and include mought (might), foard (ford), doating (doting), combattants (combatants), splinders (splinters), pannels (panels), and drap (drop — i.e., of whiskey), among others.

Soldiers wrote when they could, and they didn't always have a good surface for writing or a quiet, sunny day when they might sit beneath a leafy tree to compose their thoughts. Sometimes they were pressed for time, as Nat was when he wrote on December 5, 1863: "Too much hurried and mixed up to correct grammatical errors." And again on January 25, 1864: "My candle goes down prodigiously fast and I must keep writing — no time to meditate." Sometimes, he tried to write in terrible weather, as in a letter published December 5, 1864: "I am told it is half an hour till mail time. But indeed I have shivers so badly that I can hardly follow the lines or even keep respect-fully between them." Sometimes he wrote when a battle raged nearby, as he did on May 11, 1864, during the Battle of Spotsylvania Court House: "The great and decisive battle of this campaign is doubtless in progress now, and while I write I am so much oppressed with anxiety about the result that my hand is really nervous." Haste, unpleasant weather conditions, word usage of the period, or the nearness of battle could all contribute to spelling errors.

In many of his letters, Nat listed the names of soldiers wounded, killed, and gone missing in a battle. Where possible I have attached end-notes offering more information on these soldiers. I obtained this information largely from two sources: R. Lee Hadden's unpublished manuscript *The Bloody Fourth: The Roster of the Fourth North Carolina Regiment CSA, 1861–1865*, and the multi-volume work *North Carolina Troops, 1861–1865: A Roster* compiled for the North Carolina Division of Archives and History by Louis H. Manarin and Weymouth T. Jordan, Jr. In some cases Nat spells the names differently or uses a different initial. In most such cases, the spelling given by Hadden or by Manarin and Jordan is likely more accurate than Nat's rendering. By the time the rosters were compiled, records such as family material and official documents would have been available to check name spellings and initials.

In a very few instances where the text was garbled by the apparent omission of one or two words, I have inserted in brackets what I believe to be the missing words.

INTRODUCTION

"I stand on the summit of The Blue Ridge Mountains at the Swanan-noa Gap, on the second day of September 1857. I had just left home, expecting to be absent some years in the 'far west,' and from that lofty pinnacle, the dividing line between home and strangers, I did take a long farewell."[1]

So wrote Jacob Nathaniel Raymer, aged twenty-one years, as he paused to take a last homeward look before starting his journey toward Arkansas. He was born in Cabarrus County, North Carolina, on October 6, 1836, and was the third child of Moses and Matilda Raymer.[2] Writing to his family after reaching Arkansas, he described those last moments and his observations in the new land in a poem titled "A Last View of Home." The lines reveal an educated young man, close to his family, with a talent for writing and for keen observation that foreshadowed his later writings during the Civil War.

A Last View of Home

On that rugged peak I stood, and gazed
Long and wistfully far away,
Eastward, on that misty plain that raised
Its blue outlines against the sky,
And there forever seemed to stay.
The sun was fast sinking in a cloud
That crowned the blue hill, far westward; —
And already twilight's ample shroud
Wrapping those bright valley homes
In peaceful slumber; while heavenward
Mounted a stream of curling smoke,
From distant cottages, which bespoke
A hearty supper there, prepared
By some mountain lass so light-hearted
And gay beyond measure. — Who can guess

But on that very eve she expects
Him, who a week ago had parted,
But promised faithful to return
At the appointed time.
                    And while
Standing there I sadly thought of home
So pure,— the world before me so vile,
And me,— just entering alone — alone!
One object only, my vision
Concentrated rested on — a mound
Cloud-like on the blue horizon —
An eternal watchman near my home.
My eye ne'er tired, or wandered
Elsewhere a moment: I stood entranced,
A thousand welcome thoughts hurried
Through my o'er burdened mind — perchance
Of childhood's sports, or schoolboy plays,
Or church-bells ringing Sabbath days,—
Nights of mirth and nights of grief,
Nights of pleasure, many but brief,
All in quick succession passed.
Home with all its joys strangely rose
In imagination near that mound,
And one thought I still could see those
Relations struck with grief profound,
To know the painful hour had come,
When from their embrace should be torn
Their child — their brother. 'Twas then me thought
My father's rough but fervent grasp,
And my mother's repeated aft,—
And gentle sisters, as they passed,
All, with my brothers to the last
Blended into one seemed to press
My hand once more,— a long farewell.
But oh! I could not stay there long
And feast my eyes on distant views,
Nor dwell in sweet reflections, sprung
In my breast from fresh adieus,
So while closely scanning the lurid
Horizon,— it seemed as if that mound
Did majestic obeisance and bid
Me a last goodby.
                    Reluctantly,
I turned once more away from home,
But ne'er dreamed of that grief so wild
To be mine while abroad I'd roam,

But to which, at length I'm reconciled
Again, I bent my feeble steps westward far,
But with heavy heart, and throbbing brain,—
While the exhilarating mountain breeze—
Fresh from bold Swananoa's brim,
Fanned my feverish brow, and instilled
New life in my exhausted nerves.

                 Knowing that
Life at best, is uncertain as the wind,
And man, with death's ghostly messengers
On all sides is beset———. Nor leaves behind
A memento of his existence,
Save it be some ungrateful descendants
Who permit his name, thought once famous,
To perish, and sink in oblivion—
Or transmit it to their offspring, odious
From the source, in the world's opinion
———Nor is this the case universal,
From causes too delicate to explain—
Fame dies with the individual
Who dies unmarried, nine times out of ten.
Sister, dost thou know a thousand miles
Divide us? The thought brings sadness, and
Makes me feel lonely. A dreary road
Indeed to my one dear father's home.
Hills, and dales, and towering mountains
Are placed between us, and here and there
A busy farm, or bustling village.
And many boisterous rivers roll
Their tempestuous waves between this,
My humble western home, and the home
Of my childhood. And many dark nights
On my humble couch have I tossed
To and fro, with swift returning thoughts
Of that far off land, where plenty dwells,
And all is peace, mirth, and happiness.
Methinks I see thee, sitting calmly
Now in church, where are congregated
Numbers of the playmates of my youth,
All devoutly worshipping our God
Who is so despised and forgotten
Here, where His name is seldom mentioned,
Or only mentioned to be blasphemed,
Or profaned. O, that I were with thee!
Oft, in pleasant dreams or fancy's spell
Do I visit my own native land.

And dwell once more in father's cottage,
Or rove o'er those verdant hills and fields
So thickly covered with rustling corn,
Or waving wheat; or in the forest
Thick, and dark with shades of green oaks
In their summer prime, their lofty boughs
Mingling with the lofty pine's, are locked,
And interwoven,— forming a vast
Green arch,— the squirrels' favorite home.
Sometimes methinks I'm seated by that
Babbling brook, and quietly watching
The sparkling water as it ripples
O'er the white pebbled bottom, leaping
From rock to rock, beneath each making
Little whirlpools, where in boyish sport
Have I angled many summer days
Long, long ago.
And oft by fancy's flickering lamp
Have I seen the little lake that lies
So near our door, at evening twilight,
Calm and placid as the evening sky:
O, what is it that I would not give
To be there and sail in ____ ____
So smoothly, with sister by my side?
No sound is there to break the quiet,
Except the wild water-fowl's flapping,
The splashing oar, the owl's too-hoo-ing,
The farmyard song, on the blithe whistle
Of the plowboy, as he plods homeward
From his daily toil to rest in sleep.
And then by that happy fireside
Am I seated midst a jovial crowd
Of little brothers, while on my knee
Rests my little sister, so very
Tender hearted, yet so frolicsome.
While thus each at once is prattling
Away, entreating me to listen
To their simple tales, a history
Of their sports and plays, or childish wrongs
Which that day befell each little soul,
And which now is their joy to rehearse.
While they speak, with innocent delight
Their eyes sparkle, or grow dim with tears
Pent up, and vainly seeking vent
Till at last too full for retention
Longer they emerge and swiftly chase

Each other down their round rosy cheek
Then all are silent, and eager — wait
My decision, with which all are pleased
And satisfied. Once more all is peace,
And harmony.
                            These, and such as these
Are my midnight musings. Yet I will
Not always live on hope, — delusive
Hope! As well might I chase a phantom,
Then at once let me quell such painful
Feelings, — and forever, till the time
For my departure come, if ever —
Which surely will if High Heaven,
Yet a few weary years (to me)
Is pleased to preserve my worthless life. —
And then, O happy man! The real
Rises to my view, — so haste me on, —
On! On! the thundering rush of the iron
Horse, to me seems but a sluggish pace
Though nature's scenes are swiftly gliding
By, as if the revolving world was
But a mighty stupendous panorama.
And if I never more shall hear those
Faithful relatives bid one welcome, —
Welcome! to their fond embrace, —
Or hear trusty Fido, bay deep-mouthed
Pleasure at the return of his fond
Master, — or see him frisking around
To convince me of his gratitude, —
And if I never again shall chance
To pass the threshold of my father's
Cottage — Why then, place this little wreath
Of violets, enclosed, the first that
Bloom on this magnificent prairie,
Where each morn thousands bloom to decay,
Fade, and fall unseen by mortal eye —
— In my Bible, near the Psalm* which was
Once, and yet is, my delight to read,
To think upon, and to meditate.
Sister, thou knowest, tis marked, — place then
These flowers there, — and if their kindred
Flowers should bloom, pale in solitude,
On my grave in this land of strangers, —
Then keep them there as a memento;
And father, mother, sisters, brothers, —
Whene'er you see these withered flowers,

Think of me, and heave one heavy sigh,—
And drop one mournful tear.—[3]
*XXIII

J. N. Raymer

Nat would continue to compose descriptive passages of what he saw and what he felt about various things as he traveled about Arkansas. He wrote that these were contained in a volume of some type, but whether the writings were actually bound or just saved in a folder is unknown. This material exists now only in his private papers. He wrote the following as a preface to the presumed book:

> The pieces contained in this volume were not intended expressly for the public. I do not profess to be a "poict" [poet], and only make rhymes sometimes when I am not otherwise engaged. In other words, such writings as you may find in the subsequent part of this book I composed when seeking relaxation from study. I found it a very agreeable past time and for my own gratification preserve this collection. If they possess any merit at all it is because they are, each one of them, applicable to certain persons, or describe events which have occurred since my departure from home. An explanation generally precedes each piece, giving the circumstances under which it was written, and the sentiment of the piece is an index to my humor and feelings at that time. Though these lines are not intended for the public, yet all who lay their hands on this book are perfectly welcome to read its contents, I shall insert nothing which I wish kept secret.[4]

Nat may have changed his mind later about sending his writings out for wider reading. Among his papers is a short, three-stanza poem, titled "To

Ambrotype of Jacob Nathaniel Raymer. Writing on the back of the picture states that he was 19 years old, which means the picture was taken in 1855, when Nat was presumably living in Iredell County or nearby. Ambrotypes were the most popular form of photography in the United States by 1855. (Property of McClain Family. Used by permission.)

the Breeze," bearing the notation, "Sent North (to Cincinnati, 0) July 1, 1907."

Nat demonstrated his ability to rhyme with a colorful description of an Arkansas hoedown, titled "An Arkansas Frolic," a thirty-two stanza poem, ca. 1857:

> A jovial crowd had gathered then,
> Of Ladies fair and gallant men —
> At least 'twas so I thought,
> And each at the other glancing
> Roguish look which spoke of dancing —
> Or "will you dance or not?"[5]

The complete poem will be found in the Appendix at the end of this book.

Raymer family records do not divulge any information as to why Nat went to Arkansas or what he did after he arrived there. Perhaps he went for adventure, or to find work, or to visit friends or relatives. Only two pieces from his writing during that period identify a location and an individual.

The first was written on April 28, 1858: "At that time I was laid up with a cut foot, and living with Mr. Lorance Misenhimer in Prairie County, Ark." Actually the 1860 United States Census for Arkansas had the Misenhimer family living in Pulaski County in Gray Township. What is interesting about them is that James L. and his wife Sarah, both aged 45, were born in North Carolina, as were their five children, the oldest being 22, the youngest 13. It is possible that Nat knew them back home, which might account for his association with them. Misenhimer was a farmer, and Nat could have been working for him when he cut his foot. The last stanza of the poem "Thoughts on Wedlock" suggests this:

> ### Gracious, Stars!
>
> Oh, my foot! Such nervous twitching,
> Such pain, such dire affliction mars
> My comforts, and checks my thinking.
> You ask, — wherefore this digression?
> 'Tis plain — one morn not long ago
> I was spreading devastation
> Dreadful, in the forest, when lo!
> Poised high in the air the glit'tring blade
> Propelled by manhood's vig'rous strength,
> And which often ere this had made
> Hill, and plain, and glen, reverb'rate, —

> Fell like a mighty avalanche —
> (A high sounding word, yet 'twill do,
> I thought so then and so would you)
> And cut in twain by mere mis'chance
> My clumsy understanding. — hence
> My drollery.[6]

The second reference to a location in Arkansas was written in the summer of 1858 as an introduction to his three-stanza poem "To the Breeze":

> The following piece was written under singular circumstances. I composed it on Aug. 2nd, 1858, while I was boarding at Mr. Lou. Eggleston's, near Little Rock, Ark. I had had an attack of the Bilious Fever[7] and was tapering off with the chills. And in the forenoon of Aug. 2nd had a chill, and in the P.M. wrote this piece while I was actually lying in bed suffering from a high fever; though a pleasant breeze blew through the open window.[8]

Nat's movements in Arkansas are unknown through 1859; however, several pieces of information indicate that he had returned to North Carolina by 1860.

The first is an advertisement published in the *Iredell Express* on May 4, 1860, that indicates he was helping his father in some way, perhaps in the family business:

> NOTICE: ALL Persons indebted to Moses Raymer, either by note or account are requested to settle with me as soon as possible.
> I will be in Statesville during the week of May Court, to attend to the business.
> May 4th, 1860.   J. N. RAYMER.

In August 1860, he was attending school and wrote the following in his diary on August 1:

> At school agreeably this evening Mr. Morrison lectured us on *Going to Elections* since tomorrow is election day. We have the benefit of one or two lectures weekly from our esteemed teacher. He generally selects themes that are applicable to the class in question, his sole object being to elivate his students in their own opinions.

On the 2nd he wrote this:

> No school today. The great battle between "Advalorem & Anti Advalorem" is to be decided today. Pool the champion for Advalorem or his opponent Gov. Elis will be elected. We are anxiously awaiting the result. I spent the day in my room until 3 o'clock P.M. when we went up to Old Fort to do our first voting —**** Brady and ****. We did vote. Mr. Burgin Jno. curred [sic] us the right by fixing our taxes, although we insisted on paying them ourselves. So the matter stands,

and each of us voted the same ticket, Advalorem throughout. For Jno. Pool for Gov. Gaither for Senate. Chas. Burgin for Commons and Neal for Sheriff. **** two letters from home containing the melancholy news of **** illness, also with the appeal that I should come home immediately. I mean to start tomorrow in company with Brady. We will take stages home. went to the school house for our books. **** Brady finally gave up the notion of accompanying me — so as the stage rolled off after dinner.

The entry ends here, apparently unfinished.

Nat was counted in the United States Census of 1860. At that time the family was living in Catawba County, with the post office at Long Town. The family name is spelled Ramer on the census. According to the census, Moses Raymer was working as a millwright; his real estate was valued at $7,000, and the value of his personal estate was $1,200. Nat was unmarried, living with his parents, and teaching in the Common Schools.

Also in 1860, like many citizens in the North and South, Nat was watching the differences between the two sections widening. In the years leading up to 1860, the North and South had differed over a number of issues, such as tariffs and slavery, but compromise helped quell potential problems. It was the election of Abraham Lincoln in November 1860 that brought the issues to a boil. Fearing the consequences of the election, South Carolina withdrew from the Union on December 20, 1860.

As six other states withdrew and others considered it, the threat of war between the two sections loomed. North Carolinians were divided on the issue. The majority of citizens opposed secession. A vocal minority supported it, and they had the support of Governor John W. Ellis.

In February 1861, a vote was cast to decide whether North Carolinians should hold a convention to discuss this critical issue. On March 13, 1861, the *Raleigh Register* printed the results. The vote was 47,269 against the convention and 46,672 in favor of it. North Carolina remained in the Union by a mere 597 votes. In Iredell County, the call for a convention was soundly defeated, 1,818 to 191. However, after Fort Sumter was fired on, President Lincoln called on each state to provide regiments of soldiers to put down the rebellion. Governor Ellis emphatically refused, and on May 20, 1861, North Carolina withdrew from the Union.

Nat cast his lot in support of the Southern Confederacy.

At the age of twenty-four, he enlisted in a company forming in Iredell County to serve in the war. He was mustered in as a Private and a musician on June 7, 1861, and he enlisted for the war.

Shortly after enlisting, he wrote the following:

Leaving Mr. Stevenson's I went to Concord Church where I remained until noon — no services of any kind, but a large congregation was gathered. Mr. Barr the minister is quite feeble with consumption. At noon I **** off for Geo. Brady's — arrived & tarried some two or three hours, in the mean time did ample justice to a dinner, such as Aunt Sally Brady sets — but, precious few others.

Towards evening I came home, crossing the river at the Island ford. A most pleasant day. So clear the sky! So cool the breeze.[9]

On June 10, he wrote the following about his return to the school where he had been teaching. He was not holding classes that day and was surprised to find that many of his students had come to bid him farewell.

10th Went to Oak Grove horse back, alone. Did not "attend to my school today as usual" — But — on my arrival at the school house found very near my entire school present, — come to bid me "Goodby — Goodby!" O how full of meaning! And **** I help but love those scholars? They are dear to my heart, and sacred will I cherish them in my memory. We talked an hour and then tried to sing a few pieces — we tried none but "Mount Vernon" first; — this made us feel sad, but when we began "Unity," my voice failed — I could not sing — I felt so sad! So strange! — But my scholars, — Dear scholars! Carried each stanza through with sweet but faltering voices — Every heart beat slower, and tears moistened every cheek. Great God!

> When shall we meet again; meet ne'er to sever,
> When shall peace wreath her chain, round us forever?
>   Our souls can ne'er repose,
>   Safe from each blast that blows,
>   In this dark vale of woes — Never — No Never!

Dismissed — And spent the day riding around settling. Succeeded admirably and at sunset arrived here this evening — i.e. Mr. Dan Roseman's ****.[10]

The company was soon ordered to Garysburg in Northampton County. There it was assigned to the 4th Regiment North Carolina Troops as Company C, which was commanded by Captain John B. Andrews. Company C was known as the Saltillo Boys, so called because some of their members had taken part in the Battle of Buena Vista during the Mexican War. Adjutant General J. J. Martin mustered the 4th Regiment into service on July 2, 1861.

Nat would go with the 4th Regiment to Virginia, and later into Maryland and Pennsylvania. Except for two trips, one of eighteen days and one of twenty days, to return home with the band to Salisbury and Statesville and the surrounding area, he would remain with the regiment until they were surrendered at Appomattox Court House, Virginia, on April 9, 1865.

During his four years with the 4th Regiment, Nat became a prodigious writer of long, detailed letters to the newspapers read by the people back home. He would be witness to some of the war's greatest battles, including the Peninsula, the Seven Days at Richmond, Sharpsburg, Chancellorsville, Gettysburg, the vicious fighting in the Wilderness and at Spotsylvania Court House, the campaign of 1864 in the Shenandoah Valley, Petersburg, and the retreat to Appomattox Court House. By today's definition he would be considered the 4th's war correspondent. His portrayals of the dogged determination of the Southern foot-soldiers stand well in comparison with latter-day war correspondents. With his descriptive style and sense of immediacy, he was like a novelist who puts his readers right in the scene of action. He lived through a period that was exciting, dramatic, and tragic, and what he produced is the raw material of history, presented without a historian's comments or revisions. He signed all his letters with a single word: "Nat."

Nat's letters generally began with either "From the 4th North Carolina" or "From the Saltillo Boys," depending on which paper he was writing to; then would come the date and the location of the 4th when the letter was written. Finally, a short series of phrases listed the contents of the letter. Whether Nat did this before mailing his letter or the paper's editor after receiving it is unknown.

"Since I have promised to keep the readers of the *Watchman* and the *Express* posted in matters of general interest, why I shall do so to the best of my ability, so long as I am favored with opportunities to mail my letters."[11] Nat's letters could go home in a number of ways. By mail, postage could cost up to ten cents, but the delivery time was good; most of his letters would appear in the newspapers within a week to ten days of their composition. Soldiers going home on furlough also carried letters from fellow soldiers to their families, and individuals who brought supplies from family members to a particular company would also carry letters back with them.

"All I promise is an account of what came under my immediate observation, and such incidents as I can prove to be actual facts,"[12] he wrote. And he would be able to do this because "we always take notes as we travel through this howling wilderness, seeking not whom [when] we mought kill somebody, but something to write about."[13]

Nat's comment about taking notes is interesting. Some of his writings in Arkansas and after the war in North Carolina contain the short phrase "Refer to my journal." His descendants in Texas have told me that he kept a journal from his Arkansas days in 1857 through the Civil War till he came home. The journal was with him when he returned to Arkansas in 1883 and later when he moved to Texas. When he was quite ill in his early 70s, a male nurse lived in his house and cared for him. His relatives told me that when Nat died in 1909, the journal was nowhere to be found. They feel that either

Nat gave it to the unknown nurse or that the man just took it, perhaps in payment for his time.

The journal would be a valuable document, for I feel that what Nat jotted down later became the basis for his letters to the *Watchman* and the *Express*. I also feel that Nat might be a "Confederate in the Attic" and that one day the journal will turn up.

Nat was very observant as the 4th moved from camp to camp across the countryside. Very little would escape him, as he demonstrated in his description of Union shells falling on the town of Sharpsburg; of the appearance of Stonewall Jackson before the Battle of Chancellorsville; of the natural surroundings of fields, forests and streams; of how the people back home reacted to a concert the 4th's band played while home on furlough; of comforting a dying soldier; or of rain storming about their tent. His recordings of what he saw not only brought to life the regiment's men and their experiences for his readers back home, but it also brought home the war's harsh realities.

In a letter published after the Battle of Chancellorsville, he wrote,

> The wounded began coming in. Here is where we could see the melancholy fruits of war. Never since the war began have I seen so many men severely wounded, or so many amputations necessary. The work of butchery began about noon on the same day and continued with little intermission until ten o'clock the following day. Arms and legs were scattered and tossed about with utmost indifference, wounds probed and dressed, balls extracted, and the sufferers made as comfortable as the nature of the case would possibly admit.[14]

In spite of the harshness and grimness of war, soldiers can find humor in some of the direst moments, and Nat was no exception. Writing of the Battle of Sharpsburg from the 4th's camp near Winchester, Virginia, Nat describes an incident that he observed during the shelling of the town by Union troops:

> I saw middle aged women running through the streets literally dragging their children after them; the little fellows had to take such tremendous strides that it seemed to me they hit the ground but seldom. Then came a dozen young ladies, each with a stuffed sack under each arm, some of which in their haste they had forgotten to tie, and as they ran the unmentionables were scattered behind them. I was in need, but could get none that would fit.[15]

From camp near Fredericksburg, Virginia, he wrote:

> A small force of the enemy had crossed the river and fallen afoul of our fishing parties, scaring them out of their wits, (some I guess hadn't far to go) capturing four wagons, two of which they burned, took their nets also, and scattered the frightened fellows to the four winds, but took no provisions.[16]

Of the twenty-one men from Company C who were paroled at Appomattox Court House, five had seen only limited action in combat. They were all members of the 4th Regimental Band — William R. I. Brawley, John T. Goodman, Robert English Patterson, Jacob Nathaniel Raymer, and James Columbus Steele.[17] Regimental band members were generally noncombatants. Nat did not transfer from Company C to the Regimental Band until February 11, 1863, so it is possible he had been in action. At Sharpsburg, General George Anderson, the brigade commander, had ordered the 4th's band members back to the field hospital behind the lines. Nat's battle descriptions, however, suggest a position closer to the fighting.

Present day readers may be surprised by the fact Civil War regiments would take a band to war with them. It was a common practice. Even before the outbreak of hostilities, United States Army regiments were authorized to enlist musicians, and as many as sixteen could be carried on the rolls. When the war began, Confederate regiments followed suit. In the 4th Regiment N.C.T., nineteen men are recorded as band members.

The band's musical contribution to the regiment was in morale and inspiration. Lively music could perk up footsore soldiers on a long, weary march, or inspire them before the battle began. Concerts in the evening provided a break in the routine of camp life.

Sometimes the opposing forces were so close that they could hear each other's bands playing concerts in the evening. Bandsmen were also detailed as medics to assist surgeons in amputations, care for the wounded, serve as stretcher-bearers during and after the battles, and bury the dead.

There is one letter in this collection, written by Nat from Manassas Junction, February 19, 1862, that is in his private papers, which are the property of the McClain family. The first of the other forty-six letters appeared in the *Carolina Watchman* on July 4, 1861, and the last in the *Iredell Express* on February 9, 1865. The longest gap is between the letter of February 19, 1862, and his next one written from Winchester, Virginia, which appeared in the *Carolina Watchman* on October 27, 1862. Possibly some were written in the now lost issues of the *Statesville American*. The bulk of the letters were published in the *Carolina Watchman*, and these newspapers survived the war. Only nine issues of the *Iredell Express* from 1861 through 1865 survived the war; however, five contained letters from Nat. The reason that there are so few surviving copies of the latter newspaper is because four days after General Lee surrendered at Appomattox, Union troops of General George Stoneman entered the town of Statesville. It was a general practice for Northern soldiers to burn buildings where cotton was stored. Finding cotton on the first floor of the *Iredell Express* building, the soldiers set fire to the structure, destroying it and all contents. Nat may have had letters published in the *Express* in 1861 and early 1862 that were destroyed along with the building.

On November 2, 1883, the following letter was published in the *Statesville Landmark*. It was titled "The Record of the 4th Regiment North Carolina State Troops" and listed as "Cor[respondence] of the *News and Observer*" with a dateline of Statesville, N.C., Oct. 21, 1883:

> You ask about the 4th regiment and its history. With the exception of the small notice Col. Pool gave it in his book, "Our Living and Our Dead," and Gen Early's notice in his book, "The Last Two Years of the A. N. V.," I have never seen any mention of it. A regiment that had for its colonels G. B. Anderson and Bryan Grimes made a history that no State or people need be ashamed of. If the number of its dead is any evidence of its work, the plains of Manassas, the swamps of the Chickahominy, the banks of the Potomac, the Shenandoah, the Rappahannock, the Rapidan and the James, all have received the bodies of its men. If evidence of its courage is wanted, ask its living commanders, D. H. Hill, Early and Gordon. Commencing its work at Seven Pines, it was one of the few that held McClellan in check at Boonsboro, one of the centre at Sharpsburg, on the right at Fredericksburg, and on the flank at Chancellorsville, and was one of the regiments that charged over the gallant Virginia regiment. Its colonel, Ramseur, fought through the streets of Gettysburg and nearly to the gates of Washington; it was one of the regiments that Gen. Lee complimented when he spoke of Cox's brigade; was in the first charge at Appomattox and surrendered its colors there for the first and last time. It was but a handful from the first, but it was willing to follow "Mas' Bob" to Texas if he had said so. There were three companies from Iredell, two from Rowan, one from Davie, two from Beaufort, one from Wayne and one from Wilson. Can't some one write its history?

It was signed "R. O. L.," who was Robert Osborn Linster, a member of Company C along with Nat.

Shortly after this letter was published, a response was offered by Edwin Augustus Osborne, who was a colonel in the 4th North Carolina. The letter was published in the *Statesville Landmark* on February 29, 1884, and was titled "The Fourth N.C. State Troops" and listed as *"Correspondence of the News and Observer"*:

> Having been requested by some of the survivors of the Fourth Regiment to write a history of the part it bore in the late war, I have consented to undertake the task as a labor of love. But as the records of the regiment are nearly all lost, I shall be entirely dependent upon the survivors for the main items of the history. I therefore appeal to all the surviving members of this gallant old regiment to furnish me, as soon as possible, such items as they may possess or can obtain. If every one will furnish even a short sketch of his own history and recollections, with any incidents connected with the regiment, it will be of great advantage to me in this

undertaking, and will make the work more satisfactory to all concerned than it otherwise can be.

Address
E. A. OSBORNE, Shufordville, N.C.

Colonel Osborne did write a history of the 4th Regiment North Carolina State Troops. It appeared in the *Daily Charlotte Observer* on May 31, 1896, under the title "The Fourth N.C. Regiment: Col. E. A. Osborne's Sketch of It." It also appeared in *Histories of the Several Regiments and Battalions from North Carolina in the Great War, 1861-'65, Written by Members of the Respective Commands*, edited by Walter Clark. As he concluded his story of the 4th, Osborne acknowledged his "deep indebtedness" to those who responded to his call to share what they remembered of their experiences serving with the 4th during the war. Among those were Captain John A. Stikeleather, R. O. Linster, and a certain bandsman: "to Mr. Nathaniel Raymer, a member of the band of the Fourth Regiment, who sent me his letters written during the war under the signature of 'Nat,' in the *Statesville American*."

Nat's letters are for us, as they were for Colonel Osborne, a primary source of information about the Civil War. For his descendants they are a window through which they may glimpse the life of an ancestor in time of war. Unlike a number of authors of Civil War letters, Nat was not writing to a particular individual or family, but to a wider audience of newspaper readers. These letters depict the war as seen by the men who endured the tedium of camp life, the terror of the battlefield, the long, tiring marches, and the lack of clothing and rations. How were the boys in the 4th doing? Where had they traveled, what had they seen? How was the health of the regiment? And what were the Yankees up to? Nat answered these questions for family and friends back home; and now, many years later, those answers provide today's reader with an important and compelling story of the Civil War.

· 1 ·

FROM IREDELL COUNTY
TO SHARPSBURG

Shortly after Nat had said farewell to his students, he went out to Camp Vance about a mile west of Statesville, where the Iredell Company was encamped. The newly enlisted soldiers would remain there for two weeks receiving preliminary military instruction before boarding the train for the journey to Garysburg in Northampton County. Located four miles from the Virginia border in eastern North Carolina, the small community was an assembly point for regiments heading north into Virginia.

In one of the few pages that exist from his diary, dated June 1861, Nat recounts his trip to the place where the company was encamped.

> After a zigzag journey, equal in its mysterious turns, to the rout of the Israelites from Egypt to Canaan, I found myself at Little's ferry, where I blowed and hallooed till I was hoarse, but no ferryman made his appearance, so I wheeled my horse, went three miles round to Mock's, where I crossed right away, and struck a bee line for Statesville.— Alas! frail humanity is as liable to miss the road as to err, and the next I knew, I found myself at Alexander's Esquire barely halting long enough to eat a snack & ****. I remounted and without much direction soon found myself at Mr. Thos. Milligan's, 1 mile from Statesville and in sight of Camp Vance. Putting my horse up here, I walked to the Camp. Ay! A bone fide Military Camp, containing at this time about 150 soldiers, among whom I found friends, acquaintances, and some of *Childhood's Playmates*. By a friend (Jos. Gibson) I was introduced to the Captain, Mr. J. B. Andrews with whom as well as his Company I was so much pleased as to be induced to join his Company. And I have volunteered to serve during the War! Could we but lift that veil that hides the next twelve months!! No, let it be; the secret is God's; let us rely implicitly on Him. I go prepared for the worse, but hoping for the better.
>
> I remained at Camp till just 8 o'clock, when I bade my friends a short goodby and went to Mr. Milligan's and there spent a cosy night. All well in the neighborhood.

Soon after breakfast I mounted and went to Ross Stevenson's in order to see Sister Sallie and others. Found the baby very low (At 3 o'clock P.M. it died — aged about two months).

In late June the Iredell Company left Statesville aboard a train on the Western North Carolina Railroad line. At Salisbury they connected with the North Carolina Railroad line and continued to Greensborough, then through the state capital at Raleigh, finally arriving at Goldsborough in Wayne County. Here they headed north to Weldon on the Wilmington & Weldon Railroad. From Weldon the men rode a short four miles to Garysburg on the Seaboard & Roanoke Railroad.

Edith McClain Moss, Nat's great-granddaughter, reports that he often signed his writings with the word "Scribbler." In these first three letters, Nat writes as "Scribbler," and describes the Iredell Company's trip to Garysburg, then their trip to Manassas after they had become Company C of the 4th Regiment, and a final one that related conditions in their Manassas camp.

On June 29, 1861, "Scribbler" wrote a letter to Jacob Bruner, editor of the *Carolina Watchman* in Salisbury, North Carolina. In it he gives an account of the Iredell Company's travel to and arrival in Garysburg.

CAMP ANDERSON (near Garysburg), N.C.
June 29th, 1861.

Mr. Bruner —

We traveled all day, Saturday, and that night, at one o'clock, found ourselves in Weldon. Every where along the road we were cheered by all. Old men, and young men, matrons and fair maidens, all gave us a hearty "God speed." At Greensborough, while the cars stopped, some young ladies presented our officers with beautiful bouquets. Our journey from Goldsboro' to Weldon was in the night time, yet at every station there were crowds collected to see us pass. At Wilson, the ladies stood close to the road and showered the flowers in upon us. Long live the ladies of Wilson.

On Sunday morning, we took the train for this Camp, which is situated about four miles from Weldon, on the Seaboard and Roanoke Rail-road.

The Companies of this Regiment, (the 4th, of the N.C. State Troops,) now in camp here, are the following: The Iredell Blues, Capt. Simonton[1]; Rowan Rifle Guard, Capt. McNeely[2]; Davie Sweepstakes, Capt. Kelly[3]; Southern Guard, Capt. Carter[4]; Saltillo Boys, Capt. Andrews[5]; Scotch Ireland Grays, Capt. Wood[6]; Iredell Independent Grays, Captain Dalton[7]; Pamlico Riflemen, Capt. Marsh.[8]

Our Camp is situated in a beautiful grove bordering on the drill ground. The water, which is obtained from wells sunk on the border of the Camp, and therefore convenient, is very good. There are about five thousand troops in the vicinity of Garysburg, over three thousand at the village, Col. Tew's[9] and the eight companies of our regiment at this Camp. Those at Garysburg are, I believe, mostly volunteers, while those here are regular State Troops.

All are in good spirits; the Camp presents a lively scene in the intervals of drill exercise. Fiddling, singing, wrestling and jumping are carried on to a considerable extent. The Camp is comparatively healthy and the officers are making every exertion to keep it in that condition.

SCRIBBLER.

[Published in the *Carolina Watchman* July 4, 1861]

Eventually, ten companies comprised the 4th Regiment. Iredell County sent three — A, C, and H; Rowan County, two — B and K; Beaufort County, two — E and I; Wayne County, one — D; Wilson County, one — F; and Davie County, one — G. The regiment was under the command of George B. Anderson[10] as Colonel; John A. Young,[11] Lieutenant Colonel; and Bryan Grimes[12] as Major.

The 4th remained in Garysburg about a month drilling. The soldiers received their state uniforms, blankets, and all the other equipment of war before they were ordered to Richmond, Virginia, on July 20.

Laura Elizabeth Lee, in her book *Forget-Me-Nots of the Civil War*, includes an excerpt from a friend's letter describing the arrival of the 4th Regiment in Richmond:

"The Fourth North Carolina Regiment" is the recipient of unmeasured praise for their deportment while on leave and their soldierly bearing in the ranks. In fact not a regiment has come from our state that has not elicited unstinted commendation for their fine appearance. It does me good to stand in a crowd as I did on Sunday when the "Fourth" passed through the streets and heard the hearty words of satisfaction expressed as to the material, the "Old North State" was sending into the field. Such expressions as "Did you ever see such determined looking fellows, steady, cool and resolute looking?" "What should we fear when such as these are between Richmond and the enemy?" I assure you I felt like giving one uproarious shout for the "Old North State" forever.[13]

Richmond, July 23, 1861.

Robertson.

In a letter to the *Carolina Watchman* dated August 8, 1861, "Scribbler" writes of the 4th's trip and a visit to the battlefield:

MANASSAS JUNCTION, Va.,
August 8th, 1861.

Mr. Bruner:— It has been so long since I wrote to you, that to give you a full account of our doings would take up more space than you could spare. I will, therefore, merely give a synopsis of our movements for the benefit of our friends among your readers.

Five companies of our regiment, viz: Iredell Blues; Rowan Rifle Guard; Davie

An Ambrotype of Nat Raymer in his uniform, ca. 1861–1865. Itinerant photographers visited the camps to make photographs for soldiers to send home. This picture appears to be an outside shot and not one taken against a screen. Nat is holding his musket in the "charge bayonets" position. (Property of McClain Family. Used by permission.)

Sweepstakes; Saltillo Boys, and the Wilson Light Infantry, accompanied by the Rowan Artillery, left our Camp near Garysburg, N.C., on Saturday evening, July 20th, bound for Virginia. We went by way of Petersburg and arrived at Richmond, Sunday, about noon. We went into camp below the city, within a quarter of a mile of the river James, where we remained four days. On Thursday night we took the train for the seat of war. At Gordonsville where we arrived the next morning by sun rise, we were, for some cause or other, detained until nearly night. However, we did at last get off, and that night, about three o'clock, found ourselves at Manassas Junction. We encamped about a mile and a half north of the Junction, where we yet remain.

We did nearly all of our traveling by night, either on account of the bad arrangement of the trains or to baffle any lurking spies, who might be along the road. Be the cause what it may, it was quite unpleasant for us, for it not only kept us from seeing the country through which we passed, but deprived us of much sleep.

The next day after our arrival here, many of us visited the scene of the late battle. The field, of course, did not present as shocking an appearance as it did immediately after the fight, yet we saw enough to give us an idea of the real horrors of a bloody battle. Dead horses filled the air with a sickening odor, rendering it almost unbearable to go near the points where the hardest fighting had taken place. Numerous graves — or rather imitations, for they could scarcely bear the name of graves — were scattered over the field. In many places limbs lay exposed, and in several instances, the naked skull was visible, so shallow was the covering of the body. — Those thus buried, however, were Northerners, to whom a descent [sic] burial was refused by their own friends, and who were left to the care of their more humane enemies. The Southerners, of course, attended to their own dead first, and consequently, by the time they came to the Yankees, they were much decayed. It was, therefore, impossible to remove them or remain long enough to give them a descent burial. The ground around the graves was blackened by the life blood of the occupant, and in many instances, showed marks of the death struggle.

Despite our hatred towards those invaders of our soil, we could not but pity the fate of those who lay around us. To a person of refined feelings, there is something very repulsive in the thought of being thus buried, out of the reach and knowledge of relatives and friends. Many of those buried on this battle field doubtless left the bosom of families and started on this expedition, allured by the thoughts of wealth and renown. Unfortunately enough for them, they have scarcely enough earth to cover their dead bodies, and those, against whom they came to wage a war of extermination, had, by the unnatural conduct of their pretended friends, to give them such a burial as they received. This is war! this is glory with all its brightness. Thus may it be to all who come threatening upon the people of the South barbarities worthy of the most bloodthirsty savages. Would to God that those more guilty, — the Greeleys, Sumners and Beechers — should meet with such a fate rather than the miserable dupes they have deluded!

The health of our Regiment is not very good just now. The measles have got into camp and many are down with them. One man in the Iredell Blues, (James

Sprinkle,[14]) died with them night before last. I know of no other very serious case now in camp.

SCRIBBLER.

[Published in the *Carolina Watchman* Aug. 15, 1861]

A member of Company C, who signed his letter "Chap.," remembered in November 1883: "At this place between fifty and seventy of our men sickened and died during the warm months of August and September. Some of the best men in company C, of said regiment, died while there."[15]

Nat wrote one final letter under the name "Scribbler," in which he describes the health of the regiment and appreciation for a shipment of food from home. He began the letter "From the 4th Regiment N.C. State Troops," a form he used in many of the following letters.

From the 4th Regiment N.C. State Troops.
MANASSAS JUNCTION, VA., October 15th, 1861.

MR. BRUNER: WE have moved to a new camp but are still in close proximity to the Junction. Our move was made at the direction of the doctors for the health of the regiment. The sickest men were sent to a station some twenty-five miles up the Manassas Gap Railroad. Many of these have returned to duty and report the remainder as rapidly improving. Our men have had new spirits infused into them by our move. It had become a settled conviction among them that it was the next thing to an impossibility to get well at the old camp, when once taken sick. This belief has been dissipated by the change and a great improvement is visible among the men.

Col. Chipley,[16] of Iredell, arrived here the first of this month with three car loads of "good things from home." He brought an abundance of potatoes, cabbage, apples, blankets, clothes, honey, wine, vinegar, molasses, and numerous other articles of comfort and of luxury.

This is the second visit Col. Chipley has paid us. We are under lasting obligations to him for his self-sacrificing exertions in our behalf. Since he has been here he has been building a depot at the Junction for this regiment. The good people of Rowan and Iredell need not, therefore, withhold their hands lest their sons should be overburdened with clothing and other necessities. Many will not send things, fearing that they would be left behind and destroyed should the regiment be ordered to march. This will be the case no longer. Whatever is of any value can be boxed up and left in this depot where it will be safe until called for. Thanks to Col. Chipley, thanks — a thousand thanks — to the "folks at home" for the abundance of good things sent us. Thankful for past favors we sincerely hope for a continuance of the same. — News is scarce here, that is reliable news. Rumor after rumor has come until we no longer pay any attention to them. Somehow or other that great battle which everybody is and has been expecting for sometime, does not take place. The Yankees will not advance — they are not ready. We hear cannon nearly every day, but it is said to be the artillery practicing. Two such bodies of men, however, cannot long remain so near each other without some action. They are sick and tired of this inactive camp life, with its dull routine of never-ending and laborious duties.

We have rumors of another action on the N.C. coast in which our men were victorious. May this report prove true. Let the cowardly rascals be driven from the "Old North State."

SCRIBBLER.

[Published in the *Carolina Watchman* Oct. 28, 1861]

The 4th remained at Manassas Junction during the fall and winter of 1861–1862, doing garrison duty, drilling, marching, and learning, under the strict discipline of Colonel Anderson, how to be a group of soldiers that moved as a unit.

The winter that year was hard. Snow covered the ground, and at times sleet crusted on top of it. Winds sweeping down from the Blue Ridge were bitter and biting. The men were in winter quarters, living in log huts holding six to eight soldiers. When it wasn't snowing, it rained. Roads were rutted, and wagons had difficulty moving over them. Often the men had to leave their huts to get wood from a distance to keep their fires going.

In the spring of 1862, Union forces were massing on the Virginia Peninsula, as General George McClellan prepared to advance towards Richmond. The 4th North Carolina was also preparing to move. Nat, knowing that battle was approaching, wrote the following patriotic appeal to the citizens back home. It is among his private papers without an indication of which newspaper it was sent to.

Manassas Junction, February 19th, 1862.

Lives there a man so base; with soul so dead as to be willing to let the despot's heel crush his own posterity? If any, speak, for him have I offended or shall offend. Since we have gone this far we are determined to put it through if it costs our very heart's blood. I am aware that the prospect is now gloomy — the greater the need then for prompt and decisive action. I appeal to young men — to unmarried men. If any have married for the sole purpose of having a hobby-horse and therefore cannot come, let him stop here; read no further or your cheeks will surely grow crimson with shame; the wife of your bosom will think you are a coward, whether she says so or not, and your children — God forbid you should ever have any — will blush to call you father. I appeal to my schoolmates, my play-mates, the boon companions of my youthful days. If you have not the very best of reasons for staying at home, come now and join us. As few months may end the struggle — God only knows; and can you remain at home an unconcerned spectator? If we fail and Northern despotism again reigns supreme over our land our ghosts shall haunt you to your graves.

"Remains of a Confederate Camp at Manassas." Cabins and shanties were typ-ical winter quarters for the regiments when inclement weather brought a halt to active campaigning. For Nat and other soldiers the structures provided a 16' × 16' space where the men could cook, do soldierly chores, and sleep. Cabins had a fireplace against one wall and could hold between six and eight soldiers. (Frank Leslie, *Famous Leaders and Battle Scenes of the Civil War* [New York: Mrs. Frank Leslie, 1896]. ClipArt used by permission of the Florida Center for Instructional Technology, College of Education, University of South Florida.)

On March 8, 1862, the 4th received orders to begin the march to the Virginia Peninsula, with Yorktown as its destination. A few days later the regiment halted and went into camp near Orange Court House, Virginia, remaining there until April 8, when the march toward Yorktown was taken up again. When the 4th arrived, it was placed in a brigade with the 49th Virginia and the 27th and 29th Georgia. Brigadier General Winfield Scott Featherston commanded the brigade.

"Chap.'s" 1883 reminiscence continued:

We struck our tents and marched for Yorktown, Va., to which point McClel-lan had moved his whole command. Arriving there we found Gen. Magruder with a small command holding the enemy in check. We were placed on the front lines and were initiated into the dreadful realities of war. Here we became acquainted with the hissing music of solid shot, shell, and minnie balls. Here I first saw the novel sight of men trying to bury themselves when they heard the hissing of these missiles of death.

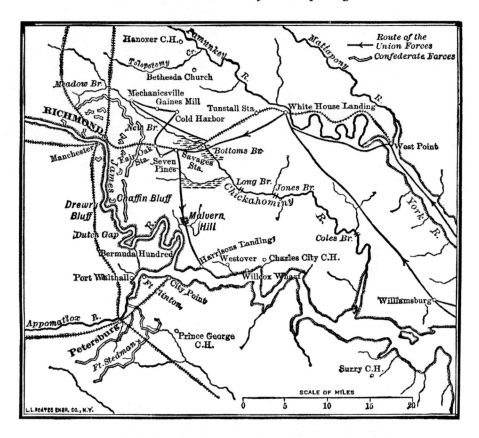

Spring Campaign of 1862. In the spring of 1862, the 4th Regiment left its winter quarters at Manassas and marched to Yorktown, Williamsburg, Seven Pines, Mechanicsville, and Cold Harbor, serving either in a reserve role or in active combat. The regiment's heaviest fighting took place at Seven Pines where half the soldiers were killed, wounded, or missing. (Robert Hall, Harriet Smither, and Clarence Ousley, *A History of the United States* [Dallas, TX: Southern, 1920]. Map used by permission of the Florida Center for Instructional Technology, College of Education, University of South Florida.)

A number of the soldiers must have reflected on the irony of the situation. Here they stood on the battlefield of Yorktown where General Cornwallis had surrendered to General Washington, ending the fighting in the Revolutionary War and beginning the first small steps toward creating the United States. Now armies were again meeting at Yorktown, this time with the purpose of dissolving the union of states.

While the regiment was at Yorktown, Nat wrote a letter to the *Iredell Express* in which he describes how Reuben Lollar of Company C risked his life to retrieve a rifle from the hands of a dead Yankee. These issues of the *Express* were later destroyed; however, the *Fayetteville Observer*, as did many newspapers of the period, reprinted material from other papers. Nat's letter was published in the *Observer* on June 16, 1862.

Reuben S. Lollar was a native of Iredell County and was 18 years old when he enlisted for the war in June of 1861. He was killed at the Battle of Seven Pines on May 31, 1862, barely a month after Nat wrote about him.

One night our pickets were charged upon by pretty heavy squads of both infantry and cavalry — signal guns were fired, our reserve brought up, and the clatter of musketry began. The signs for a general battle were propitious, but all soon vanished when our heavy cannons on the forts opened on them. The incessant thunder from our guns was really appalling to us, how much more so to those in whose ranks the shells were making such a direful havoc. They could not stand it, and in fifteen minutes withdrew, taking their dead and wounded with them, with the exception of one dead man, lying with fifty yards of our rifle pits, who was probably overlooked. There he lay during the balance of our stay at Yorktown, a week or more, and for aught I know may be there yet.

As remarked before, he lay not more than fifty yards from our pits, not further from the Yankees, and in full view of both. For these reasons no one ventured out to bury him, and as no flag of truce was sent out he was permitted to stay. As a matter of course there was much conjecturing as to what he might have. Innumerable surmises concerning his gold, silver, pistols, &c., went the rounds of every camp-fire in our regiment. Among all they were sure of but one thing, and that was that he had a gun of some sort which could be seen distinctly; and under the circumstances that gun would certainly be a valuable trophy. This subject was discussed several nights; — the excitement ran high; many fellows boasted that when it came their time to go on picket they would get that gun, that *they were sure;* perhaps spin out an oath to it. But their turns came, and so came they back to camp without the gun. After all their boasting the risk seemed too great. The dead man was watched with hawk eyes by the Yankees, nor could our boys raise their heads, or an arm above the bank of earth that concealed them, but a shower of balls whistled about them. Finally an intimate friend of mine allowed curiosity to become his master; perhaps not so much curiosity either as recklessness, and his "don't care a continental" sort of way; be that as it may, he resolved to get the gun or let the Yankees get him in the scrape. For half an hour he watched the Yankees with one eye above the parapet; he said they were not so much on the lookout, and taking advantage of the opportunity he got out of his "hoill" as he called it — lay flat on the ground and began "making the trip" snake fashion. He began to think it was half a mile instead of fifty yards, but lay low, lower than he ever lay before, and kept crawling. "Oh," said he, "Nat, you can't imagine how fidgety I felt about the time I was going to lay hold of my stiff customer. Ay, Yes, and stink — the g-e-e buck." Did you turn him over? "I had no time for inspection; I thought the air was full of Yankees, all coming at me with bayonets fixed; so grabbing the gun by the muzzle I began to crawfish. But it would not come —

the fellow had hold of it too tight; I had to get back to him and absolutely tear his hands loose. At last I had the gun, and I knew very well that I had no time for fooling, but crawling was too slow, and jumping up I made the fastest time on record back to my pit." But were you not fired on, I asked? "O yes," said he, "when I was halfway back I was discovered and several balls whistled close to my ears, they only made me git quicker." And he did "make the trip," as he called it, and has for his trouble one of "Colt's five shooter army rifles," in fact a splendid gun. It excited considerable wonder in camp, and could be sold at any time for $150—$200 has been offered. He returned his Minnie rifle to the armory and uses "the one wrenched from a dead yankee" altogether. Perhaps you would like to know the name of the fellow who ventured so far? I will give you "the first letters" viz: *Reuben S. Lollar* of the Saltillo Boys.

The Regiment left Yorktown on May 4, 1862, heading for Williamsburg. "Chap.'s" letter continues:

Remaining at Yorktown about two weeks, we began that retreat toward Richmond known as Gen. Johnston's "famous retreat." We marched and countermarched through mud and rain, and while there was some hard fighting at Williamsburg, our regiment arrived on the field only in time to see the enemy repulsed.

The brigade continued moving back towards Richmond. On May 13, the 4th Regiment reached the Chickahominy River and went into camp. They remained there until the Battle of Seven Pines.

On May 30, the day before the battle, the men sweltered in the high temperatures as they moved about under arms. As evening approached, orders were given to prepare rations for the coming day, an activity that kept them up until the late hours. Finally the tired soldiers turned in, some without blankets to cover them, others with only a blanket propped on a pole or a small tent. No sooner had they settled for the night than thunder and lightning exploded across the sky. Torrential rains poured down upon them, adding to their misery.

James Columbus Steele, who was perhaps Nat's best friend in the regiment throughout the war and also shared a cabin with him when the 4th was in winter quarters and a tent during shorter camp stays or during marches, remembered the night before the great battle. "That night it rained in torrents, but Nat and I slept soundly under our little Yankee tent, which consisted of two pieces of canvass 8 × 8 feet, buttoned together and stretched over a temporary ridge pole. Each of us carried one side of this tent."[17]

General Joseph Johnston's plan called for the battle to begin early on May 31, but complications began to arise. Johnston had given oral rather than written orders, and some commanders misinterpreted them; some commanders argued over who had seniority; divisions went down the wrong roads; the element of surprise was lost.

General D. H. Hill had his division, to which the 4th Regiment was attached, under arms from 8:00 in the morning until 1:00 in the afternoon. In that time he had not heard any cannon or musket fire; nor had he received any orders. Deciding not to wait any longer, Hill gave the order for his men to attack.

Less than a quarter of a mile away stood enemy artillery batteries and redoubts. Between them and Hill's division was a daunting abatis, an obstruction made by felling trees and piling cut limbs throughout it. Adding to the formidable defenses were pools of water and muddy ground from the heavy rains of the night before.

As soon as Hill's men were spotted coming through the abatis, the batteries opened on them. The men went forward into a storm of shot, shell, and canister as they climbed through the downed trees and branches, unable to return the enemy fire. Then they were through the abatis and onto open ground where they began returning the enemy fire with such intensity that the enemy momentarily stopped shooting. The North Carolinians advanced toward the enemy, getting within fifty or sixty yards of them.

Colonel E. A. Osborne, then a Captain, remembered the moment:

> We halted near a zigzag fence. The men were falling rapidly.... It was evident that the regiment could not remain there without being utterly destroyed. Major Grimes was near, sitting on his iron-gray horse, with one leg thrown over the saddle bow, as afterwards so often seen in battle. "Major," I shouted, "we can't stand this. Let us charge the works." "All right," said the Major, "Charge them! Charge them!"[18]

The regiment surged forward and captured the works. Captain Osborne was wounded near the breastworks. The regiment retired back to the fence to await reinforcements, then charged again over ground that was littered with the bodies of their dead and wounded comrades.

Grimes led the charge on horseback; suddenly a cannon ball tore off his horse's head, and horse and rider went down hard. The dead animal pinned Grimes' leg to the ground. Seeing him fall and thinking their commander killed, the lines faltered, but Grimes rose up and waved his sword and shouted for them to keep going. Several soldiers rushed to his aid and pulled the dead animal off him. "Upon regaining his feet," Colonel Osborne wrote, "he saw that his color-bearer was killed.... He seized the flag himself and rushed forward, waving his men on to the charge."[19]

The 4th's band members were sent into the fight as litter bearers, and as the regiment moved forward, the men were in position a short distance behind the charging troops, accompanied by the assistant surgeon. Cannon balls eight inches in diameter hissed overhead, smashing trees trunks or bounding crazily through the ranks. This was the band's first experience under fire. Soon the men began to encounter wounded soldiers walking toward the rear lines.

James Steele recounted the intensity of the Yankee fire as the band followed the Regiment in the charge:

> We came to a grove of small gum trees and here a Yankee battery had our range exactly, firing grape and canister as fast as they could load. I lay down behind a gum tree six inches in diameter, with my head toward that battery, saying, this is a small tree, but it may turn a ball. I had just struck the ground when a grapeshot like a walnut just missed me. I got up to look for a wounded man, the limbs of gum trees were dropping all around, being cut off by minnie balls. [20]

Wherever the fighting raged, bandsmen serving as stretcher-bearers were in the line of fire just as much as the regular infantryman.

"Chap." commented on the battle:

> Early in the morning we were ordered out and preparations began for the attack. The 4th Regiment, with others which I now cannot name, were placed in front. The order was given, "charge," and then the work of death began. The rattle of musketry, the booming of the cannon, the shrieks of the dying, the shouts of the victorious, rendered the scene frightfully grand. The enemy was driven from his works at every point; but he succeeded in getting his reinforcements across the river, and Gen. Johnston withdrew his forces from the field after burying his dead. On this battlefield lie bleaching, the bones of many of North Carolina's truest and best sons. Here the blood of some of Iredell's noblest sons was shed — White, Simonton, Hill, Waddell and many others we might mention.

During the battle the band members found themselves in an unusual situation. James Steele relates:

> Our surgeon was on a horse and we were ordered to follow him, but at the first exhibition of shells he was making a beeline toward the rear. Some one pointed to him saying "shall we follow him?" but all said no. He was not seen after that during the fight. I am not alluding to myself when I say the band did not show the white feather in this fight. It was no one's duty to look after the band to see whether we did our duty or not except the surgeon, and after he left everyone did the best he could without orders. [21]

The 4th went into the battle with 678 men and had 77 killed, 286 wounded, and six missing. The regiment was shattered in their bloodiest charges of the war with a casualty rate of over 50 percent. For Nat and the

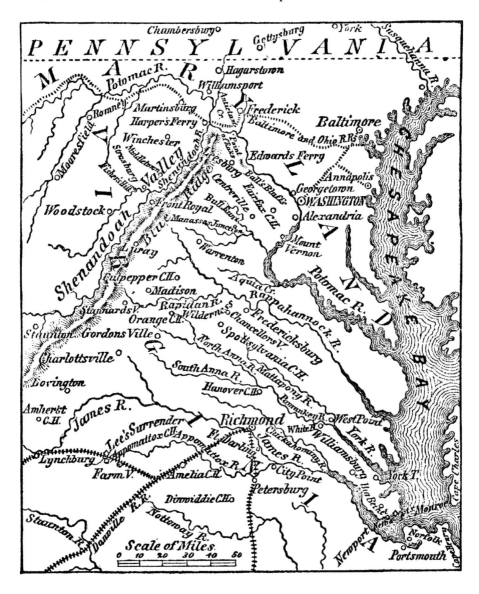

The Seat of War in Virginia. With the exception of two furloughs home, this area was the center of Nat's life from June 1861 until the surrender at Appomattox on April 9, 1865. He would write his first letter from Manassas and his last from Petersburg. (Marcius Willson, *History of the United States* (New York: Ivison, Blakeman, 1872. Map used by permission of the Florida Center for Instructional Technology, College of Education, University of South Florida.)

rest of the band, "did the best he could" meant picking up the wounded and getting them to the field hospital as quickly as possible and then burying the dead.

A major result of the Battle of Seven Pines was the wounding of General Joseph Johnston. This forced President Jefferson Davis to eventually appoint a new commander for the Army of Northern Virginia — General Robert E. Lee.

At Mechanicsville, Virginia, on June 26, the 4th could call to arms only 150 officers and men. Major Bryan Grimes received orders from General D. H. Hill to hold the 4th in readiness to charge should the other troops assigned to take a battery fail, but the troops captured the battery, and the enemy was driven off.

At the Battle of Cold Harbor the 4th sustained heavy casualties. Carrying the colors, Grimes led the charge on horseback, until the animal was shot out from under him. Of the 150 officers and men who attacked with the other regiments, 11 were killed and 54 were wounded. Among the wounded was Nat's company commander, Captain John B. Andrews, who died shortly afterwards.

Because they were assigned to bury their fallen comrades, the 4th Regiment did not take part in the fighting at Malvern Hill and escaped the disastrous assault on July 2.

After the close of the battle for Richmond, the 4th Regiment was assigned to an all North Carolina Brigade, along with the 2nd, 14th, and 30th regiments. These four regiments would remain together for the rest of the war. They were under the command of a newly appointed General — George B. Anderson. Bryan Grimes was promoted to Colonel of the 4th.

Now Anderson's Brigade, along with the rest of General Lee's army, moved toward Maryland, crossing the Potomac River on September 4–5, near Leesburg and going into camp near Frederick City, Maryland. From here they would advance toward Boonsboro.

It is at this point that Nat's letters to the newspapers above his own signature begin.

· 2 ·

SHARPSBURG

General Lee entered Maryland with an army of 55,000 soldiers. General McClellan awaited him with a force of over 90,000, a 2 to 1 superiority. The war had been ravaging Virginia for over a year, and supplies were low. Lee had hopes of recruiting Marylanders to the Southern cause but was sadly disappointed by the coolness of the citizens. A number of his troops lacked shoes and blankets, and were subsisting on green corn and apples, but there would be no outpouring of aid and supplies in sufficient numbers to meet his needs.

Nat's letter to the *Carolina Watchman*, written after the Battle of Sharpsburg and published on October 27, begins with comments about the little enthusiasm shown for the Southerners.

News from the 4th.
CAMP NEAR WINCHESTER, Va.,
Oct. 6th, 1862.

Camp near Hagerstown, Md., — Fight on the Mountain, Sunday, Sept. 14th — Retreat to Sharpsburg — Battle of Wednesday Sept. 17th — Flight of the citizens from town — Ludicrous scenes mingled with the most heart-rending — Another retreat — Fording the Potomac, &c., &c.

Saturday night, the 13th of Sept., we were encamped five miles West of Hagerstown in Maryland. I cannot say whether or not we were on our own soil; — once we pretended to claim that vine-clad State, with its clay ovens and ancient churches, as a part of the "Sunny South," but the serious impression is that we have not much business there, judging from the cold reception and little sympathy manifested towards us. In some sections, it is true, we met with persons who hailed our advent with rejoicing, but the majority shouted over our exit. The expedition was an experiment the results of which may not be made public in all their minutia for years to come. But whether in Dixie or not the sun went down — unobscured by the fragment of a cloud, and the dark blue hills of Pennsylvania stood out in bold relief against the sky. Every thing was remarkably quiet, — no

36

stir in camp nor any sign visible of a deadly contest approaching so near. The thousands of weary soldiers around us stretched themselves beneath the tall trees and were soon wrapped in profound slumber.

The Southern army had been either fighting or marching since spring. Consequently, their clothing was worn, ragged, dirty, and infested with lice. The appearance of the men as they marched through the towns and countryside was not the army the people of Maryland were expecting to see. Were these the soldiers who defeated the North's armies battle after battle?

When the soldiers marched through Frederick City, one Maryland woman, a Union supporter, recorded her impressions in a letter to a friend in Baltimore. All that is known of her is her signature, "Kate." Her letter was intercepted, and it provides a description of the appearance of Nat and the other soldiers. Alexander Hunter later included it in his "A High Private's Account of the Battle of Sharpsburg," published in 1882.

Frederick City, Maryland, September 13th, 1862.

I wish, my dearest, Minnie, you could have witnessed the transit of the Rebel army through our streets a day or two ago. Their coming was unheralded by any pomp and pageant whatever. No bursts of martial music greeted your ear, no thundering sound of cannon, no brilliant staff, no glittering cortege dashed through our streets. Instead came three long dirty columns that kept on in an unceasing flow. I could scarcely believe my eyes; was this body of men, moving so smoothly along, with no order, their guns carried in every fashion, no two dressed alike, their officers hardly distinguishable from their privates — were these, I asked myself in amazement, were these, dirty, lank, ugly specimens of humanity, with shocks of hair sticking through the holes in their hats, and the dust thick on their dirty faces, the men that had coped and encountered successfully and driven back again and again our splendid legions with their fine discipline, their martial show and color, their solid battalions keeping such perfect time to the inspiring bands of music? I must confess, Minnie, that I felt humiliated at the thought that this horde of ragamuffins could set our grand army of the Union at defiance. Why, it seemed as if a single regiment of our gallant boys in blue could drive that dirty crew into the river without any trouble. And then, too, I wish you could see how they behaved — a crowd of boys on a holiday don't seem happier. They are on the broad grin all the time. Oh! they are so dirty! I don't think the Potomac River could wash them clean. And ragged! — there is not a scarecrow in the cornfields that would not scorn to exchange clothes with them; and so tattered! — there isn't a decently dressed soldier in the whole army. I saw some strikingly handsome faces though; or rather, they would have been so if they could have had a good scrubbing. They were very polite, I must confess, and always asked for a drink of water, or anything else, and never think of coming inside of a door without an invitation. Many of them were barefooted. Indeed, I felt sorry for the poor misguided wretches, for some were limping along so painfully, trying hard to keep up with their comrades. But I must stop. I send this by Robert and hope it will reach you safely. Write to me as soon as the route is open. ****1

General Lee had divided his army into three groups: General James Longstreet was at Hagerstown, Maryland; General Stonewall Jackson was sent to capture the Union troops at Harpers Ferry; and General D. H. Hill with five brigades numbering 3,000 men was to guard Turner's Gap at South Mountain. Protecting the Gap was considered a precaution; no action was expected there before the three groups reunited. However, during the night of the 13th, General Hill had received a message that great numbers of Federal campfires had been seen beyond the Gap in the valley on the east side of South Mountain. The usually cautious McClellan was coming.

Nat's letter of Oct. 6 continues:

> Before the break of day Sunday morning the drums beat reveille. In a few minutes all were under arms and slowly groping their way out to the turnpike. Scarcely half awake we were marched eastward at a quick pace, without food, water, or rest and in clouds of suffocating dust until 10 o'clock, A.M., when we reached the summit of the Blue Ridge (so called there; whether indeed it be that ridge or not I cannot say.) Soon after our arrival we were sent off to the right, that is ours (General G. B. Anderson's) and General Garland's brigades, and before we were aware of it came in contact with a pretty heavy force of the enemy. A fight ensued which lasted perhaps an hour, in which Gen. Garland was killed, together with a good many men in his and our brigades, and a considerable number wounded.

On the 14th, Anderson's Brigade would take 1,174 men into the fight at South Mountain. The 4th Regiment, which had sustained heavy losses at Seven Pines and in other fighting afterwards, had less then 200 men.

Colonel Bryan Grimes, in crossing the Potomac River on September 5, had been kicked in the leg by a horse. Unable to walk much or even ride, he traveled with the regiment by ambulance. On the morning of the South Mountain fight he was riding in a wagon as the Brigades marched toward Turner's Gap.

Two of General Hill's brigades, Alfred Colquitt's and Samuel Garland's, had gone through the Gap earlier in the morning, and were in defensive positions on the eastern slopes of South Mountain. At 9:00 o'clock General Garland's troops were engaging large numbers of the enemy who were climbing towards them. General Hill ordered Anderson's Brigade to his assistance. Lieutenant John C. Gorman of the 2nd Regiment North Carolina Troops recounted the moment in a letter to the Raleigh newspaper *Spirit of the Age*:

The enemy have thrown in their whole force on the right flank. The men become restless and uneasy, and the light of battle is seen in every face. But here comes one of Garland's aids, galloping furiously — "General, send us reinforcements — we are falling back, and the enemy are pressing us hard in heavy force. General Anderson, hurry your brigade to Garland's assistance." And we are faced to the right, and away we go up the side of the mountain double quick. We pass lots of wounded limping down the mountain, trickling blood at every step, then again a stretcher containing more desperately wounded, and as I bend over one, I catch the pale face of the gallant Garland, who is being carried down desperately wounded in the breast. He died before he reached a surgeon. He was killed on the first charge of the enemy, while gallantly rallying his men before their superior force.[2]

Grimes called for a horse. Despite his painful leg, he mounted with assistance from his men, and led the 4th up the slopes of South Mountain.

Nat's letter continues:

Our troops held their positions while the enemy fell back to change position to meet which ours had to change theirs also. The day was spent by brigades and divisions marching and countermarching through deep ravines, dense thickets, and over abrupt hills and rocky precipices, in order that we might always have a force at any pass to oppose the advance of the Yankees. Meantime our artillery kept up an incessant fire in reply to theirs, making every hill top and mountain gorge resound as if the very elements were at war. Our batteries were placed in advantageous positions on the top of the mountain, commanding full range of those of the enemy planted at the base about a mile and a half away. During the entire day the fire from both was terrible. Shells were constantly hissing through the air in every direction, and towards evening a dense cloud of smoke settled down on the plains completely shutting out Lincoln's hosts from view. But they were not inactive as we afterwards discovered. Finding that they could not turn our right they concluded to try our left and at sunset, that wing of our army was attacked furiously. Fortunately Longstreet had just arrived from Hagerstown and his whole division was sent to support our weak and flinching force. They rallied and with greater fury attacked the enemy and drove him down the mountains. Night was coming on, — reinforcements kept pouring in for our adversary while we could get none; our centre was giving way and the right in a perilous condition; then to save the army a retreat was necessary and accordingly ordered. To get information to the various brigades scattered over a space of four miles in those mountain passes and peaks was, in reality, a very difficult undertaking, — it was done though, and as the night advanced our troops retreated by various by-paths down the mountain and into Sharpsburg turnpike. It was impossible to prevent straggling to a great extent. The men were exhausted, hungry, and foot sore. It is surprising that more of that class were not captured, — the greater portion of them managed to struggle through incredible hardships in getting back to Sharpsburg, and not a few continued the retreat on their own responsibility until they were safe across the Potomac and on Virginia soil. Not withstanding these, the number kept together were sufficient to put a wholesome dread on the Yankees, and keep them at a respectful distance in our rear. During the night the road was blockaded for miles with trains and wagons, artillery, &c., but by patience and perseverance all were moved out of danger before daylight on the morning of the 15th. Our only regret was that we had to leave our dead in the hands of the enemy. 'Twas a vain regret and we silently plodded on our way until we reached Sharpsburg. Here our entire force was drawn up in line of battle about a quarter of a mile north of the town, where we calmly waited the advance of the enemy. The day passed away and towards evening the minions of the North hove in sight. That night, and the next day and the next night we spent lying on our arms inactive but in anxious suspense. The citizens of the town, some five or six hundred, were ordered to quit their homes and seek safety in the country. The majority, however, paid little attention to the order, believing it impossible that the roar of battle should disturb their usual quiet. It was evident, though, to us, who had been accustomed to seeing preparation made for a battle, that a storm was approaching. All day Tuesday we could see detachments of the Yankee army marching thro' fields and skirts of timber selecting their positions.

During the fighting on South Mountain, Grimes' horse was shot out from under him, the third time that had happened since May. He was forced to lead the 4th on foot. By the time darkness brought a halt to the action he was exhausted. General Anderson, seeing how worn out Grimes was, ordered him to the field hospital, and four litter bearers carried him there. Grimes was taken across the Potomac River to Shepherdstown and was there during the battle of the 17th. Command of the regiment passed to Captain William T. Marsh.

McClellan was only eight miles from where Nat and the men were resting and watching the movement of the Federals, but it took them forty-eight hours to get into position. By then General Lee had his regiments ready for McClellan's advance.

James Steele related what the band was doing as the battle opened on the 17th:

Next morning about 10 o'clock General Anderson, who commanded the brigade, formed line of battle on a big long hill parallel with his line of battle and marched almost to the foot of the hill. Then he told the Band to go back to the field hospital, and as we marched up the hill we could see the Yankee army column coming on the side of the other hill facing us and filing off to their left, forming line of battle fronting our Brigade. We stopped on the crest of the hill to look, but General Anderson saw us and spurred his little bay horse up the hill and told us again to go to the field hospital, and just then a bouncing shell came from a Yankee battery, and struck nearby, so this and General Anderson, together, got us back to the hospital, where our place was during a fight.[3]

Nat's letter continues:

The night passed away quietly, but on Wednesday morning Sept. 17th, as the sun rose fiery and gloomily midst dust and smoke, the booming of cannon begun. Shells and solid shot came whizzing into town shattering the houses and creating a sudden and frightful panic among the inhabitants who flocked in squads together and took their flight from the town. It was sad to see so many people deserting their homes, especially for that reason, but in all the uproar and confusion I could not restrain a hearty laugh at the many ludicrous sights presented. Narrow souled men were seen nailing up their cellar and smoke house doors to prevent starved soldiers from taking advantage of their absence and helping themselves to something to eat. It was useless,— I verily believe every door in town was broken open, and, everything that could be eaten was consumed. I saw middle aged women running through the streets literally dragging their children after them; the little fellows had to take such tremendous strides that it seemed to me they hit the ground but seldom. Then came a dozen young ladies, each with a stuffed sack under each arm, some of which in their haste they had forgotten to tie, and as they ran the unmentionables were scattered behind them. I was in need, but could get none that would fit. Of course the most valuable articles were taken, but it is often difficult to determine which was more valuable; and frequently when they would be half a mile out of town they would think of something that must not be left, and here they would come tilting back for it. Regardless of this consternation the battle waxed warmer, and the cannon shot from the enemy literally raked the streets and battered down the houses. Men and horses fell dead and wounded at every step. The women and children, still in town, were running, crying and screaming so loud that their combined voices could be heard above the roaring battle and the bursting of shells around us. Still our troops pressed on to reinforce their comrades. The enemy fought obstinately, more so than they ever did in Virginia or any where else. They held their positions for the most part, so did ours, until late in the evening by the falling back of both parties at different points the line of battle was somewhat changed, leaving the greater portion of the battle ground in our possession. Night came on and by mutual consent the firing ceased. The wounded were cared for as far as possible, yet their sufferings were most intense. For several days preceding the battle our rations had been very short, and many had nothing save apples and corn and such crumbs as they could pick up by the way. Water too was inconvenient, but the greatest suffering was caused by the intolerable dust. Late in the evening some barns were fired by exploding shells. The flames spread rapidly, and soon the scene of carnage was illuminated by the glare of half a dozen burning buildings, presenting a picture too horrible to attempt description. A gloomy and sleepless night succeeded the day, and a day full of painful anxiety succeeded the night. While the commanders were parlaying over a flag of truce a portion of our men were busily engaged burying the dead and taking care of the wounded, while the main army was retreating across the river, although at the same time, it is said, our Generals challenged the enemy for battle. That night, Sept. 18th, our whole force retreated across the Potomac. Fording it in the pitchy darkness and floundering among sharp and dangerous rocks, we succeeded in getting across without the loss of a single man save the few stragglers that were captured, and our wounded to a considerable number. At 10 o'clock

A.M., on Friday our rear guard crossed without serious molestation. Since our arrival in this State we have had comparatively an easy time — plenty to eat but little marching. For two weeks stragglers have been arriving daily, which with the men are coming in from home and various hospitals, is materially augmenting our regiments, brigades and divisions, and our army is again presenting quite a formidable appearance.

NAT.

[Published in the *Carolina Watchman* October 27, 1862]

Captain Marsh was mortally wounded.[4] Captain Edwin Osborne then took command, but, he, too, was wounded.[5] The officers continued to fall. Near the end 2nd Lt. F. H. Weaver commanded, and he was killed while carrying the regimental colors.[6] As the battle drew to a close, Orderly Sergeant Thomas W. Stephenson, of Company C, commanded the 4th. He survived.

After the battle, Colonel Grimes went into the hospital at Winchester for treatment of his leg. The 4th went into camp on the Opequon Creek near Bunker's Hill, Virginia (now called Bunker Hill, West Virginia), about ten miles from Winchester.

FROM THE 4TH N.C.S. TROOPS.
CAMP NEAR WINCHESTER, VA.,
October 21st, 1862.

Smoke, wind, dust, and a thousand and one rumors are whirling about our ears,— all agreeable enough, but the dust and smoke. We cannot avoid it or find a place where it does not come. Our eyes are sore — our nostrils are clotted, "bunged up," as the boys call it. We sneeze, cough, and hiccough, all to no purpose — matters grow worse, if possible. There is no use growing angry either, but "grin and bear it," is the best philosophy. Not all the rumors are so very agreeable. We have just received the news of the death of our General, George B. Anderson, and Ashe Fraley,[7] Lieutenant in Co. A. Our General died from a wound in the foot, apparently slight, too, received at Sharpsburg. Fraley died of disease, at Staunton, I believe.[8]

During the fighting in the Bloody Lane, a minié ball struck General Anderson in the foot near the ankle joint. The regimental physician did not consider the wound dangerous or life-threatening, and General Anderson went home to Raleigh to recover. In the weeks following, an infection set in, and his foot was amputated. He died shortly after the amputation, on October 16, 1862, almost a month after the Battle of Sharpsburg.

Nat's letter continues:

Aside from this, we have intelligence from the West of the most cheering nature, in consequence of which, our troops are unusually lively. It is true, times are right hard with us; our rations are short and consist of nothing but beef and flour without a particle of salt, excepting about twice a week. These nights are chilly, and our clothing is not sufficient to make us comfortable, with a host of minor privations, each of which, is greater than we ever experienced at home. Still we have abundant reason to be thankful that it is no worse. I need not recapitulate the news from the West — they got to North Carolina before they reached us, and have undoubtedly caused a thrill of rejoicing to arouse every indifferent soul in the old North State. Aye, there may be many indifferent, and no doubt inclined to rejoice over our reverses, but thanks to our Congressmen, the conscript law is a most valuable institution for them. It may compel many of them to see a little service, though they should desert and make their homes in caves and rocks and the mountains; an experiment which a dozen or more from our regiment are trying now. It is even so, and this is how it happened. Three or four days ago we received orders to get ready for a march at short notice. Our small rations were cooked, knapsacks packed, cartridges given out until every man was supplied. Companies A and F were sent out on skirmish, and the remainder of the brigade was held in readiness to march at an instant. Besides these preparations, the wagons and sick, cooks, &c., were sent to the rear. — Thus things remained until near sunset, when we were relieved, partially, by orders to "rest on our arms that night." The time passed on, but little sleeping was done. The darkness was intense, and a fine mist was falling; every thing favored the deserters. They decamped about two o'clock, on the morning of the 18th inst., and have not been heard from since. Various conjectures are afloat as to the motives that induced them to leave. Some think they are gone to the lick for salt, — some that they are attempting a flank movement on the enemy on their own hook; — others think they are bound for home, since one of them has been much distressed about a gourd full of whiskey he left there, and "his wife might drink it all before he got back, if he staid till the war ended"; another wanted to train some young hounds to hunt possums, and so on. But the most plausible theory is, that they did not like the signs of the times during the day preceding. Well, in truth, those cartridges, burnished bayonets and gun barrels, and whetted swords, did look suspicious; but the next day passed quietly, though ready to march, and that evening brought the welcome news that the enemy had retreated across the Potomac, and the unexpected news that a parcel of our conscripts, including two or three old soldiers retreated "the way Ward's ducks went."

NAT.

[Published in the *Carolina Watchman* November 3, 1862]

· 3 ·

CAMP NEAR STRASBURG

Nat's letter to the *Watchman* from the Strasburg area, published November 24, covers a period of approximately three and a half weeks.

From the 4th North Carolina.
ENCAMPED IN SIGHT OF STRASBURG, VA.,
Nov. 14, 1862.

During the month past we have been kept marching constantly, so that we have scarcely had time to drop "a few lines" to our "duck," much less time to write a letter to a newspaper. But I shall attempt it this morning, though I doubt very much whether I get this page full, with all my haste, before the drum rolls to fall in. D. H. Hill's division has quit soldiering and begun working out railroad contracts. It is a fact; we have made "a clean husking" of the Harpers Ferry and Winchester railroad, not having left a cross tie or straight bar of iron on it: Nothing remains of it but ashes and bent rails.[1] About Charlestown, famous for being the place of John Brown's execution, we had to be right sly about it. The work of tearing up and burning was done one rainy night while a heavy force of pickets and skirmishers were sent out ahead. We ventured within two miles of the Yankee outposts, within six miles of Harpers Ferry, and from that point to Winchester utterly demolished the road.

Destroying a railroad track is hard, backbreaking work when done in ideal conditions and is doubly so when done in a cold November rain that soaked the men's uniforms and chilled their bodies. Rails were pried loose from the crossties, and then the heavy wooden ties were placed in piles of twenty to thirty. The iron rails were laid on top with a few crossties to hold them in place. The piles were then set ablaze, warping the rails in the intense heat and making them entirely useless.

Nat continues:

Whence we went by a number of circuitous marches to Front Royal, where we were kept three days and nights hourly expecting a battle. On the last evening of our stay in Front Royal, Nov. 6th, we were drawn up in line of battle on a knoll about a mile North-west of town on the Winchester turnpike, and within a quar-

Strasburg, Virginia, in the Shenandoah Valley, was under Federal occupation in March 1862. Like many other small towns in the South, this rural community was suddenly thrust onto the national stage when northern and southern forces clashed there. (Frank Leslie, *Famous Leaders and Battle Scenes of the Civil War* [New York: Mrs. Frank Leslie, 1896]. ClipArt used by permission of the Florida Center for Instructional Technology, College of Education, University of South Florida.)

ter of a mile of the Shenandoah river to our rear. The evening was exceedingly cold and disagreeable. Black flying clouds were scuding across the sky from the range of mountains westward, while a piercing wind chilled us to the bone. It was almost impossible for us to get any kind of wood to burn, everything having been consumed by both Federal and Confederate soldiers who had occupied the ground at various times from the time the war first broke out. Still we managed to gather up a few old rails from the desolated plantations around which served to give us a glimpse at least of a fire. There we stood, shivering around our small fires, expecting every moment to hear the first cannon fire that should announce the opening of the contest.

The regiments were standing in the cold, in line-of-battle, because the division commanders had received word that a Federal force was advancing on the town of Paris, and the soldiers were in readiness for a rapid advance to meet them.

Nat continues:

> The sun went down and as the night grew dark and cheerless, the vast amphitheatre of mountains around us were dark and dismal, except a few spots occasionally illuminated by a few straggling rays from the half moon, which now seemed more distant and colder than ever. Our fire did us but little good, since gust after gust of wind would scatter the blazing pieces of light wood like sky-rockets in the air. At 9 o'clock at night a muffled drum was rolled and we were ordered to fall in quickly, we did so, wondering what in the name of Heaven could be up now. But we were not long kept in suspense; soon the dark mass ahead of us were moving toward the river, and then for the first time it flashed across our minds that we would have to wade the stormy river. Horrible idea! But there was no use halting and talking; the fact is we were allowed to do neither until we were on the bank of the river when an ominous pause was made. Col. Grimes (now in command of the late G. B. Anderson's brigade) rodd [sic] across the foard and back again several times in order to find the most shallow place. Soon he had found the best foarding, when he came back to the same side that we were on, and two rods from the land he sat on his horse full five minutes, dreading to give the command, and we dreading as sorely to hear it. Delay was useless, and reluctantly the Colonel gave the order "forward" upon which those in advance plunged in; we soon followed and, — oh! ugh! Nah!! It takes my breath to think about it. Well — if we are ever immersed it must be in the summer time when —
>
> > "The pool beneath the weeping willows,
> >   Looks cooler, fresher, purer,
> > As the drooping shrubs, and withered corn,
> >   Beseech the clouds for water."
>
> Once across — and that was indeed a serious business, the river about one hundred yards wide and on average two feet deep — we were marched double quick about two miles, halted, told to camp and build fires of anything we could find.

Crossing the Shenandoah River created hard feelings between Grimes and General Robert E. Rodes, and it would be 1864 before the two patched up their differences. Unknown to Grimes, General Hill had placed Rodes in temporary command of the division while he was away. At the river Rodes had ordered the men to keep their pants and shoes on while wading the river. Grimes thought the order impractical, feeling the men should carry their clothes so they could quickly have dry garments on the other side. Thinking they both held the same rank — brigade commanders — Grimes expressed his opinion to Rodes and received a sharp rebuke. In effect, Grimes had questioned the orders of his division commander, no matter that the rank was temporary.

Nat continues:

No sooner were the arms stacked and accouterments off, then a fence close by began to disappear. Everybody was scrambling for rails and "in less than no time!" the fence, as a fence, was numbered with the things that were. An amusing incident occurred during this rush for rails that will bear relating. Every body thoroughly wet and shivering with cold; then of course the main object was to get a fire as quickly as possible, and it was evident that a few rails would not extend very far in a brigade of men. Quick as thought one of our fellows fixed his bayonet, placed himself in front of two pannels and commenced walking his post; soon quite a number of boys out of our and other regiments pitched in for the rails, but the words, "Halt, you must not take them," rather surprised the boys, especially so since Col. G had told them to burn them if they chose to do so. Most of them were satisfied with the "halt," but the sentinel had to bring his piece to a charge bayonet occasionally and threaten to report his visitors if they persisted in taking the rails. Finally the fence was swept for hundred of yards on both sides and to the two pannels still untouched. The self proclaimed sentinel was still pacing to and fro before ****while the crowds had dispersed and were gathered in groups, gents di disiabile around blazing fires scattered in all directions thro' the woods. "The Col. surely wants them for some particular use," though I, although, had some suspicions:—A minute later I was convinced of the sentry's motive when he called out lustily, "Ben I say you, Ben. Tell those boys in our mess to come up and get these rails; I've had a h__ll of a time with them; I'm freezing and want to warm some." Presently Ben and some half dozen other fellows made their appearance and carried away every rail. There was not much sleeping done that night. We were up all night drying our be-drenched clothes and fixing for the snow-storm which was evidently approaching. As daylight dawned on the next morning everything presented a dreary aspect. A dead calm prevailed while the clouds hung out, dark and lowering. By 8 o'clock, A.M. thin flakes of snow began falling a few here and there at first, but before noon the air was filled with snow falling thick and fast. At first we had not a shelter of any kind whatever, but towards evening a few tents were brought in; not enough though to give more than half of us even their frail protection. Those of us who had comfortable clothing and good shoes fared bad enough, God knows; how much worse then for those who were barefooted and but thinly clad, and that number was not a few. We have never known, until now, what suffering was. We have never before experienced any thing to compare to it. Surely the soldiers of the old revolution of '76 could not have had it much worse. Is it any wonder they should ardently long for the restoration of peace! That they should sigh for the luxuries and comforts of home, and above all, its quiet! Still at the present time, and under the present circumstances there is no possible chance for us to realize those blessings; and to all indications it is not likely that we will soon however much they may be desired. But we hope a brighter day is dawning. At any rate we can considerably mollify our condition by submitting patiently to our ills.

This distressing war can surely not last forever, though it may in all probability last for a year or two longer. We have borne it thus far, can we not bear through to the end? We may expect great hardships and suffering and must prepare for them at home and in the army. Our rations may yet grow shorter, our little allowance of salt may fail entirely, prices may go higher at home, and it may become more common to see helpless children begging bread for themselves and widowed mothers, but we pray God in mercy to expand the hearts of the wealthy in proportion as the wants of the poor and destitute increase. We know there are speculators and avaricious men throughout the South who are sucking the very life blood of the poor — God for some wise purpose allows it for the present; while he holds poised over their heads the most direful vengeance and fearful retribution.

NAT.

[Published in the *Carolina Watchman* November 24, 1862]

Nat's words are a sad commentary on the human condition that in the direst circumstances of war, when everyone should be working together for the good of the country, there are those individuals who seek to make money at another's expense. The following article, which was published on February 24, 1863, in the Raleigh newspaper *North Carolina Standard*, comments on this:

A Good Example. An esteemed friend writes us from Stanly County, that Mr. Alexander Misenhimer and Brother, who own mills in that County, and have a good supply of wheat on hand, are grinding it up and selling it to soldiers' wives at ten dollars per barrel, when they could get thirty-two dollars for all they can grind within sixteen miles of their mill. This is practical patriotism. Honored be Alexander Misenhimer and his Brother, and their children and their children's children! The poor soldiers whose wives and little ones they are supplying with bread, will hear of this and bless them. And when the battle is joined again, as joined it must be, they will strike with a steadier arm and a stouter heart, for they will feel that they have some friends who remember them, and who are caring for their families while they are risking everything for their country. Our friend adds that the two gentlemen above referred to, were both Union men up to Lincoln's proclamation.

And now for A Bad Example. A correspondent informs us that on the 13th day of this month, in Catawba County, at an administrator's sale by E. Yount, Esq., administrator, some wheat was put up in lots of two bushels each to accommodate the poor women who were present, when a certain person bid against the women and bought the wheat for speculation — thus taking the bread out of the mouths of the poor. We are also informed that this person who bid off the wheat owns a share in a mill, and as soon as the exemption bill passed, he discharged his regular miller and crept into the mill himself, in order to avoid the conscription.

It is useless to denounce such a person as the one above described. His hide is as thick as a rhinoceros, and his soul, if he has any, could easily waltz into the skull of a mosquito.[2]

As the months passed, the *North Carolina Standard* instituted a column called "The Honor Roll," which highlighted individuals who sold items at very low prices to the wives of soldiers, while at the same time refusing the higher prices from speculators. The Honor Roll contained many names.

· 4 ·

CAMP NEAR FREDERICKSBURG

On November 27, 1862, the brigade was camped near Gordonsville, Virginia. Brigadier-General Stephen Ramseur had replaced Grimes as brigade commander. No one questioned Grimes' ability to lead or his courage on the battlefield, but General Lee preferred trained West Point graduates as his brigade commanders. Grimes remained in command of the 4th, and because Ramseur was absent wounded, he also remained as temporary brigade commander until Ramseur arrived in early 1863. The two men would become fast friends, and when the brigade was in winter quarters, their wives would join them.

On December 3, Jackson's Corps moved to Port Royal, Virginia, and remained there until December 12. Nat's letter describes the snowfall experienced there. The Corps marched the night of the 12th to reach Fredericksburg. On the 13th, the day of the battle, General Hill's Division was held in reserve. The 4th did not engage in the action, but suffered twenty-five casualties from Federal artillery fire.

Following the fight, the 4th went into winter quarters on the south bank of the Rapidan River. Nat's following two letters begin at this point.

FROM THE FOURTH NORTH CAROLINA.

A squall approaching — Cooking Stove — Unexpected Orders — Taken down a button hole — Preparing to comply — Slightly sentimental — Domiholes — A catastrophe — A smashed horn.

There is something in the wind; whether or not it proves to be all "wind" and "entirely without foundation," we shall see, — For the last two days and nights, we have heard occasional firing to the Northeast, the direction of the Rappahannock. Sometimes at the dead hours of midnight, these ominous sounds disturb our slumbers; 'tis then that it makes us feel uneasy. During the day time we pay no attention to them. The weather has been cold, windy, rainy and every other ugly feature imaginable; and to make ourselves more comfortable, we (my mess) bought us a capital little cooking stove just one week ago, around which we were gathered to-night at eight o'clock, congratulating ourselves on our good fortune and good times generally, when to our utter dismay, a courier stepped to the door of our tent, and said, "Pack up and be ready to march at a moment's notice." Gracious! how our feathers were clipped! Such a crew of black countenances and chop-fallen faces it is hardly possible to conceive. Our jolly chat was suspended, the smoke ceased to ascend in "dizzy wreaths" from our pipes, and we sat full three minutes staring at each other as if we had been doomed to perpetual night. "That's the dickens again," says J. as he mechanically took his stumpy pipe stem between his teeth. "Now that we are comfortably fixed and can laugh a stormy winter, we cannot get to enjoy it." "It is too bad — too bad! But this is war for you, and when shall it be any better?" "There is no necessity for grumbling, boys," I remarked, "and the best we can do is take it philosophically, and make the best of a bad bargain. It will not always be so, and the day may not be far distant when these hard times will be over, and we can look back with pleasure to the fortitude with which they were borne by us. Cheer up, and let's get to work." And we did "get to work;" — cooking rations, packing our knapsacks (throwing away such articles as we cannot possibly carry, besides being of little service,) burning our letters, &c. Now, "Nat" has one, (a letter of course,) — no, he cannot commit it to the flames yet, — he don't think its time has come; at any rate, he will risk "one eye" on it for a few days. It is now ten o'clock at night, orders to march are not yet issued, but we are momentarily expecting them. We need not conjecture about the future, the past is a sealed book, from whose pages we can blot nothing, — the present, then, is all with which we have to do. But, judging from our past, we have reason to look forward with dread forebodings. Not that our army is not brave, or may be defeated in battle, or any thing of the sort; but the suffering, hardships, and the heartrending scenes incident to battle, all of which we are compelled to witness, that make us quail at the thought of an approaching conflict. I would caution my readers to be prepared for any kind of news; the storm may blow over without a fight, but I do not think it. Though we are poorly supplied with tents, yet most of the men have constructed shelters of some kind. Most of them are caves dug in the side of a hill on which we are camped, and covered with sticks, leaves, dirt, &c. But these holes are right dangerous things, as one of our boys found out to his sorrow. This was the way if it: A few nights ago we were requested to go serenading some distance from the camp. To be sure we went, and a magnificent time we had too. The small hours of midnight were creeping on as we entered camp on our return; but as our quarters were on the opposite side, we had to pass through the entire regiment to get to them. It was intensely dark, and knowing the hill to be full of uncovered caves, (domiholes not finished,) we had to be very careful where we set our feet. But with all our caution, my dear friend, John T., made a misstep and tumbled heels over head in a hole about six feet deep. I heard the rumpus, and turned to render assistance, but being fearful of a similar fate, I "cooned" it up to the verge of the "hoil," as they are generally termed, and bawled out, "Hello! Who's down there." "Oh, Nat" said he, "I believe I've broke my leg." "Plague take your leg," I replied, "what about your instrument?" He only gave a doleful groan, and handed the instrument up to me. It was enough,—if it had been mauled a week, it could not have been mashed flatter. Don't think that my friend was top-heavy—not that—but he will run into such places sometimes.

Nat.

Near Fredericksburg,

Jan. 23, 1863.

[Published in the *Carolina Watchman* February 2, 1863]

From the Fourth North Carolina.

The old fourth is still in the neighborhood of Fredericksburg. This week we made a move which for suffering beats anything we have ever seen. Fortunately for us, it was soon all over. On Tuesday last, at 3 o'clock, P.M., we were ordered to get ready to march immediately. An attempt to describe our feelings would be useless, enough to say we were awfully bored. During the night and day snow had been falling without a moment's intermission, and at the time we began our march the ground was covered six inches deep, and still getting deeper. But there was no use trying to shirk it, (and I am proud to say but few attempted it,) the trip must be made. As darkness began to settle on us we set out, loaded like jack mules, and trudging in snow half knee deep. "Good God," thought I as I went half bent against the wind and sleet —"this is soldiering in earnest." "How much more could a man endure and live?" "All my philosophy avails but little now. Something uncommonly must be up or they would surely not take us out on such a night as this. But if I only knew where we were going; hope we will travel all night, if we don't, and have to make our beds in this snow and tempest, besides, some one will freeze sure." Thus I soliloquized, and a great deal more. I verily believe "a preacher would have sworn." I looked around on the desolate hills and plains covered with a vast winding sheet of snow. I could see dark masses of troops moving in front and rear of us, and could not help contrasting ourselves with the French army in Russia. "Can this be America, the boasted land of freedom, or is it the domains of a military despot." "Are these the peaceable citizens of America or the tools of some tyrant." Such reflections were spontaneous, I could not banish them from my mind. I confess that I came nearer "caving in" than I ever did before, but with a mighty effort I was able to quell these rising feelings of discontent, and, in short, succumb. The labor necessary to get us through the snow soon brought on copious perspiration; mile after mile was slowly counted off as hour after hour of the night wore away. We were not allowed to halt for rest, which was certainly a wise precaution, though it bore dreadfully hard on us.

Finally, we came to a bold running creek with icebound banks, but it proved no obstacle. Without slacking our gait we plunged in, stumbled across and crawled out on the opposite side, considering it a capital thing. What a pity our dear mamas didn't know we could stand water so well; for lack of knowledge they have certainly missed a wonderful chance of rare fun. But wouldn't it have been rich for them to play "mother duck" while we would have been goslings—ducklings, I should say; if I mistake not, a gosling is a little goose, except when we mean human goslings, of which I have seen a few for sartin. But this is the wrong road;—

ah, that is my failing, I hope my readers will excuse, and in the future I will endeavor to stick closer to my text; though a bad one, yet I will expatiate from firstly even unto seventhly — I'm sure they are at liberty to leave church in case they become wearied. Away we went, (after we got across the creek,) not such a breakneck gait either as you might imagine, but we toddled, I'll say that, but I doubt anybody knows how fast that is. Well, we toddled on some two miles further when we were turned into shanties already built, and recently vacated by a portion of Hood's troops. Our surprise was great and agreeable — the move was, after all, decidedly to our advantage. I very readily took back all that I had thought or said during the march, and made a firm resolve never again to be dissatisfied with anything, no matter what, which I did not fully understand. Roaring fires were built from the wood prepared by those who lately occupied the cabins, and in half an hour after our arrival all hands were snoozing comfortably. The next morning we awoke, and at first thought that we had got home on furlough, or were out visiting, or something of the sort. Things presented such a comfortable appearance that we were right sure we were not dreaming, or the subjects of some trick; but soon we were convinced that all was bona fide; a glance out of the doors was sufficient. The snow lay deep on the ground, but the air was milder, and rain was falling in one of your regular drizzles-doozles. So was it the next day and the next. The snow disappeared leaving a world of mud and water, and an hour by sun on Thursday evening, February 19th, the last vestige of a cloud disappeared from the sky, and the atmosphere, though hardly pure, was perfectly transparent. We could see Fredericksburg, poor Fredericks! about a mile distant. We could trace the meanderings of the Rappahannock, and on the bluffs and table lands, occupied by the Grand Army of the North, wondering no doubt whether this is the road to Richmond. Old Burnie tried this rout once; it didn't pay. Fighting Joe Hooker now has a notion of trying it awhile. I should not be surprised, if six months hence, he should exclaim as did the Arkansas belle at the close of a frolic — "Here I've sot, and sot, till I've about tuck root, and nobody didn't come." Richmond, I guess, will be like the grapes were to the fox, sour, therefore not worth striving for. Our regiment is at this time on picket down on the banks of the river — they will return to-morrow. True, the pickets are not allowed to shoot at each other, but all intercourse is forbidden, — both wise policies. The former is barbarous in the extreme — the latter can be productive of no good in the long run — none to our enemies at least. A month ago our boys were on picket near the same place; then free intercourse was allowed. As might be guessed, the rebels made it pay, and any quantity of tobacco was swapped off for five times its worth in coffee. Newspapers were exchanged, canteens and overcoats bought for a trifle, paid in tobacco, of course — the yankees are crazy as bedbugs for it. A good many letters were sent across to be mailed; New Yorkers and North Carolinians would discuss "the prospects" for an hour, then shake hands and part mutually well pleased with each other. The yanks say they are heartily tired fighting for the d____d negroes, and don't care how soon the affair is wound up; and if the privates had the management they would soon wind it up. In a tour from camp, I discovered many traces of the battle recently fought here. The trees are shivered by shells and cannon shot; the saplings, in many places, are riddled with bullets —

some were shot entirely off; fences scattered, houses demolished, and everything looks like it is fast hastening to ruin. The most revolting sight of all is the half buried men. These are of the enemy — our own were decently and well buried. There is a place, not very far from our camp, where seventy-seven of the enemy were tumbled into one hole — a few shovelsfull of dirt were thrown on them and that is all; their partly decayed bodies now lie exposed to the gaze of passers-by. What a shocking thing! If they have been our enemies, they now certainly deserve the respect due to dead men. How many whose bones are bleaching there, not long ago left home full of lusty life, and left there, too, mothers — doating mothers, loving wives, gentle sisters, or little prattling boys and girls, or lisping infants.— Harrowing thought! Go, leave me!

The night is fast going, and gusts of wind have caused my candle to melt and run down the bayonet, used for a candle stick, thus depriving me of at least an hour's light. A bright fire is sparkling in the chimney, and as it burns that strange phenomenon, "tramping snow" is going on briskly. I should not be surprised if we should have more snow to tramp before many days, but no matter, we are well prepared for it, provided we get to stay here. We do everything according to military science out here; we have musket barrels for pokers, (there are not a few scattered over these plains,) ramrods for pothooks, parch wheat and pound it in a skillet with the breech of a gun — in fact, a gun has something to do with almost every thing we do do. No wonder the boys seem so much attached to them, and spend so much time keeping them in order. Still the time is not more than half occupied with all necessary duties. The intervals are spent snow-balling when there is snow on the ground, if no snow then "Bull pen," "cat," etc., is the order of the day. I hardly ever hear any one say, "I do wish this war was over"—"When do you think we will have peace" and such like; we don't bother our brains about it, well knowing that anything that we can do will have but little effect towards shortening or prolonging it. We have an easy time, (except on marches — I must admit that it don't pay to have our feet clogged with snow) we get rations abundant, and good, too;— pshaw! If nobody were suffering more than we, why we would consider it a happy time generally. But the trouble is I can't get to see Gemima, nor can Gemima get to see me, and I'm afraid she will take a fool notion to pitch into somebody else or somebody else into her.

NAT.

Night of Feb. 21st, 1863.

[Published in the *Carolina Watchman* March 9, 1863]

· 5 ·

HOME ON FURLOUGH

Camp Near Fredericksburg, Va.,
April 1st, 1863

Left Salisbury — Behind times — Raleigh Seminoles — The effect — Richmond — In Camp — All O.K. — Concert and Ball in Salisbury — More rude boys — Times dull — The Dance — Why I didn't — A surprise ended with a night's march — Who ought to dance a Schotish — Jemima again.

It would interest my readers to know something about our trip home to this place, and about this I shall write first, though I have many other things about which I must say something as soon as an opportunity presents itself. Well, then, on Tuesday night the 24th ultimo, the whole 4th N.C. Band, with the exception of Charles _____,[1] who procured an extension of ten days, got aboard the train at Salisbury bound for Raleigh. We traveled "slow march tune," and, as was expected, fell behind and "missed connexion" at the place, the Weldon train having left an hour before we drove up on Wednesday. — When we found that there was no help for it, we sagely concluded to "lie over" till eleven o'clock that night; accordingly we jumped aboard an omnibus, and at half past eleven A.M., alighted at the Exchange, a fourth of a mile from the depot, and for the ride, don't you think the cussed mullato had the audacity to charge each of us one dollar; — no use to growl about it, so the best we could do was to pay the yellow scamp — thank our stars it was no worse, and determine to walk back that night. — That's economy for you. We got a right good dinner reasonable enough, ($1.25,) and the afternoon every fellow spent according to his own tastes, some, I fear, rather on the wrong side, others not altogether so bad. For my part, I desire to see the strange, the wonderful and the beautiful, induced me to visit, first, the Lunatic Asylum,[2] then the Institution for the deaf and dumb and blind, and lastly, the Capitol. I'm not so sure that Dr. Fisher[3] thought that I was going to take lodging in the first, but I guess I didn't though: — any way, I consider myself richly paid for my afternoon's trouble, and in the future will have something to say about each. At sunset in the evening, according to agreement, the Band met at the Exchange and began playing. Before we closed the second piece the side walks, yards, gardens, pailings, and even the very streets were jammed with an appreciative audience. Not gentlemen and ladies, nor men and women, nor white nor black, nor man, nor

beasts — what in the name of common sense were they then? you ask; — a cross
between wise-acres and — and — and, our "colored brethren" — an amalgamation
of two races, the extremes of color and intellect — Raleigh Seminoles, or what will
convey the idea better, Mongrels — in short, good reader, Mulattoes — not a "brack
nigger" was to be seen among them all, and if I should say five hundred souls of
the aforesaid species, were congregated, I don't think I would "stretch the blanket." What a slamming encomium on our Capitol and the vultures who flock there!
Nevertheless, I speak truly; we always take notes as we journey through this howling wilderness, seeking not "whom we mought kill somebody," but something to
write about. Since I have promised to keep the readers of the *Watchman* and the
Express posted in matters of general interest, why I shall do so to the best of my
ability, so long as I am favored with opportunities to mail my letters. I know that
many of my friends have never seen the Capitol of our State. I mean the town
around the capitol building, (it is well worth a trip) and no doubt many would
like to visit the place; not in the capacity of legislators, senators, governors, or
even editors, or their wives, but merely a social visit, or one for curiosity's sake.
Now, take a bachelor friend's advice, and if you ever do allow such a fool notion
take possession of you, don't fail to provide yourselves with an abundance of "torch
pine," it is plenty round there, and "light up" when you enter; if you don't, you
will think a perpetual twilight reigns there, or the sun is in an everlasting eclipse,
or something of the sort, all the effect of so many copper-colored descendants of
Pochahontas strolling about. Apart from these, there are, doubtless, many pure
Anglo Saxons residents in the town, but unfortunately, they kept themselves close
while we were sojourning in their midst. It is true, a score or two of "genuine
white" ladies and gentlemen ventured within sight of the outskirts of the yellow
rabble around us but the fact is, they had no showing at all, and retired, satisfied
with a "long range" peep at the elephant — so did we at the close of the third
piece. Ate supper, took a nap, (very much needed too) and at midnight found
ourselves comfortably seated in the ladies' coach and whirling on towards Weldon. At eight o'clock, Thursday morning, we arrived in W____, took breakfast
off an empty table, and plates filled with the same stuff. Half an hour's rest, and
we were again rolling on for Richmond, where we arrived at sunset the same evening. Ran the blockade of guards, put up at the Spotswood,[4] got transportation
and passport, and after all, found ourselves seated in the theatre before the per-
formances began. I am sorry that I didn't have an opera glass, for the lack of one
I certainly missed the cream, at any rate, a tall, lank, half witted, bushy headed
Confederate officer sitting in front of me, seemed highly amused with one. Wonder what he saw when peeping through it? But then it was the first he had ever
had in his hand — I'm sure of it, because he invariably put the wrong end to his
eyes. I think I shall get a pair of chuck-a-luck boxes, or some pieces of tin gut-
tering, and use them with results equally satisfactory the next time I visit the theatre in Richmond. However, an ear trumpet would be much more useful; this
jumbling, and muttering, and lisping, and disgusting affectation in some of the
actors and actresses, is absolutely insufferable. The show closed at midnight, we
returned to our quarters, slept, and early on Friday morning we were aroused to
make the train for Fredericksburg. The morn was cool and frosty, but the large

crowd on board kept our bodies comfortably warm. At Ashland, seventeen miles from Richmond, we stopped and got a hot breakfast, bolted down, then on again. At 11 o'clock A.M., we were landed about a mile and a half from camp, walked out, and on our arrival were greeted with shouts from the old 4th, that made the welkin ring.

And now we are in camp once more, right glad of it too. We find it the same as of old. The time is spent drilling, guard mounting, dress parade, trying experiments in cooking, singing, telling yarns, &c., and it passes rapidly. I am sometimes bothered considerable to determine whether I have in fact been at home, or whether it was all a dream. But it must be; we have surely been somewhere — if not at home, why close about there. We have distinct recollections of the concert and serenade in Statesville, and also of the concert and ball in Salisbury; and frequently speak and dream about them. They constitute the source of the most pleasant recollections which will surely accompany us to our graves. But I should devote one page at least, to the "spree" in Salisbury — it richly deserves notice. And, before I forget it, or not have room, allow me, in behalf of the Band, to return our warmest thanks for the efforts made by friends, both known and unknown, to contribute to our happiness and pleasure. It seemed as though they could not do enough for us — they spared neither pains nor expense. Individually, they made lions of us; collectively, a herd of them.— There was too much flattery, and certainly more than we deserve. But say, Julia, don't you think there was one bear in our crowd?

"Oh, yes, that party, I must close
What I've begun while genius glows,
And prompts within to write."

We were much pleased to see so large an audience of youth and beauty, and middle age, assembled in Murphy's Hall on Monday night the 23rd ult., to listen to a specimen of the music we have in the 4th N.C.S.T. We are, no doubt, a hard looking set of customers, (who would not be after a two years' life in the woods) but music has a wonderful effect in soothing down a rough exterior.— we hope it did so for us. The concert was put through in a creditable style, each player performed his part admirably, and the audience, I presume, was stupefied with our sublime music. Hard to tell though which produced the greater effect or drew the most attention, the band, or the gang of illbred, noisy boys in front of the stage,— to say the least, a very bad comment on the parental training of the rising generation in Salisbury. With the exception of these precious boys, our audience was mute as statues — no cheers, no clapping of hands, nor throwing flowers, like in Statesville, where the music seemed to have an exhilarating effect, here, it seemed rather depressing. And this feature existed — this feeling of unconcern prevailed during the entire night. This was the case with a large majority of those present, while the minority were in a state of feverish anxiety to have the concert over, and the dance begun. That time came at last, to the joy of many who were anxious to

"Trip the light fantastic toe."

My limbs did not feel very supple, from the fact that I have been trudging a knapsack for a long time; and if they had been, why, my army brogans was an obstacle unsurmountable, so I contented myself with the more profitable, if not more agreeable occupation of forming new acquaintances and renewing old ones; with all of whom, I was exceedingly well pleased, and finally, with one of the latter class, undertook a night march, of which I fear some of the incidental results proved rather mischievous. "All right," we say, and here goes. Upon my return to the Hall, I found everybody, in general, dancing with a vengeance. "Perhaps you only thought so" says somebody; well, I do know there was a considerable uproar in the house. The Band struck up a schotisch when half a dozen couples or more "pitched in." I admired the attitude, the steps, the giddy whirls, the collapsing of crinoline, etc., etc., but grew light-headed, wondering why they didn't, so wisely come to the conclusion that it would never do for me to attempt it, until I was first put through "squad drill." Since then, Jemima and I have been practicing the attitude, and other preliminaries alone, and verily, I believe we have improved on the inventor. This, of course, was done privately; we are resolved never to appear before the public until we are both on the same side of the broom stick, feeling assured that none but such should dance a schotische. At the peep of day, or may be a little while before it, the ball busted up, and

> "Ere noon are closed those hazel eyes,
> While beauty's self in slumber lies,
> And dreams that all is well;—
> But first, that braid,—that golden foil—
> Those scallops, ruffles, garments, all
> In grand confusion fell."

NAT.

[Published in the *Carolina Watchman* April 13, 1863]

· 6 ·

CAMP NEAR
FREDERICKSBURG AGAIN

In the first letter below, Nat expounds on the line of poetry, "I resolve to be merry and gay," and speculates what the next three months will bring — "our land will tremble with the shock of mighty armies." In the second he describes remembered scenes of home that are contrasted with a severe downpour and the desolation he calls "these battle-farmed plains around Fredericksburg." When he composed the first letter, the Battle of Chancellorsville was almost a month away. When he wrote the second one, the battle was only four days away, and the 4th was doing picket duty on the banks of the Rappahannock River.

> **From the Fourth North Carolina.**
> **Near Fredericksburg, Va.**
>
> "To be happy, and pass life with pleasure,
> Is a secret 'twere well all would treasure:
> If the sky be serene, or o'er shaded,
> If the bloom from the roses has faded;
> Tho' of fortune the Fates may bereave me,
> I resolve to be merry and gay,—
>   Time travels too fast
>   To be sad or o'ercast,
> It is wisdom to laugh while we may."

This is our logic — it ought to be of every soldier. What is the use of fretting of things over which we have no control. Contentment is truly the great secret of happiness. Though it is hard for us to bear up under many of the crosses we have here, yet it is undoubtedly best for us to wear a cheerful exterior, and make the best of our lots under all circumstances. Here, if a man is humorously inclined, he can always find something to laugh at; on the other hand, if he is of a morose and gloomy temperament, rest assured that he can find enough to render him most miserable every day of his life for ten years to come. He will grumble about his rations, consider them not half enough; he has to perform a great deal of unnecessary duty,—his officers use partiality, or neglect him entirely—his company of sergeants and corporals are a set of "bigheads," he could do better himself, with a thousand such foolish notions. All nonsense; they are the instruments of their own unhappiness, and are not to be pitied. It is no wonder that such fellows have never had any favors shown them. They do nothing to accommodate their associates, are even ill and overbearing in their dealings with them.—They are half hypochondriacs; and when they do in fact get sick, the surgeons, disgusted with their former hypocrisy, pay very little attention to them, and to talk of getting a furlough is absurd. These are the men who write those "doleful letters from the army." But the effective portion of the army is composed of such men as think—

"Let the wide world sit as it will,
We will be gay and happy still."

They are the first on duty, always cheerful, popular with their comrades, and first when favors will be shown. Depend upon it, the man who maintains an even temperament in the army will do to tie to.

Every thing remains quiet on the Rappahannock. True, we have had orders to send all our surplus baggage to Richmond, i.e., all that we cannot carry, and make ready for an arduous campaign. We are expecting marching orders, but where to, is impossible for us to tell. The tents of the Yankee army are as thick as ever beyond the river, and almost every afternoon a huge balloon ascends from their midst. The man in the basket takes a peep at the rebels and then descends to communicate some valuable intelligence to Fighting Joe, no doubt. Whether he is pleased or not with all he sees, we can't tell, but he takes good care to keep out of range of our guns along the river hills. A storm is gathering evidently, and not here only, but at several other places in the South. Ere another three months roll around, our land will tremble with the terrible shock of mighty armies. Oh, how anxiously we look forward to the result! Our destiny is in the hands of an all-wise God—we can but hope that in the future He will favor us as He has done in the past. If our cause, indeed, be just, we will surely come off conquerors in the end, through we may yet see much tribulation, and "wade through seas of blood."— We cannot expect Heaven's blessing on the ground that we are universally a God-fearing people, or even because a majority of us are so, which is certainly not the case; but a certain city was once spared because a few righteous persons were found within its limits; so, with our nation—our homes—may they be spared because of the few pious souls still left in our midst. I hope to God that not all are gone astray—not all become filthy. God's hand now lies heavy upon us—His chastenings are sore and grievous; but surely we are not all Pharoah's or his descendants that our hearts should grow harder! Our trust lies in the christian people at home—what if the large majority should be women, our mothers, our sisters? On their prayers hangs our salvation.

It is so now that we can hardly realize our situation. We have so long been in the army that we are almost induced to consider it a necessary part of life; and the wickedness heard & witnessed every day has grown familiar, it does not shock us now as it once did, we pay no attention to it. To say anything about it is folly, instead of doing any good it brings down a cursing on our heads; the best we can do then is to stand aloof ourselves, hoping that the day is not far distant when we shall be more agreeably situated.

    April 8, 1863.

NAT.

[Published in the *Carolina Watchman* April 20, 1863]

From the Fourth North Carolina.
CAMP NEAR FREDERICKSBURG,
April 28th, 1863.

    Storm and sunshine — Visitors from the South — A stray butterfly and its message — All quiet on the Rappahannock — Fish cutting and the result — Don't be alarmed — Advice wanted — Alarm in camp — A demoralized tent — The alarm accounted for — Scenery around camp — Yankee outrages — Sunset — More conscripts — Universal good health.

    After two days and nights of storm and rain yesterday dawned on us clear and pleasant enough, except a blustering gale from the South West. But during last night even that shifted, and calmed down to a pleasant breeze directly from the sunny South, which to-day brings us the sweet odors of the lilacs and violets; — of the orange tree and hawthorn bush. Accompanied too by visions of green meadows, blooming orchards, verdant landscapes, and impenetrable forests clad in their luxuriant summer foliage. We can hear the glad songs of the ploughboy at his work, and the merry tinkling of the cow bells on the green hills; and can imagine that we see swarms of butterflies one of which has certainly strayed beyond its latitude and paid a visit to these battle-farmed plains around Fredericksburg. Ah, my pretty yellow fellow! You have come to cheer us in our troubles, and speak words of encouragement to our hardy solders. Faith, and you are a fit emblem to represent the fair daughters of our dear country; and I opine if you could speak, your sentiments would be about the same as theirs, would they not? You love flowers and sunshine, — so do they, and your flitting noiseless way of getting from place to place reminds me much of the sweet human butterflies at home! You say, "courage brave boys; our souls are with you though our fragile bodies are not, " so they say, and we are proud of our company and feel honored by it. But go; beautiful insect, go to your flowery home; the obscene songs of camp, the thunder of artillery and clash of steel is not fit music to you, neither is it for the fair creatures you represent. Go, but carry this message for us and deliver it safely to your gentle keepers when they chase you from the morning flowers to pluck them for their own bosoms, —

"Thine eyes will see these flow'rets fade,
    Thy soul, its idols melt away;
But oh, when flowers and friends lie dead
    Love can embalm them in decay;
And when thy spirit sighs along
    The shadowy scenes of hoarded thought,

Oh listen to its pleading song —
  Forget me not, forget me not!"

But the all absorbing question with everybody is "What news?" — none of importance. The old 4th is now on picket five miles below, near the banks of Rappahannock. They will return to-morrow and re-occupy the same old quarters I presume. We have indeed a fine time of it, not much to do, and abundance to eat, the two most important items with a soldier. Each morning every seventh man in the regiment is allowed to go fishing, and when they return at sunset, the same number are allowed to go for the night if they choose. A few are caught with hook and line, but the great mass are caught with dip nets, which are bought from the citizens around. The result is fish in superabundance, mostly shad and herring, the former weighing on an average four pounds, the latter about one. We draw from the commissary enough fat bacon to fry them, which being "done up brown," with light bread, rice, coffee made from the same grain parched, and sugar, make a capital meal. We do not fool away time to pick the meat from the bones, but swallow all together; if they lodge, an old moldy biscuit (a lot of which are always kept on hand for the purpose) forced down with a ramrod removes all obstructions; besides checking a digestion too vigorous, and thereby producing a wonderful sense of relief. Numerous minute fish bones are protruding all over the surface of our bodies, so much that we look like huge cylinders for music boxes. There is no danger whatever of being "scourged" at night, (it will be better before we come home on furlough again) but what in the world are we to do about changing our linen? This is a mystery that we cannot solve, and would like to have the advice of sympathizing friends on the momentous subject.

One night last week our camp was thrown into a blaze of excitement about the rumored advance of the enemy below us; and it was said that they were crossing the river in heavy force. Orders were issued to be ready to march at a moments notice, (that is the general way of expressing it) upon which the usual consternation was visible. A frightful storm was howling around us which made it almost certain we would march, — such is invariably our luck. We lay down and slept, well knowing the long roll would wake us, provided they would want us to march before day. The wind slashed our old demoralized tent about until it was as badly torn as Lou's dress was when a "black racer" chased us in the strawberry patch, but now the consequences were of a more serious nature. The rain dashed on our faces, the little ditch around our tent was overflowed, and if we had not set our feet against small stumps we would have been washed to the foot of the hill; but we pulled the blankets over our heads, turned over for another snooze, and when we awoke it was daylight, or as nigh as it could be beneath such black clouds. The rain had not slacked a particle, but our suspense was in a measure relieved by others for the brigade to go on picket, which it did at 9 o'clock A.M., leaving the band in camp a favor for which we are under obligations to Col. G. The preceding alarm was not altogether false, but greatly exaggerated. A small force of the enemy had crossed the river and fallen afoul of our fishing parties, scaring them out of their wits, (some I guess hadn't far to go) capturing four wagons, two of which they burned, took their nets also, and scattered the frightened fellows to the four winds, but took no provisions. After the rascals had done all this mischief, which upon the whole was rather ludicrous, they beat a hasty retreat to the other side of the river. Since then all is a profound quiet; no warlike demonstrations, nor anything indicating a move. Far in the distance beyond the Rappahannock may be seen whole plantations full of yankee tents, and every day that everlasting balloon is up. Our camp is located on a piece of high-lying land, I can hardly term it a hill, but from my tent door I can see over a very large scope of country. Partly because I am some what elevated, but more because the timber is swept clean from the surrounding neighborhood. Due North six miles lies Fredericksburg, the spires of which may be seen rising about the intervening pines. In flourishing times the town looks like it might have contained seven or eight thousand inhabitants, now not more than two or three hundred of the original denizens can be seen. The lower part was burnt a few days before the late battle; nothing is left but some blackened walls and solitary chimneys. The reminder of the burg is riddled with shot and shells, the upper part especially looks like a ruin, a few words will convey the whole idea, a grave yard and bat roost. The citizens are refugees scattered throughout the Confederacy.

On the right of the town for a distance of six or eight miles we can see the opposite bank of the river from our camp, extending like a wall in an easterly direction. Immediately beyond the river and rising abruptly from it are the barren hills recently vacated by the enemy. On this side is the low-land; it extends down the river as far as it is possible for vision to reach, and up to a point just above the village where the hills close in. The plain, or rather the upper end of it is the battle field, and lies about four miles from the spot where I am now standing. Westward is an extending tract of that country, now grown up in weeds and grass, but in times of peace it groaned beneath the weight of grain. There is at this time a large field of wheat about the centre, and green as a meadow, but not a vestige of a fence around it; however, that matters not, there is scarce an animal in this section save such as belong to the army. Just beyond this plain rises a chain of undulating hills, barren now from necessity, but evidently covered with a rich soil. This range extends from Fredericksburg to Guinea's Station, near twelve miles and at intervals of half a mile or such matter are fine farms, (or have been, they are deserted now) on most of which are dwellings that once well deserved the title costly; the out houses, fence pailings, &c., are, in almost every instance, demolished. Along the base of this range, and in full view runs the Richmond and Fredericksburg Railroad, at the nearest point about a mile distant. Beyond these low hills and further to the right rises another set, higher, but destitute of the fine groves of oak which crowned them a year ago; they are now covered with rebel tents which at this distance look like an immense flock of sheep. South of us dense thickets of dwarf pines and cedars obstruct the view beyond a quarter of a mile; but eastward the scene is unbroken, and for miles we are greeted with the sight of gently rolling hills and fertile valleys, sprinkled over with neat farm cottages. The citizens were as a general thing, quite wealthy, and cultivated their farms in a skillful and scientific manner. Their homes and the pleasure grounds around them were decorated with clambering vines and the most beautiful shrubbery which nature produces; the waving wheat and rustling corn imparted an air of thrift and comfort to the whole land, and the people were happy. But alas! all has been swept away from the scorching breath of the god of war, and now this looks more like a desert than a habitable portion of the globe. A few nights ago I spent two hours with Mr. Dickerson, a wealthy citizen, living a mile from this place. He says that near a year ago the enemy took from him twenty young negro men and eight women, leaving some thirty old decrepit men and women and useless little children. They took also every horse, mule, ox, wagon and cart that could be found on his plantation, besides killing his poultry, hogs, cattle and sheep. This they said they did out of revenge, because the old gentleman's son piloted Stewart's cavalry on their famous raid on the Pamunky last spring.

This is not an exception by any means. Mr. D told me of a particular case in Stafford county (just across the river) — A gentleman whose wealth was considered almost unlimited had every thing he had in the world stolen from him, and now, said he "The old man has to toat his fire wood upwards of a mile."

But these outrages do not spoil the beauty of the landscape, or mar the sublimity of these charming sunsets. The last rays of the King of day as they linger on these romantic hills have a soothing, a sweet influence on every lover of the beauties of nature which is absolutely indescribable. O, I love these scenes, I dearly love them! In spite of my hardships and disagreeable mode of life I love them still!

Yesterday we receive thirty-six conscripts in one regiment — and I hope the last installment from the Old North State, for a season at least. Like the fellow who got drunk on punch — I say "too much of a good thing is enough any time." These men all from the western part of the State, though but two or three from Iredell, and perhaps the same number from Rowan. I am not personally acquainted with a single one of them all. They do not look so hearty and fresh as our soldiers, and from all appearances I hear but few will prove to be of much service. The officer in charge said he started with forty-two, but six escaped from him by jumping from the cars while they were running.

I hear but of a few cases of sickness, and the alarm about the small pox has entirely subsided. I never saw men in better health and notwithstanding the gloomy prospects of an early peace the troops are cheerful and full of sport. The flattering indications of an abundant crop, and the assurance that their families will be provided for, tends greatly to produce this effect.

NAT.

[Published in the *Carolina Watchman* May 11, 1863]

· 7 ·

CHANCELLORSVILLE

Two of the following three letters were written for the *Carolina Watchman* and one for the *Iredell Express*. Nat's disgust at the harrowing scenes and brutality of the battle is evident, as is his compassion for the dying soldier in his care. He describes Stonewall Jackson's appearance just before the battle.

From the Saltillo Boys.

On Picket — Unexpected Orders — Fog — Turning the Flank — Battle Line — Stray Shells and their Effect — Yankees After Us — A Close Shave — A Night in the Pines — The Wilderness — Great Battle at Chancellorsville — Wounded and their Merits — Woods-fire — Men Burned Alive — The Battle Field, &c., &c.

The regiment had been on picket a week, the band, cooks, &c., left in camp as usual; when at ten o'clock on Thursday night, Apr. 30th, we very unexpectedly received orders to join our regiment with all possible haste. We bundled up, and after an hour and a half's rambling in the thickets bordering the Rappahannock, we found our boys, all busy fixing for a march. During the day preceding heavy cannonading had been kept up, and a few of our men killed and wounded. — On Friday we expected a great battle; — it is no wonder then that we were astonished at the unmistakable signs of an intended evacuation. Orders had been issued in camp to burn and destroy every thing that could not be moved; and the troops I discovered were throwing away every thing they had except for the clothing they had on, and a change of linen in their knapsacks; also excepting their arms and seventy-five rounds of cartridges. Besides these they carried their haversacks, stored with three days rations. Who couldn't "smell a rat?" Feeling very tired I lay down and the next moment I was sound asleep. At 2 o'clock I was aroused — Oh, Heavens! my kingdom for a little more sleep! 'Twas useless to think of it, but shaking my stupor off I shouldered my knapsack and began the march with the others. Some thought we were going to Guineas, some to Hanover, others to Culpepper and so on; but when we took the road for Fredericksburg all came to the conclusion that we did not know where we were going. — Some asserted that the road led to a certain nameless place full of sulphurous odors; — if so, this was not the broad way, but a kind of by-path, as yet unexplored, and full of holes, into which many a poor fellow stumbled. To add to our difficulties a thick fog made the darkness almost visible,—but ere long day dawned, which indeed we had a reason to thank God for his kindness in shrouding us with such a dense covering. We discovered, too, that none of our conjectures about our route was correct, and that instead of going to any of the towns above mentioned, we were only endeavoring to outflank the enemy; and had it not been for the friendly fog a tempest of shells would have met us at every turn. The Yanks could not see what we were up to, neither could they hear, since every man was cautioned to make as little noise as possible. While the thousands were passing, a person two hundred yards from our road would not have had the least intimation of it. By noon on Friday we were out of any great danger. We were halted and drawn up in line of battle, say a fourth of a mile from the enemy. One of our regimental surgeons was sent with his retinue (consisting of the band) to a house half a mile back to await orders, or the arrival of wounded. So far everything was perfectly calm,—the quiet was even oppressive,—it foreboded no good. We remained until 4 o'clock P.M., when orders came to move forward. The surgeon left, telling us to come on as best we could. We traveled about five miles, making inquiries of every one we saw, but none could give us any satisfactory information concerning Rhode's [Rodes'] division. Night came on, and with it an irresistible desire to rest and sleep. All agreed, and some fifty yards from the road we built a huge fire, around which we piled ourselves promiscuously, and slept profoundly until daylight on Saturday morning. Soon we were up and off again; and three miles further up we got wind of our division, which we learned, was lying in line of battle about a mile ahead. Knowing the aversion which doctors generally have for these unwelcome visitors usually called shells or bombs, we felt sure that our surgeons would come back and make their headquarters at the dwelling at which we were then halted. So confident were we in this belief that we remained there until 3 P.M., when having not seen or heard from our brigade we concluded to go forward on the line. Meantime two or three small battles had been fought since noon, in sight of our position, and near the exact spot where we thought our brigade was placed. Battles they would have been termed in the days of the old revolution, but now it is nothing but skirmishing. We do not apply the word battle now-a-days to anything short of a "skrimmage" where not less than ten or fifteen thousand men have been killed or wounded. Fast people—we are, truly! But to resume;—when the firing somewhat abated we took up our beds (and board) and walked out within a few hundred yards of the battle ground. We had scarcely halted ere we learned that our division was eight miles to the left and still going double quick. The command "right about" was useless, for the next instant a shower of shells were thrown at the ordnance train (ammunition wagons) standing nearby. They (the bombs) exploded above our heads, scattering fragments uncomfortably near us. These had a wonderful **** and concluding at once that the atmosphere was unhealthy about there, we "cut grit" and made remarkably good time for about two miles; urged on for the first half mile by messengers from the same quarter bringing the same news. When well out of danger we reined up, blowing like young steamboats, and for an hour took it more moderately.—When three miles from the scene of our glorious charge to the rear, we halted in a nice shade beneath some cedars, slung knapsacks, lit our pipes and lay down for a rest. We had been there perhaps half an hour, when we were alarmed by the clatter of musketry a short distance in our rear, and soon afterwards a hundred skirmishers came snorting along, and bawling out to us — "Run for life, — the Yankee cavalry are after us in sight." They never slacked their gait, but tumbled on, pell mell, in worse confusion and more frightened than a flock of sheep when chased by hungry wolves. And let me assure you, kind reader, we did not need a second bidding. The chase that followed was more amusing than the first; — it might well be termed "scientific skedaddling," and was kept up for the next mile and a half, when we came to a place known as the "Old Tavern" or "Wilderness Tavern."[1]— Here we came up with reinforcements, unfortunately, of the same stripe as ours, viz: frightened skirmishers. But our force was sufficiently strong to repel any attack which a squad of Yankee cavalry might see proper to make. This, in Virginia's palmy days, seemed to have been quite a public place.— Four roads met, the first leading to Spottsylvania [sic], the second to Orange, the third out to the plank-road and up to Culpepper [sic], and the fourth back to Fredericksburg. On each road couriers were sent to order back all wagon trains, which by night were congregated in considerable numbers around the cross roads. Danger threatened us from all quarters; but soon after nightfall our squad ventured up to the Orange road about a mile, then turning square to the right, we entered a dense pine thicket which we penetrated some two hundred yards, where we spent the night in dread apprehension of a fight or surrender before morning. During the afternoon we had heard distinctly the roar of battle but a few miles to our right and front; and not knowing exactly what to make of it, and dubious about the result, it is not surprising that our slumbers were none of the sweetest. But Sunday morning, May the 3rd, dawned on us, clear and serene, and we were still living rebels. At an early hour we set out, and by a circuitous march found our brigade hospital about 10 o'clock A.M. The great battle at Chancellorsville was then raging in all its fury; the very hills shook with the thunder of cannon, and the sun was clouded with immense columns of smoke rising heavenward. Our hospital was located at "Wilderness Church," around which had been a very severe battle on Saturday evening preceding. Dead men, and horses, shattered artillery carriages, clothing, and, in short, every conceivable article of plunder lay scattered thick over the adjacent fields. It was but a mile down the plank-road to where they were then fighting. It was Sunday, but no one thought of it, or cared. Fresh troops were hurrying up to assist their exhausted comrades, and among the thousands that went pouring forward, not a straggler was to be seen; all seemed cool and determined. They had been well fed, well rested, well clothed, and now they felt ready, willing and able to plunge madly into the bloody work before them. The artillery went rattling on, raising clouds of dust as they rushed along — even the horses seemed "to smell the battle afar off." All was excitement, hurry and tumult. At noon the firing ceased — the wind bore the tidings onward — The victory is ours. An hour later, and the wounded begin to arrive,— the butchery begins, and amputated limbs are tossed carelessly about,— wounds are probed, balls extracted, the blood besmeared soldiers are washed and all made as comfortable as circumstances will allow. My dear readers, you can never do enough for these brave fellows, never! never! If you could once see a battle field, or a hospital near by;— If you could see their faces burnt with powder,— broken arms dangling by their side,— clotted masses of blood hanging in their hair, or the life-tide gushing from ghastly wounds on their bodies;— or hear them beg for help, or one drop of water;— then would you think them more worthy of love and kindness?— I have seen it, and more than I dare attempt to portray.

The enemy was driven back, but obstinately contested every inch of ground. At 1 P.M. the fight was resumed, and continued with unabated fury until long after night's dark pall was spread over the blood stained earth. Then to add untold horrors to the scene of carnage the woods in which the battle raged after noon caught fire, and being very dry burnt rapidly. Many dead bodies were scattered through the thick underbrush, and not a few wounded. These could not be brought out, but were left to their horrible fate. True, the greater portion of the dead and living who were thus burned in one awful funeral pile were our enemies, but, that signified nothing.— Their bodies burned with a crackling noise and a **** that resembled many pine knots; and the screams, the unearthly shrieks made the night hideous. Great God! Is this war! Then deliver us! Oh, spare us another such harrowing scene.

On Monday morning I visited the spot where our regiment fought. The fire had not got on that side of the road, and they lay as they fell;— in every posture imaginable, but mostly

> "With their back to the field
> And their feet to the foe."

The greater portion of them I could recognize, but some were so mangled as to render recognition impossible. The woods through which they charged was torn up with shot and shell most frightfully. A hurricane could not have slashed down the timber worse. Some have told me that the crash of falling trees could be heard above the dread roar of battle. Scarce a shrub or sapling is left standing, all are shot away.— The wonder with me is, how a single soul could pass through and live.[2]

NAT.

Fredericksburg, May 11th, 1863.

[Published in the *Iredell Express* June 4, 1863]

From the 4th North Carolina.

The Battle at Chancellorsville — The Charge — Destruction among men — Hospital and wounded — An affecting incident — Suffering — What becomes of the whiskey?

Soon after sunrise on Sunday morning May the 3d, 1863, the first cannon fired that announced the opening of a most terrible at Chancellorsville, ten miles above Fredericksburg. I shall not attempt a precise description of the country, or define the positions of the various brigades and divisions of the Confederate army; all I promise is an account of what came under my immediate observation, and such incidents as I can prove to be actual facts. On the two days preceding the great battle the two armies were marching about three-fourths of a mile apart and prob-ably, each endeavoring to out-flank the other. Incessant skirmishing was going on between them as they advanced in a south-westerly direction from the river. At this point our division (once D. H. Hill's, now Rhode's [Rodes']) being in front succeeded, by a night march, in turning the enemy's right flank, and on Saturday swept like an avalanche down on their rear. After a sharp contest the yankees fell back some four miles to the heights at Chancellorsville where they strongly entrenched themselves during the night. On Sunday morning our division received orders to storm the heights. They advanced in solid column, presenting a scene awfully grand. The lines extended at right angles with the plank road running from Fredericksburg to Orange Court House, and the left of our brigade rested on this road. Our regiment was on the extreme left of the brigade, and as they advanced came directly in front of the enemy's batteries. The first Virginia, or "The Stonewall brigade" was in front of ours; and on Saturday evening, I am told, did good fighting; but on Sunday morning could not be induced, by threats or promises, to budge out of their position. Ours (Ransom's brigade)[3] was then ordered to charge over them which they did without waiting for second orders.[4] The woods through which they ran — literally ran in the charge, was thickly set with trees of ordinary size, saplings and underbrush, and gently descending to a brook, immediately beyond which were the breastworks. As they advanced the roar of artillery and small arms was deadening; and the shower of shells, grape, canister, solid shot and minnie balls that were hurled among our boys was truly appalling. Men were falling on all sides — sometimes whole ranks were swept away, but those who were unhurt rushed on heedless of the groans and piercing cries around them. The crash of falling timber could be heard above the combination of unearthly noises; shells bursting in the face did not intimidate men, nor impede their progress, and not until they were within ten paces of the earthworks did the hosts of the enemy turn and flee from them.

After the firing (which lasted about two hours) at that particular point ceased, I went to the hospital three-fourths of a mile back, and by 11 o'clock A.M. the wounded began coming in. Here is where we could see the melancholy fruits of war. Never since the war began have I seen so many men severely wounded, or so many amputations necessary. The work of butchery began about noon on the same day and continued with little intermission until ten o'clock the following day. Arms and legs were scattered and tossed about with utmost indifference, wounds probed and dressed, balls extracted, and the sufferers made as comfort-able as the nature of the case would possibly admit. Details were sent on the bat-tle field to pick up blankets and yankee tents, overcoats, and in fact anything in the world that would prove useful. Such articles lay scattered in the greatest con-fusion over the surrounding hills and fields. Our hospital was located at "Wilder-ness Church" around which was a fine grove of pines. Outside these were large fields, cultivated last year, but now fenceless, desolate, and torn into great fur-rows by the maddening wheels of artillery hurrying to and fro; and lying at inter-vals of a few rods over these fields were dead men and horses, slain in the battle on Saturday evening. The few of our men who had been killed were buried, but those of the enemy (and there were not a few) lay festering in the sun. Half a dozen of these loathsome sights lay within fifty yards of the spring out of which we procured water for the use of our men at the hospital. I noticed on the various battle fields that nearly all the enemy's dead were stripped of everything save their underclothes. This is a barbarious practice against which I have ever protested. Sometimes it may be excusable, but certainly not now, since our men are abundantly supplied with the very best of clothing. This hankering after "yankee blue" is not a good sign by any means. Taking off a pair of good boots or shoes, I don't think, is an unpardonable sin, but to go further in the stripping line smacks too much of Canibalism.

But to resume:—A sufficient number of portable tents were brought off the battle field to shelter our wounded, and blankets enough to make all comfortable. The night was spent ministering to their wants as best as we could, but I could very easily perceive that we were all miserable comforters; sweeter voices, gentler hands, more assiduous attention than ours were needed, and often piteously longed for. How often were my feelings harrowed by such expressions as these:—"Oh, if I only were at home;" "I would give all but my life for a soft bed;" "something to eat!—can't you give me something besides meat and crackers to eat?" I thought my feelings were thoroughly steeled, and that I could stand anything unmoved, however shocking it might be; but I must confess that one man made me feel awfully bad, and ere I was aware of it I felt a warm tear rolling down my cheek. This man belonged to the 14th N.C., but by some mistake had been placed in the department of the 4th. I first saw him late in Sunday evening, but was so much engaged with others that I paid no particular attention to him further than to see that he was resting apparently easy, and to examine his wound. I found the ball had entered an inch below the breast bone, and at a glance I felt convinced that he would die, perhaps before morning. His mind was clear, and he seemed to talk with ease; he did not consider his wound dangerous — said he felt no pain, and expressed a great desire to sleep. I carefully adjusted the blankets around his body and left. During the night I went to see him two or three times, but always found him as I left him at first. Once I drew down the blankets and felt his breast, to see whether he still lived. I found that he breathed as calmly as though he was in good health and enjoying a refreshing sleep. Soon after daylight on Monday morning I called on him again, he was awake and in quite a lively humor, though much weaker than I had ever seen him. His features struck me, as being very peculiar and really handsome. His face was rather long, a fine mustache, close set but short whiskers, and silky hair, all coal black, and the last, longer than is usually seen in the army, clustered in curls about his temples, and high forehead now bloodless and white as marble. From appearances I would suppose him to be twenty-three years old — I made some inquiries about his welfare, and was assured that he was doing finely. After a few jocular remarks, I was called away and did not see him again until two o'clock in the afternoon, when he called me to him as I was passing near. From the moment I first saw him he had been lying on his back with his legs perfectly straight; he had never so much as expressed a wish to change his position, but now to my question.

"What will you have?"

"Turn me on my side, please," he replied.

"No, my friend, you cannot stand it; try and content yourself the way you are."

"Well then, wont you raise my knees up, and draw my feet towards my body?"

"O yes, I'll do that," and went to work; but I knew from his restlessness that his last hour had come. I put my hands under his left knee and raised it well up; when I released my hold his foot and ankle remained stationary, but the remainder of his leg slid away over it, and struck the ground beyond. I was perfectly shocked; it was the first intimation I had had of a broken leg besides the other wound.

"Some how that leg wont stand," said my friend, "try the other." The other sat up very well. After a short pause he said,

"Is my left leg broken?"

"It is, but don't trouble yourself about it now."

He covered his face with his hands and heaved a sigh that seemed to tear his heart strings. A moment afterwards he locked his hands across his breast, and said in a faltering voice,

"My leg shattered — a ball through my breast — I must die — what will Fanny do? — poor Fanny!"

"Come now, be quiet; you —

"O God! what will Fanny do when I am gone?"

I saw that he was fast going, but all I could do to console him was of no avail. He could scarcely speak above his breath. I ventured to ask,

"Say, tell me, who is Fanny?"

"She is my wife — a-a noble wo-wo —. I married her last winter — while I-I-I was at home on fur-fur-furlough —"

He lay as if he were dying — he gasped for breath — then rousing himself, he took my hand, and in a whisper, barely audible, said,

"Good by — you've been my best friend — Tell-tell her — Fanny — Fanny" —

'Twas the last he ever said. — I have never learned his name, but he was a whole-souled man. His blanket was his winding sheet; we wrapped him in it and the next morning his body was buried beneath a tall pine that grew near by.

Towards sunset, Monday evening, a heavy thunder shower fell on us. It continued raining all night, and Tuesday and Tuesday night, and on until Thursday evening before it slackened, and then continued cloudy and cold until Saturday. The wounded suffered sorely; we could keep no fire, had precious little eat, and a chilling rain falling incessantly. We divided ourselves into reliefs, one of which was ever among the wounded. The men called for spirits, brandy or whiskey. I went to the Surgeon myself for it; he gave me one quart bottle full, and left two others like it; he said that was all he had — indeed, I knew it was, but he should have had a great deal more. How far will three quarts go among 150 wounded men in a four day's storm of cold rain? Temperance is a good thing in its place: — so is whiskey, and on such occasion as above referred to, it should be used freely. It nerves the men, and enables them to bear up against the despondency which is almost certain to follow under such circumstances, and which, in the absence of stimulating drinks, frequently proves fatal. I don't understand how it is that for the last six months provost guards have been stationed at every depot for a hundred miles around Richmond, with instructions to examine every box that passes the roads and take out any liquors that may be found — ostensibly for the use of hospitals; and now when the hospitals need it most, scarce half a gallon can be found. The guards did their duty well — scarce a box go through without being ransacked. But who got the liquor, the guards or the Surgeons? How long will the people submit to such outrages? Let the men who bring cargoes to the army go well armed, and, if any man dares to open one of your packages, shoot him down — every soldier will back you.

NAT.

[Published in the *Carolina Watchman* May 25, 1863]

From the 4th North Carolina.
CAMP NEAR FREDERICKSBURG, VA.,
May 16, 1863.

All quiet up this way — Stonewall Jackson — some of his peculiarities — Universal grief — The gloomy prospects in Mississippi.

Since the late bloody battles everything has again sunk into more than usual quiet. Once only have we been annoyed with orders to march immediately, and that has been a week ago. The enemy was reported crossing the river at two points, one at or near Port Royal, the other above us some twenty-five or thirty miles. The rumor, like a thousand others in daily circulation, proved to be entirely without foundation, which was ascertained before we began a march, upon which our orders were countermanded. We needed rest, and were very loth to begin another week's campaign, how gladly then did we hail the tidings, "Make yourselves easy; it is all a false alarm!" I need hardly say another word with reference to the battles fought here in the early part of this month. Ere this every circumstance, from the most important to the most insignificant, has appeared in print, and of course eagerly read by the thousands at home who feel interested. The most lamentable event of all of the death of our old hero Jackson. I should not say old either, since he was but thirty-nine, but then his name was familiar to every man in the army of the South as well as the North; to the former a word full of hope and the utmost confidence: to the latter a terror and foreboding some dire calamity. In courage and sagacity few were his equal, none his superiors. In his conduct he exhibited these qualities in a wonderful degree of perfection; hence he is called old. The only time I ever saw him was on Friday of the present month, when I perceived that he had bestowed more than usual attention on his dress, a sign of an approaching battle which I never knew to fail. His coat and pants were of the usual greyish blue, but of the finest quality, and the gold lace fancy work sleeve looked as if it might have been put on the day before; his boots were well glossed and his spurs looked like burnished gold. He wore buck gloves with cuffs that came halfway up to his elbows. I barely got a glimpse of his hat since he carried it in his left hand as he galloped past, while I was on his right, but it was black felt, the height usually worn by officers. I would suppose him to be a little over six feet high, or that much at the least; well proportioned, but not corpulent by any means, and would weigh about one hundred and seventy pounds. He kept his hair and whiskers (very black) neatly trimmed, his moustache nicely curled to the sides of his mouth, but had not made use of a razor for months past. His complexion very fair, blue restless eyes, in fact quite a restive temperament generally;— and a prominent though not a large nose; altogether he was a fine looking man besides being a very good one. He never would have his troops to march or fight on Sunday if it could possibly be avoided; he never failed to attend divine services when an opportunity offered, and on such occasions I have been very near to him, and of course did not fail to scan his features closely. At two o'clock on the morning mentioned above we began the memorable march, by which it was designed that we should out flank the enemy, who thought we were gloriously retreating. A fog had settled down so thickly that we could scarcely see a man a hundred yards away, and marching very quietly we eluded the enemy, and an hour after daylight we were five miles from Fredericksburg, on the Orange road, and eight from the picket lines, our starting point. The whole division was moving, and now, that the greatest danger was over, it was concluded that we halt, stack arms, and rest an hour, during which we would eat breakfast. When troops move from place to place they are marched in "close column four ranks deep" that is four abreast, and as well closed up as it is possible to be. Marching in this manner a division extends along the road about a mile and a quarter, perhaps a little more. Mudholes, creeks, &c., are not regarded at all, and when the command "rest" is given, the arms are stacked at one side of the road. Just so on Friday morning of which I speak. The arms were stacked, and the soldiers lying about at their ease; some were smoking, others washing their faces, or taking a snack of breakfast and chatting gaily over it. Presently we heard a yell in the rear of our division;— nearer it came, nearer — nearer — nearer — "It's Jackson coming," said some one — and the next moment he emerged from the timber on the hill two hundred yards behind us, and came dashing furiously towards us. But two of his staff were with him, one of whom rode ten or fifteen steps behind the hero of a score of battles, the other an equal distance further back; all spurred their horses to their utmost speed. Hundreds of hats were flying in the air, and wild shouts from the troops, as he literally flew onward. He held his own hat in his left hand, and kept continually turning his face first to the right, then to the left, and as he disappeared over the hill in our front, his bald crown was the last we saw of him; little did I think that I never would see him again in this world. He often passed through the army while we were on the march last fall and winter, and his way of going through was always as I have described above. The greatest enthusiasm prevailed among the troops, and the most lusty cheering which moved like a spirit of the wind with him. As a general thing, other generals of equal or superior rank were cheered but very little as they passed along the lines. But the hero is gone,— may his successor prove worthy of trust.

Everybody mourns the death of Thomas J. Jackson, "Stonewall," and the melancholy is made deeper and more lasting when we reflect that his wounds were inflicted by his own men. It seems that Providence has so decreed, and we bow submissively to His will. A mighty pillar is taken from under us, but his death will be bitterly avenged by the thousands of devoted hearts still in the field.

We know not what the result of these battles will be: It appears that our foes are only exasperated by their repeated misfortunes; and now instead of visible signs of a peace feeling at the North, that government, "in its great agony," calls for 500,000 more men! Affairs about the capitol of Mississippi look gloomy; a terrible battle will be fought there, — I cannot see how it can be avoided; and if the Confederate forces should be defeated, and Jackson taken, then Vicksburg must be evacuated or surrendered. — God, defend us!

NAT.

[Published in the *Carolina Watchman* June 1, 1863]

· 8 ·

NEAR FREDERICKSBURG

There is a timelessness in Nat's words in his first letter as he writes of the victory at Chancellorsville and of its terrible toll and the blighted hopes of those who remain at home.

> **From the Saltillo Boys.**
> **CAMP NEAR FREDERICKSBURG, VA.**
> **May 16th, 1863.**
>
> **All quiet here — Our feelings and the feelings of those who more bitterly wail their loss — Broken engagements and blighted hope — Our duty — The return from the battle field — Change camp — Enchanting scenery — Wild flowers — Carried home by music, &c.**
>
> Although nothing of an alarming nature has transpired here since the great battles in the early part of this month, yet I am aware that letters from the army are ever read with the most lively interest by the many thousands who have relatives and friends here. What though their dearest treasures lie buried beneath the clods on the Rappahannock hills; still the hearts of the people fondly cherish the memory of their loved ones, — sad recollections fill their bosoms, — their tearful eyes turn wistfully toward their newmade graves on the battle field, and the names of these dark and bloody spots sink like burning lead into their souls. Ere this sad news of the direful conflict and our victory have been spread in every nook and corner of the Southern Confederacy; while on the other hand, the defeat of the enemy has sounded like a knell through every section of the North. Thousands now wail for the slaughtered dead; — parents for their sons, — wives for their husbands, sisters for their brothers, — what more? But there is an agony greater, a pang keener, a grief more poignant than any of these. When the bright hopes of a brighter future have buoyed up tender hearts during a two years absence, and often soothed at midnight the lascerated feelings, and cheered them when all else was gloom, — to have these hopes blasted in a breath, and the cup of bliss, sweeter because expected, not enjoyed, thus dashed away forever when almost within their grasp. Heavens, it is too bad — too bad! Is it any wonder that young hearts should be crushed, — that reason should totter, — that the young, the beautiful should be clad in the habiliments of the deepest mourning, not to say the most hopeless

despondency? "But," says some one, "it was a great victory." I admit it, and give God the praise; but what shall we say to comfort those who only waited the advent of the white winged god of peace that the nuptial torch might be lighted, — their happiness complete? But now their hopes are wrecked. The past to them seems but a dream, an infant's sunny dream; — the present brings the reality, the fore-taste of blighted expectations; — the future too awful to contemplate. The bonfires, the shouts, the roar of cannon, the delirious joy that will resound through our land when peace is proclaimed will not bring back some of those who left home bound in sacred promises sealed with a holy kiss. That last parting is impressed indelibly on many a broken heart. How oft when the evening dews grow chill, and twilight's shades grow darker, she looks back and with pensive thought dwells on his last good-by: —

> "He turned and left the spot, oh, do not deem him weak
> For dauntless was the soldier's heart, though tears were on his cheek;
> Go, watch the foremost ranks, in danger's dark career,
> Be sure the hand most daring there, has wiped away a tear."

It is impossible to suppress such thoughts; I have but given them vent with my pen. — No one can deny but the rejoicing over the late victory on our part will be dampened by the lamentations of widows and the orphan's disconsolate wailings. How much greater the tribulation among our foes? But in spite of all this tribulation the war does not cease, the carnage is not stayed; and before the people, who have been robbed of their earthly hopes, recover from the shock produced by the first intelligence, the nation will again be plunged into mourning for the loss of more of her brave sons. In all probability ere this reaches you the breezes from the West will waft to your homes the news of another terrible battle — more blood shed, more lives sacrificed. And what can we do to avert the storm now gathering? Nothing — absolutely nothing. All that we can do is prepare to meet it like brave men; God will yet take us safely through — the right, not might, will prevail. These are troublesome times, and we must bear with them resolved to do our duty faithfully.

Since the excitement and uproar incident to battle have died away here, we have been resting — and such sweet rest as only a soldier knows. We returned to the very same spot we occupied for six weeks preceding the battle, and remained there four or five days. The sun shone hot on us; not a shade tree, not even a shrub was left standing; the little firewood necessary to cook our rations was hard to find, and worse than all the water which we were obliged to use was getting very bad, as the warm weather drew nearer. For these reasons, Col. Grimes moved us to a beautiful forest about half a mile distant, a favor for which we shall be under last-ing obligations. This is indeed a charming place; the regiment is encamped in a romantic valley, through which ripples a sparkling brook, while the field and staff, including the band, are tented on the summit of a hill rising abruptly some hun-dred feet above, and completely overlooking the regiment. The little valleys around, and the abrupt round hills are thickly shaded with majestic chestnut oaks, now clad in their richest summer foliage. Twilight is gathering now — it is already so dark that I can scarcely see to write; but still I keep on. The tree frogs and whippor-wills have begun their serenade — we feel like we were at home. No troops save our regiment are in sight, and this Saturday evening everything is so calm, so quiet that we can easily imagine ourselves in a land of peace and plenty, far from the desolating breath of war. Thousands of wild honey-suckles, daises, blue-bells, and other gayer flowers perfume the evening breeze with their sweet odors; — we lack but human flowers to make this a paradise. — An hour hence and we will awake the slumbering echoes among these hills with music that for the time will transport us to the happy throng that once assembled in the town hall in Statesville — God bless and spare them.

NAT.

[Published in the *Iredell Express* June 4, 1863]

From the 4th North Carolina.
CAMP NEAR FREDERICKSBURG, VA.,
May 27, 1863.

Prospect in the West — News expected — the great importance of Vicks-burg — Review of Early's Division — Gen. Lee — On picket — Deserted farms — Once in a while a woman — What sort of a dinner?

The summer is passing away and not much doing in our department. But while we are lying about resting ourselves here, desperate and bloody work is going on elsewhere. At Vicksburg especially; how the balmy air over many Southron homes in that quarter has been jarred by the booming of cannon; how terrible and des-perate the conflict; of what more momentous importance to us and to the enemy, is the fate of that beleaguered city, and oh! with what deep anxiety do we wait for the result. But before this reaches you, you will know all, and we humbly trust that a thrill of joy will vibrate in every Southron patriot's heart; that exultant shouts over another victory won will resound from the sea to the mountains, and from the mountains to the sea again; and that every hill top, and valley, and level plain in our sunny land will re-echo the glad tidings of the dawn of peace, for such it will be if Dixie's boys are successful. Under no conditions, upon no con-sideration should that strong hold be evacuated. We can better afford to lose Rich-mond or Charleston, or Mobile, or all of these. Not that Vicksburg is of such vast importance to us directly, but inversely, because it puts the enemy to so much inconvenience. Ere long you may look for stirring news from this army. Though we are inactive now, yet it is evident that extensive preparations are making for a march. It would be imprudent for me to state when where and how, but before another month passes we will certainly be on the move. Gen. Lee is reviewing the entire army by divisions, and, I am told, has expressed himself highly pleased with the condition and appearance of the troops. Yesterday Gen. Early's division passed in review. Early in the morning Gen. Gordon[1] sent our band a note, stating that he would be under obligations for our services in his brigade, on the occasion, as he had no band of his own. Not having much to do we concluded to go, and at noon reported at his quarters. A little cogniac, the General thought, would be good for our frequent infirmities, and accordingly placed a huge decanter full at our disposal, — of course it was monstrously slighted and treated with silent contempt, but somehow there was some tall blowing done during that evening. An hour later we played for the forming of the brigade, and at the head of the column began our march for the lowlands bordering on the Massapony, distant 2 miles. We arrived in the plain at 2 P.M., and in a field one and a half miles long by one wide the various brigades formed in parallel lines about one hundred yards apart, and leisurely awaited the orders for review. Four brigades belonged to Early's division, each brigade numbering between three and four thousand but this I believe is the smallest division belonging to the army on the Rappahannock. In the course of half an hour Gen. Lee arrived and took his position.— arms presented, drums beat, flags waved, and in one moment this part of the ceremony was over. Next he began his round, and followed by his staff, he galloped along the whole brigade, during which the bands played lively airs. When the General had made his last round he resumed his position in front of the whole division. Each regiment was then wheeled into companies, music in front of each brigade, and thus the entire division marched in front of the old hero, who saluted each flag as it passed by taking off his hat, and exhibiting his cotton scalp to the admiring throng around him. I have never had an opportunity to scan Lee closely. I have frequently seen him, but generally during battle, when everything was so upside-down that I scarcely had time to take care of myself. But I have seen enough of him to know that he is what the soldiers term him, viz: "a bully looking man"— that sentence, in the army, conveys the idea of perfection in full, and is applied to all things indiscriminately. He is rather tall, heavy built, through not fleshy;— pleasing countenance, but few wrinkles, and his hair is as white as a lamb's fleece, not bald at all, but thick set and fashionably shingled; his whiskers and mustache are thick the usual length, and perfectly white. He is an idol with the army, though Jackson was scarcely subordinate in the affections of the soldiers. When Lee is seen on the battle field nobody has any fears about the result. It is said that he has some notion of paying a visit to his home one of these days, provided old Abe has no objections — I will only add that the said home is on Arlington Heights.

Ramseur's brigade is on picket at this time,— left yesterday, and will be absent five days. All intercourse with the enemy is forbidden, no firing at each other, nor shelling is allowed, consequently picket duty is a mere frolic. The weather has been cloudy and cool, but to day the sun shines clear and warm. The few crops cultivated in this region look well, but as a general thing grass and weeds grow rank and tall over the deserted farms. A few citizens are scattered around here, and among the female portion of the population we get to see once in a while a young lady who can still lay some claim to beauty, honesty and decency,— they are exceeding scarce though and keep themselves close; half a dozen ventured out last Tuesday to hear Dr. Wm. J. Hoge, our division chaplain address our brigade.

There is some little sickness scattered through the camp, but so little that it is hardly worthy of notice. I have just recovered from a short spell myself, and feel under a thousand obligations to my companions, to your Surgeons, and especially to Col. G. for their numerous favors and kindnesses.

Dinner will be ready in a few minutes, not so good altogether as we might get at home, but for all that it is first rate, if you call bread, meat, and a camp kettle full of polk and dock[2] anything; it is "bully" in the army. And to-day it comes the turn of two of our boys who are capital cooks, one from Salisbury, the other not far above, and if we may judge from the way they have been swearing and sweating round the fire for the last two hours we may expect a dinner that is "bully" in the superlative degree.

NAT.

[Published in the *Carolina Watchman* June 8, 1863]

· 9 ·

A DEATH IN THE BAND

William R. Gorman was transferred to the band from Company I on February 11, 1863. The muster roll for February–May 1863 states that he was home sick on furlough since November 1, 1862. He died on May 24, 1863. Nat wrote this tribute to him on May 30, 1863.

WILLIAM R. GORMAN.

The subject of this paragraph departed this life in Concord, N.C., on Sunday, May the 24th, 1863, after a protracted illness of seven months. He was about twenty six years old, and, before the sickness, which terminated in death, he ever enjoyed the most robust health. Many weary days have we marched side by side — but he is gone, gone, gone! O, that my eyes were a fountain of tears, and they would flow like a brook; I would then be relieved of this awful weight pressing on my heart. Oh! it seems but yesterday when we strolled over the hills around Manassas, or sported on the beach at Yorktown, or sat by moonlight on the mossy banks of the little stream near the Chickahominy; how can I forget it or him who seemed half my soul. No warmer love than ours ever linked David and Jonathan. How strange that we should have our preferences so distinctly traced in our affections! That we should meet with a few of our own sex, during a whole life-time, whom we love with a brother's devotion. There seems to be an affinity of soul — something inexpressible and incomprehensible. I can boast but three such friends — alas! I could once, now all are gone to that unknown land from whence no traveler returns. The first died of a lingering disease incurred by exposure in the Valley; the second fell in the hottest of the battle at Chancellorsville, and now the last lies cold and low beneath the sod. Gorman was taken ill while we were in Maryland, but with an unbending will he refused to report sick. "A mere brush," he would say, and zealously discharged every duty. He grew worse, and by urgent, and the most importunate entreaties, was at last induced to go to the hospital in Winchester. He remained but a short time and was taken to Staunton, thence to Richmond where he was confined to his bed three weeks. At the end of that time, being "a little on the mend," he said, he succeeded in making his way to Salisbury, his home.

We kept up a regular and highly interesting correspondence from the time he left us until his death. The physicians pronounced his disease chronic diarrhae, and it proved so obstinate as to baffle the skill of the most learned and successful among them. But we hoped — ah, so fondly hoped that he would get well again. His own letters, from time to time, encourage the hope; but under all we could see a current of despondency that often embittered the pleasure felt one moment before.

Words are empty sounds — they can at best bring little comfort, but now they fail entirely to express our feelings. It is vain to speak of what might have been; no storied urn will mark the last home of my departed friend; his body will rest in obscurity beneath the green turf, his name forgotten by his thoughtless summer friends, but his memory shall live enshrined in the hearts of all who knew him as he was.

NAT.

[Published in the *Carolina Watchman* June 15, 1863]

The band members then met to pass a Tribute of Respect. A small committee or one person usually composed these. Nat could either have written it himself or have been part of the committee.

TRIBUTE OF RESPECT.

The deepest gloom and sadness was cast over our small band last evening when the intelligence reached us that Wm. R. Gorman, our fellow member, was no more in the land of the living. Every spirit was so depressed that we felt but little inclined to conversation or amusement; the usual concert at night was omitted — we had no heart for music, and to-day the following resolutions, embodying the sentiments of every member in the band, are adopted without a dissenting vote:

Resolved, That in the death of our dear friend we recognize the hand of an Omnipotent God, and now realized more forcibly than ever the uncertainty of life — the certainty of death, and our utter inability to stay the dread messenger when once sent forth on his errand.

Resolved, That though we are surrounded with the "pomp and circumstance of war," yet we shall mourn for our comrade, and grieve only as brother grieves for brother. We have lost a tried friend — a boon companion — ever jovial, ever kind and generous, whom to know was to love, and one whose talent for music had won our highest admiration and the applause of every officer in the regiment.

Resolved, That we sympathize with his bereaved relatives; — verily they weep not alone for him, who, in the prime of his manhood, has been locked in death's cold embrace; his own bright anticipations wrecked, and with them, fond hopes crushed, and tender hearts broken.

Resolved, That these resolutions be sent to the *Carolina Watchman*, with the request that they be published — though poor, it is the best we can do to testify our regard for him, who has been taken from us.

E.B. NEAVE,

NAT. RAYMER,

CHARLES HEYER,
M.J. WEANT,
J.C. STEELE,
R.E. PATTERSON,
J.G. GOODMAN.
W.A. MOOSE,
T.P. GILLESPIE,
J.Y. BARBER,
W.R.I. BRAWLEY,
G.W. JACKSON.

Members of the 4th N.C. Band, camp near Fredericksburg, Va., May 30th, 1863.

Spirit of the Age please copy.

After the Battle of Seven Pines, William Gorman had written of the dark aftermath of the fighting and his work in the hospital. In reading his words, one can easily picture his fellow-soldier-bandsman Nat serving in the hospital in the same capacity.

After going about three-fourths of a mile I came to an open field behind which death was playing dreadful havoc with our boys I remained some time there, shells and grape and minié balls whistling a lively air around the while, until I saw men to me seemingly countless — coming back. I concluded the thing was up and we were compelled to give way, and I went back to my charge. But I was mistaken. The tide of battle went Yankee-ward. So I went to the hospital and did all I could to alleviate the horrible suffering of the wounded until late at night. Heavens! What sights I witnessed! Piled in heaps lay arms and legs amputated — an awful scene; — while from the bloody masses of flesh went up such piercing cries that the blood almost chilled around the fountain of life.... One hundred, or nearly, of the devoted 4th sleep today the sleep that knows no waking, and 260 are hors de combat, wounded in every conceivable shape and place. Oh! the misery of this fratricidal war! Would to Heaven it would end and that speedily![1]

An excerpt from a letter Gorman wrote that same month:

How calm and still is everything since the grand battle of Seven Pines! Nature smiles so sweetly, the breeze sighs as peacefully, and the birds sing as enchantingly, as though no deeds of blood and carnage have been perpetuated near this now peaceful spot — deeds so dark that angels doubtless wept over the men — for such scenes as I witnessed were enough to make the angels of darkness weep, were such a thing possible. I can't say I was in the battle, but I feel confident that I could have passed through it and not felt half the horror that I did at the hospitals. I remained at the hospital as long as wounded were brought from the field. When I first reached there, several had already been brought in. I noticed quite a number with wounds exposed, and horrible ones, too. One I saw — I don't know his name — had been hit by a shell on the right leg, just at the knee, taking away half his leg; not cutting it off, but nearly splitting it half and half, from six inches above to six inches below the knee — a horrible spectacle indeed. He lay, however, seemingly perfectly easy — not a groan escaped his already ghastly lips. Several lay with wounds exposed, pierced through and through the stomach with minnie balls, upon whose features death had already set his seal, and they too died without a groan. Some had both legs torn off by the shells, from who arose heavenward the most piercing cries. God of Mercy! Such cries! Why the very blood chilled around the fountain of life, and I felt as though I would rather myself suffer their pain than stand and listen at their dying groans. I saw arms and legs amputated, and though chloroform was administered, the pain was so intense it had no effect, and the poor wretches broke the stillness of the night with cries so heartrending that it seemed the very corpses around them trembled. And such shocking sight when the surgeon's task was done — arms and legs piled up like cord wood. No matter how strong your imagination you can't for your life picture a scene so horrible as the terrible scene I witnessed. The regiment lost 375 killed and wounded, and to-day can't start 400 men for duty.[2]

· 10 ·

ON THE MARCH
TO PENNSYLVANIA

After the Battle of Chancellorsville, Ramseur's Brigade was transferred to Major General Robert E. Rodes' Division. The four North Carolina regiments still comprised the brigade. On the night of June 3 the march toward Pennsylvania began.

From the 4th North Carolina.
CAMP NEAR CULPEPPER, Va.,
June 7th, 1863.

Under circumstances most unfavorable that can be imagined, I will briefly and hastily inform you of our whereabouts and how we happened to get here. On Thursday morning, the 4th instant, at half past one o'clock, we were aroused from our profound sleep, not by rattling drums, but quietly, and told to make our way towards Guinea's Station as speedily and as noiselessly as possible. It was vain of us to grunt and growl, or complain of broken rest, or anything of the sort, but knapsacks were bundled up in a twinkling, slung on our shoulders and away we went. At daylight we were near the station, and leaving it in sight to our left we pushed ahead for Spottsylvania Court-House. As the sun ascended the heat became oppressive, and the dust intolerable. But at 3 P.M., we arrived at our company ground, one and a half miles west of the above mentioned Court-House, having traveled about sixteen miles. After taking a cold water bath we lay down for a night's rest with sore joints and aching bones. The next morning we were aroused ere the stars ceased to shine, fell into line, and marched in dust and heat worse than the day before, with a rest of ten minutes in every hour, until 4 o'clock P.M. We were moving in the direction of Culpepper, and at night found that we had marched about eighteen miles that day, through a country mostly level, sandy, not exceedingly fertile, but overflowing with pretty girls who stood along the roadside and enthusiastically cheered us. Of course we had to play occasionally for them, and once a squad of them generously donated to the band a basket of pies, biscuits, and boiled ham. We are called "Tar Heels," and I am proud of the appellation — North Carolina heels, from their adhesive properties, are always put to the most important posts in battle, and they stick or advance; but I am not sure but by-standers would have thought our fingers tarred as well as our heels if they had seen the good things getting out of that basket. It was emptied in the "twinkling of a cat's eye." So, so, we had no time to parley, and away we went in a cloud of dust, munching at our fists full of delicacies, and as saucy as monkeys with red apples. At night we encamped in a cluster of underbrush, and near a stout creek. Half an hour after arms were stacked hundreds of men were in bathing — it is equal to a night's rest. Many feet were swollen and blistered, and every muscle in our bodies was aching from the effects of our unusual exertion; but after the refreshing bath, our nerves were reinvigorated, our spirits revived, and at dark we stretched ourselves on the ground, grateful to God for the little shower that was then falling. The following morning (yesterday) we were up and off at four o'clock. The little rain that fell that night had laid the dust and made fine walking. We drove rapidly for five miles, when we were very unexpectedly turned into camp to await further orders. Some movement of the enemy caused this, but no matter what brought it about, we got to rest our tired limbs. We remained in that beautiful forest until an hour before day this morning (Sunday) when we took up our line of march anew — two hours brought us to the Rapidan river, but it was no obstacle, we pitched in and waded across it as though it had been a spring branch. It was about 100 yards wide, and on an average knee deep. Once across we traveled on without any detention save the usual rest for ten minutes every hour, and at 1 P.M. passed through Culpepper, (town) three miles north of which we are now encamped, having traveled fully eighteen miles to-day. We have recovered from the soreness felt at first, and are now in good plight to travel. The men march remarkably well, not a straggler is to be seen, and so much cheerfulness I have never before seen on a march. I hear but little complaint of sickness, everybody is eager to see what is up. The campaign is open in earnest, and until its close my readers need not be surprised at anything they hear. Something important is in the wind — I know but little of it, and dare not tell that which I do know. But if my opportunities for mailing continue the same as now, you may not lack for information after things have happened — it would not be prudent to tell them before. This country is a perfect ruin —

both armies are trying now, and have been for the last twelve months to make the destruction complete, and they have well nigh succeeded. The enemy is in strong force beyond the Rappahannock, half a day's march from us. A battle is expected to open hourly.

NAT.

[Published in the *Carolina Watchman* June 22, 1863]

Nat completed his letter on June 7. On the day the *Carolina Watchman* published it, June 22, the division was crossing the border of Pennsylvania. In the fifteen intervening days, the division had been in the following places: On June 9 they reached Brandy Station to assist a cavalry action, but the battle had ended by the time they got there. By June 12 they were in Cedarville. On June 13 they moved on Berryville, but the Federal soldiers escaped. Before the Martinsburg defenses on June 14, Rodes ordered his brigades to charge the enemy. Ramseur's Brigade led as the Confederates chased the Federal soldiers on a two-mile run, but again the Yankees got away. Ramseur's Brigade and two others were sent across the Potomac River on June 15, and on June 19 the division was advancing toward Hagerstown, Maryland, where it rested two days before taking up the line of march toward Pennsylvania. On June 27, they reached Carlisle, and on the 28th, raised the Confederate flag over Carlisle Barracks, the Federal Army cavalry school. The barracks would be the northernmost military installation captured by the Southern army. Shortly thereafter the soldiers were recalled to Gettysburg.

· 11 ·

RETURN FROM GETTYSBURG

From the 4th North Carolina.
Camp near Hagerstown, Md.
July 9, 1863.

The last two weeks are big with events of the greatest importance; what the next two may bring to light we cannot even imagine at the present. But of the first I shall attempt to sketch a brief and hastily written outline. I am aware that the readers of the *Watchman* are waiting impatiently, and in the most painful suspense for news from the bloody battlefields in the North and to relieve the anxiety in some degree I will give at the close of this letter a list of the casualties in our regiment, kindly furnished by my friend, J. E. Steele.[1] On Monday the 22d of June, we entered Pennsylvania, by way of the Cumberland Valley, and a more magnificent country I never saw. It looks like a well cultivated garden, and so thickly settled that we were continually travelling in the suburbs of some city it seemed. The citizens are German almost universally, and in politics of the copperhead stripe, that is, for peace at any cost. They live in substantial brick or stone dwellings generally, and on every farm you may see commodious and elegant barns. Small grain is the staple, wheat, rye, barley and oats; but little corn is raised. More luxuriant fields of wheat cannot be imagined, and while we were there it was fully ripe and falling down. The harvesting machines were lying idle in the very spots from which our scouts unhitched the horses and drove them away. Thousands of bushels of small grain will be lost for lack of means to save it. The horses, mules, wagons, cattle and, in fact, everything that could be of any use to us was pressed in for miles on each side of our line of march. The horses, though, are not suitable for cavalry use as a general thing. They are too fat and clumsy for any use, but are peculiarly adapted to the farm. The citizens were frightened out of their wits, whether they had far to go or not I do not pretend to say. Many fled before us and left all they had in the world at our mercy, and those that remained threw their doors open and told our foraging parties to take what they wanted. The consequence was that we fared sumptuously. Our corps (Ewell's) penetrated the State as far up as Carlisle, and some detachments ventured within a few miles of Harrisburg. It was generally believed that the Capitol was the point we were aiming at, but on the last day of June we changed direction, and began our march

86

for Gettysburg; that night we encamped near one of the many small towns in that country, and within eight miles of Gettysburg. During the night some skirmishing was going on, and our troops lay on their arms, ready to move at short notice, but the night passed away and nothing unusual occurred. Early next morning, July 1st we moved forward, and after some manoevering formed line of battle about noon. By two o'clock P.M., the ball opened in earnest and lasted until nearly night, through the burg, and up to the base of a small mountain South-east of the town. The next day the fight began early, and raged furiously until dark. The inhabitants of the town, terrified almost to death, fled in confusion in every direction, seeking safety in cellars, in stone houses, behind chimneys, &c. The window shutters, door signs, and such like in some places were riddled with bullets, but the town was not shelled. If it had not been for the sick and wounded Yankees in town, it would have certainly burned, because union men fired on our boys from the windows. At the close of the second day's fight the position of the two armies was precisely the same as in the morning. During the greater portion of the day I was standing on an eminence on one end of the battle line along which I could see for three miles at least. At the point where the fight was hottest dense columns of sulphurous smoke would rise above the tree tops, shutting from view everything beyond. The roar of artillery and small arms was incessant and appalling to one not accustomed to such sights. But on the next day, July 3d, the last desperate effort was made to dislodge the enemy from the mountains on which they had entrenched themselves during the night preceding. The forenoon was taken up deploying troops and giving the various batteries position. About two o'clock in the afternoon everything was ready, and the order given to advance. The firing began, and for three hours three hundred cannons thundered their death messengers in the opposing ranks. The best writer in the universe could not give the faintest idea of the horrible conflict. The enemy held their position, though our men rushed upon them in their trenches and cut them down with their swords; — bayonets clashed together, but in vain. Our forces were ordered to fall back, and they did it in good order, but had suffered severely, though at the same time they taught the enemy a terrible lesson concerning the valor of Dixie's boys. The loss I suppose is almost equal, though Northern papers set down their loss greater than ours. 30,000, I think will cover all, including both parties. Below is a list of casualties in the 4th N.C. Regiment;

Com A — Killed — Privates M B Mayhew[2] and R. M. Brawley[3] wounded, Eli Day,[4] thigh severe; J Massey,[5] left leg amputated; M. T. Clark,[6] both legs fractured below the knee; J A Cohen,[7] side slight; M. Snow,[8] shoulder slight; F M Morrison,[9] head slight.

Com B — Killed — none. — wounded — Capt J F Stancil,[10] slight; J M Sides,[11] leg severe; Wm Rainey,[12] head severe; T S Lyerly,[13] leg slight.

Com C — Killed — W M Chipley.[14] Wounded — A M White,[15] slight; I N Crotherton,[16] shocked; M L Arthurs,[17] slightly; H L Lollar,[18] jaw severe; Wm Dobson,[19] shocked; C S Sharpe,[20] slight; C L Johnston,[21] leg severe; J H Hartness,[22] leg severe; J M Rickett,[23] slight.

Com D — Killed — none. Wounded, W H Gurley,[24] leg broken; W Barnham,[25] Andrew Sauls[26] and Jas Scott,[27] slightly.

Com E — Killed — Private J D Litchfield.[28] — Wounded, W F Beal,[29] head severe.
Com F — Killed, W B Nolly.[30] Wounded — Capt. Thompson,[31] slight.
Com G — Killed, G H Cunningham.[32] Wounded, W Clary,[33] slight.
Com H — Killed — Lt J B Stockston;[34] pr Burgess Campbell.[35] Wounded, John Farr,[36] slight.
Com I — None killed or wounded.
Com K — Killed, none. Wounded, O Holtshouser,[37] arm severe.
About twenty missing out of the regiment, supposed to be prisoners; among them are Hugh Hall,[38] Jack Mayhew,[39] _____ Weisenfeldt,[40] A F Goodman,[41] Jas Norton,[42] and Michael Hennessy.[43] On Sunday 5th we fell back to Hagerstown.

NAT.

[Published in the *Carolina Watchman* July 27, 1863]

Lee's army began the withdrawal from Gettysburg on the evening of July 4 and reached Hagerstown, Maryland, by July 7. During these days the 4th Regiment was part of the rear guard and engaged in several brief skirmishes with the enemy. Nat refers to this in the following letter to disprove statements that the army "retired in great confusion from Gettysburg." A line of battle was set, but the Federal army made no attempt to attack Hagerstown. On July 14, Federal soldiers probed the lines, but were driven off by Ramseur's Brigade. The division then waded across the Potomac River that night and went into camp near Bunker's Hill [now Bunker Hill], halfway between Martinsburg and Winchester. Just before the army had advanced into Pennsylvania, the western part of Virginia had broken away on June 20, 1863, to form West Virginia. Bunker's Hill and Martinsburg now lay in another state. .However, the locations on Nat's letters never changed — every letter was always written from Virginia, whether it was withdrawn territory or not.

From the 4th North Carolina.
Camp Near Bunker's Hill, Va.,
July 20th, 1863.

For more than two years the Confederacy has been floating on a current comparatively smooth; nothing has impeded our progress save here and there a snag in the shape of Yankee armies, a few gun boats and such like, but all at once we are plunged into a whirlpool from which I fear we shall never be able to extricate ourselves. The news of the fall of Vicksburg and Port Hudson has started us like a clap of thunder on a cloudless day. We were not prepared for such intelligence. Why have we been told that those places were impregnable, — that they were abundantly supplied with rations and ammunition, and that the garrisons were in such splendid trim? Why have our journalists attempted deception when they knew that the truth must eventually leak out? As yet we have learned none of the particulars; we only know that one of the main pillars under our new government has been removed, and that its removal has caused a mighty tottering among others, the most serious of which is the stagger this blow has given to our currency; it is evidently tumbling, and there is no reason why our officials should shut their eyes to the fact. But it is not expedient for me to proceed farther on this subject at present, still I must say to every observant mind a depreciating currency is the first sign of decay. During the last two weeks a wonderful change has been effected on our men in ranks. — I did not think it possible in so short a length of time; then, bright hopes and prospects buoyed them up and spurred them on; now, desperation seems to have settled on every countenance, and a determination to push affairs to a speedy, perhaps a fearful crisis.

In our department battle has become quite an every day thing. Fighting does not seem to do a particle of good, for no sooner is one bloody struggle over than preparations are made for another. No strategical points are gained by either party, and this way of standing off and firing into each other for days and nights at a time, or rushing on batteries through the horrid hissing of a thousand death missiles don't pay the South: with the North it matters but little; there, armies spring up like Jonah's gourd vine, in one night, — they seem to rise like mushrooms out of the earth. There they have lost near half a million men, but what of that! Their places are filled to a great extent by fresh importations from Europe, while we might as well expect reinforcements from the moon as to look beyond the confines of our own territory for help. This morning I heard "intelligent contraband" say that "de white in de Souf would soon be played out, and de white army was goin' to bust up, den dey would have an army ob niggers an' I's goin to be a major general, yah, yah, yah!" There is no doubt that the negroes in the army hate Yankees just as intently as our soldiers do. While we were in Pennsylvania if any had desired to do so they could have left us, but instead of that they were afraid to venture beyond the sight of camp for fear they would be kidnapped. What conclusion shall we draw from what has been said above? Several; first, that our situation is growing alarmingly critical; second, it is high time some method was adopted by which our men might be saved, and not needlessly sacrificed; and, third, since butchery and loss of life seems to be doing no good whatever, why is it that diplomatists are not at work to bring about a settlement. It is folly for the North or any other people, to talk about conquering the spirit of the South. We admit that by overwhelming numbers we may be temporarily subjugated; and it is a fact indisputable that those who are laboring to depreciate our currency are doing more for our utter ruin than the whole Yankee nation; but granting that they succeed in establishing their abhorrent rule over us, will it be than as a union? The people of the United States remind me of a man who whips his wife to make her love him. In the event of a failure to establish the Confederacy, allow me turn prophet for a few moments, and acting in that capacity I would predict no peace for the South for the next twenty years. Our newspapers would be filled with accounts of foul murders, insurrections, plots and rebellions, — and the deplorable state of affairs generally would be too horrible to contemplate.

But let us turn from the future to the present. It has been said that Gen. Lee's army retired in great confusion from Gettysburg. This is not so, because I constituted a mite in that army myself, and I believe that my opportunities for seeing and learning were as good as those of any man in the army. Some of the divisions suffered severe losses, but I can assure my readers that our loss in killed and wounded was no greater than the enemy's, while his loss in prisoners was much heavier than ours. The principal reason for the falling back was that our lines of communication in the rear of the army were too long and too much exposed, which we learned to our cost. Another reason was the immense number of prisoners in our hands. They refused paroles on the field, or any where else except at Richmond, consequently they had to be guarded back to that place. I saw not less than ten or twelve thousand, and was told that there were other gangs on their way Southward. Instead of "confusion" the whole retreat was conducted with remarkably good order. We seldom traveled more than eight or ten miles in twenty four hours, but those marches were made mostly after night. The main body of the Yankee army attempted to cut us off before we reached Hagerstown, Md., but failed, while small detachments were continually harassing our rear, doing no damage, however, but rather a favor, by hurrying up our wagons and the few stragglers who were behind. One day while we were yet in Pennsylvania I noticed the road blockaded with wagons for two miles. A pelting rain was making the mud and things in general worse every moment. But there were, and had been for two hours waiting for the wagons to get out of the way. The men were getting impatient,— wagon masters were galloping about whooping and hallowing, swearing at the drivers and hurrying them up, but it did no good. Presently a Yankee battery hove in sight, took its position on a hill and began "tossing" shells at the whole train; they bursted and whizzed and sparkled about uncomfortably near, which, some how, impressed on the minds of the wagoners the idea that the atmosphere was unhealthy — and such an everlasting getting away never was heard tell of,— it is well that the train was not loaded with glass ware. The horses were whipped into a gallop, and the wagons seemed to bounce half a rod without touching the ground. In twenty minutes not one could be seen, but this and similar skedaddles no doubt gave rise to the reported confusion. The infantry, the bone and sinew of the army, was in no instance hurried or hard pressed.

Near Hagerstown we lay in line of battle for two days and nights waiting for the enemy to attack us. Instead of advancing on us they crossed the Potomac below us, thus endeavoring to cut us off again. Lee kept his eyes open, and pushing his own army across headed them and beat them at their own game. But armies now confront each other near Bunker Hill, a small town midway between Winchester and Charlestown. We expect an engagement daily.

NAT.

[Published in the *Carolina Watchman* August 3, 1863]

· 12 ·

CAMP NEAR ORANGE COURT HOUSE, VIRGINIA

By the first week of August, Ramseur's Brigade was in camp near Orange Court House, Virginia. It would be a welcome respite from the marching and fighting of the past several weeks that had included Chancellorsville and Gettysburg. The 4th Regiment remained here for the next six weeks, spending most of their time drilling, doing picket duty, and generally resting from the rigors of the past. Nat's next three letters describe that period.

> **From the 4th North Carolina.**
> **July 31st, 1863.**
>
> **Camp near Madison Court House — Expected to remain some time but left at short warning — Fight at Manassas gap — up the Shenendoah — Recruits — Something about deserters — Hot work — distressing thirst — Our fare — new clothes.**
>
> A day's rest affords me an opportunity to write again for the gratification of my numerous friends; hitherto incessant marching has prevented it. After scrambling among mountains and wading creeks and rivers for ten days in succession, we are at last within three miles of Madison Court House, where it is possible that we will remainder of Early's, Rodes' and Johnston's division.[1] The remainder of Lee's army is in the vicinity of Culpeper it is said, but I doubt very much whether a single man in our corps knows its exact whereabouts. We have had no fighting since we left Front Royal, near which, on the evening of the 23d inst., we had a sharp skirmish with some Yankees who had the audacity to attempt to cut us off. In the fray we had one sharp shooter out of our regiment killed, viz: Mark Hall,[2] member of Co. A. The fight took place at the entrance of Manassas gap in the Blue Ridge, and though it was very serious business, yet the scene was something more than ordinarily exciting and beautiful. At midnight we were aroused and marched quietly five or six miles up the road to Luray which follows the wanderings of the charming Shenendoah. — The men were exhausted and could go no farther. During the day preceding we had marched upwards of twenty miles, and

then the fight in the evening, and the marching at night, was positively more than we could bear. I never before saw men so thoroughly worn out, and it was 9 o'clock the next day before all arrived. When we stopped to lie down it lacked but an hour or two of day break, and not more than fifty men of our regiment were up with us. About 9 A.M. on the 24th we moved on up the river, and have been moving ever since until the 29th inst., when we landed here. Our brigade has recently received considerable accessions from home and the hospitals. The larger portion reached our camp yesterday, having wandered two or three weeks in these mountains or endeavoring to get home. Still we would have it distinctly understood that all deserters are not from North Carolina; though the old state has had a bad reputation in that respect, yet more is imputed than she really deserves. There is a trick prevalent that should be made public, and now is as good a time to do it as I will ever get. Yesterday an old member of Co. C, arrived in camp, who had been detailed as a scout to arrest deserters. He was assigned to duty in the neighborhood of Fairfax, Va., where, by keeping a vigilant look out, he soon succeeded in capturing several fellows who belonged to the "Wood's Rooster Battalion." He asked them where they were from, their reply was, North Carolina. Others made like inquiries and received the same reply; but when they were brought before the proper authorities, and the truth forced out, the very officers examining them were astounded to learn that they were genuine Virginians and belonged to the 23d Va. Regiment. A few days later a squad of more North Carolinians were arrested, but in the end they turned out to Georgians. Scarcely a day passed but deserters were taken up, who invariably reported themselves from North Carolina at first but afterwards proved to be from some other state. A few, perhaps one-fifth, my friend says, were indeed from the old North State, but by far the larger proportion were from Virginia. These facts can be proved beyond a doubt. I do not make these statements at random, simply to tarnish the fair names of our sister states, but I do it to vindicate our own honor. I am sorry that a single soul has ever deserted from the Confederate army; but since men will go, it is not right that they should travel for hundreds of miles under assumed names and on North Carolina credit. It makes our blood boil to hear North Carolina denounced as a harbor for deserters and traitors when in fact there are fully as many in other states. One man has just arrived from Salisbury, he says that the last call takes the few men who have been lawfully left in his section of country. Some are brought out whose legs have been broken, others their arms broken, some out with their hands off, one man had his neck disjointed; and he says it is a fact that blind men have been taken to Raleigh, their eyes operated on, and then sent to the army. He is my authority — of course it is generally believed.

ORANGE COURT HOUSE, VA.,
August 2d, 1863.

Most unexpectedly as I finished the last sentence above, orders came to move immediately. The sun was hardly an hour high, the men about half done cooking, nearly every man had been washing his clothes and they were still wet, but no allowances were made, and in fifteen minutes all were ready, and on their way to Madison, through which we passed at dusk. Taking Orange road we went about four miles farther and at 10 o'clock at night struck camp, having travelled about seven miles. At four next morning we moved; the morning was warm but as the sun rose higher the heat became most intense, to which add the suffocating dust, and you have some idea of our trip. Many men failed from exhaustion, sunstroke, insufferable heat, &c., and never did the heart pant after the water brook more ardently than we did; such thirst, such intolerable thirst none can know until they experience it. At 1 P.M. we went into camp one and a half miles from Orange Court House. To-day we have rumors of a skirmish near Culpeper, and the enemy advancing. We have just received orders to remain in camp and be prepared to march at a moment's notice. It is too extremely hot to fight, but if we must we must though our pewter bottons should melt and drop from our coats.

We fare sumptuously on beef, bread and blackberries, the last constituting the larger half of our living by far; and wherever we go we find them in the greatest abundance — it is a most fortunate thing for us, though the fact betokens a country going to wreck. Briers, thistles and thorns grow luxuriantly where a few years ago the fields were covered with golden wheat or rustling corn. We have but little sickness, and what we have is caused by the oppressive heat. To-day we received an abundant supply of clothing and shoes and none to soon either, for we were needing them badly. When we march from here the rag pickers would do a profitable business by going through the woods and picking up what is left.

NAT.

[Published in the *Carolina Watchman* August 17, 1863]

From the 4th North Carolina.
CAMP NEAR ORANGE C. H., Va.,
August 22, 1863.

Negligent Commissaries make soldiers steal — Our fare, Who is responsible — Fast Day and its observance — Religious exercises.

All goes on smoothly and quietly with us. The only complaint I hear is concerning the quality of our rations. Nothing but corn meal and beef, with a little bacon once in awhile, is rather hard diet during the dog days. It might be better, and could be, if we had a brigade commissary worth his room in purgatory; but as it is, he is too hopelessly lazy to make an effort to procure the articles prescribed by order No. _____ which says brigade commissaries are authorized to purchase green corn, potatoes, &c., from the farmers in the neighborhood, &c.— or something to that amount.[3] Now, Dole's brigade,[4] which lies near us, has been feasting on these things for a week, procured by an energetic commissary, while we have been endeavoring to keep a protracted fast on this loathsome corn-bread. As might be expected, the result of this gross mismanagement is stealing; scarce a day or night passes but roasting-ears and vegetables are clandestinely brought into camp. The men grumble every where, and some are so bold as to threaten desertion as a last resort to get food appropriate to the season, when such food could be had in abundance if our commissary thought less of his own ease and more of the comfort of the soldiers generally. The officer whose business it is to provision the troops has one of the most arduous and responsible positions in the army;

thousands of men feel the least neglect of duty on his part, and bitterly curse him for such neglect; we can see the profusion of luxuries on his table and turn with disgust to our own meagre diet, yet we are helpless; we have neither money nor credit, and at once our consciences become accommodating and our appetites incontrollable. The blockade is run, sentinels eluded (which, by the way, does not require much shrewdness — they generally wink at it, or keep both eyes shut,) and thus a change of diet finds its way into camp. Or place the disgrace, or sin, whatever it be, where it properly belongs — we are guiltless. A new hand at the wheel for the last two weeks, probably, has been the cause of our meagre diet; — we look for better things since Major Miller has once more resumed the discharge of his duties.

Yesterday was fast day — the observance of which was almost a necessity with us. The camp was profoundly quiet, as much so any Sunday I have ever witnessed in the army. All labor and duty was suspended, and the men assembled in large congregations to hear and participate in divine service. We have two chaplains in our brigade, Mr. Betts of the 30th, and Mr. Powers of the 14th, both Methodist I believe. They delivered very appropriate and affecting sermons both in the forenoon and in the evening, and at night the solemn ceremonies of the day were concluded with the Holy sacrament administered to upwards of two hundred communicants. I never saw a scene of the kind more deeply impressing, and humbly trust that great good may be the result. The condition of our country was brought vividly before the minds of the hearers, and so eloquently and touching that tears were soon chasing each other down not a few sunbrowned cheeks. Our land is waste; bright and smiling farms are trodden under foot; black ruins mark the spots where once stood beautiful cottages with their thousand pleasant associations; family circles are broken, some of the once happy members lie unburied in a foreign land, or fill bloody graves in our own, and the very atmosphere is burthened with the wails and prayers of disconsolate widows and orphaned children. Such were some of the appeals made to the hearts of the soldiers; — who would not be affected? Still scarce a ray of hope sheds its light upon us; reverse after reverse attends our arms, — calamity after calamity befalls our nation — all, the just chastisements of a righteous God for our national sins. O! when will it be said enough! Peace! — and the same mighty voice, that stilled the ocean's storm, will ere long, still the tumult in our own unhappy land. Let us patiently bide our time, and do our duty faithfully. Let us renounce every evil way, and sincerely follow the dictates of a pure conscience; then let come what will, whether success or misfortune, be assured that in the end all will be for good.

NAT.

[Published in the *Carolina Watchman* September 7, 1863]

From the 4th North Carolina.
ORANGE C. H., Va., Sept. 9, 1863.

In the absence of all excitement whatever, of a military nature, or political either at present, we have nothing to write about unless we light on the great revival again. It seems to be gathering strength daily and nightly, growing wider and deeper, and now I learn from reliable authority that the religious excitement prevails throughout the army of Northern Virginia, and also in some divisions of the army of the West. It is truly encouraging, and from its effects we hope ere long to see the welcome dawn of peace. During three weeks past scarce a day or a night has passed in which we have not had divine services in camp. At first a small arbor was constructed, sufficient to accommodate two hundred persons, but from time to time additions and improvements have been made, until now, at least two thousand persons can be comfortably seated; and yet large numbers are obliged to stand around the outside or squat like tailors on the ground. Some four or five scaffolds have been erected around the hallowed spot on which blazing fires of pine knots are kept burning during night services, and many of the night scenes presented are of the most affecting and thrilling nature. Soon after sunset squads from other brigades come in — they flock together from every quarter, and by the time the drums are done beating tattoe, every seat beneath the arbor is occupied as well as every foot of room about the firestands on the outside. And the men listen to what is said, they are not prompted by curiosity or the vain notion of seeing and being seen, a most wonderful motive power in some sections. Here we see no gaudy dress or jewelry, no hooting and howling and yelling of fast young men on the outskirts of camp — nor fast young ladies either. The altar here is not an improvement on the Ancient Roman Amphitheatre, like we have seen in bygone days, where the gladiators and gladiatoresses made night hideous with unearthly shouts and disgusted every sensible person with their — shall I say it? — cavortings. We have no loafers or pleasure seekers, nor shriekers, nor game-making — all feel an interest in the great work now going on, and all alike express themselves as convinced of its thoroughness and sincerity. Notwithstanding, the addition of an equal number of females might bring some evils, yet we painfully miss them, and listen in vain for a lady's voice when a thousand rough soldiers begin to sing a hymn or spiritual song. And such singing — Oh! it is indescribable! It is overwhelming. It seems like a flood of the most seraphic music is bearing on us. So grand! So sublime! I cannot account for it, except it be the feeling with which the men sing, and that feeling seems to be imparted to all within hearing distance.

The meeting goes on — the interest unabated. Some night near a hundred penitents come forward to the altar; it does seem that it is going to work a thorough and most happy revolution in the morale of the army and may we express the hope that the good influences of this "revival in the army," may reach the hearts of the massy people at home and work a beneficial change there, where it is certainly as much needed as here.

Content reigns supreme among the soldiers — our bill of fare embraces all we can expect once more — we have good health, well shoed and clad, and four months wages in our pockets — I mean what is left of it, after liquidating our debts, and paying for a watermelon at the present.

NAT.

[Published in the *Carolina Watchman* September 28, 1863]

· 13 ·

ON AND NEAR THE RAPIDAN

During the summer of 1863, a peace movement was growing in North Carolina. W. W. Holden, the publisher of the Raleigh newspaper *The North Carolina Standard*, was a leading proponent of it. A group called the Heroes of America spearheaded much of the movement, and the *Standard* reported the activities carried on at a number of the meetings. The *Standard* circulated among the North Carolina regiments in Virginia, and the resentment of the soldiers toward Holden and this group was intense. As many as thirty of the regiments met and passed resolutions that denounced Holden and the meetings as being detrimental to the army. These were sent to other North Carolina newspapers where they were published. Several of the generals felt desertions were increasing because of Holden's activities, and one soldier, just before he was executed for desertion, said he would not have deserted had it not been for Holden's writings. Still, even against this background of home and the violence of the battles at Chancellorsville and Gettysburg, the esprit de corps of Ramseur's Brigade and Grimes' 4th Regiment remained high.

RACCOON FORD, RAPIDAN, VA.,
September 16, 1863.

At early dawn on Monday morning last we bade adieu to our quiet camp, taking up our march for this place where a battle was expected hourly. The enemy in heavy force (we are told) advanced from Culpepper C. H., and, perhaps, would have crossed at this ford but for the obstructions placed in the way by the rebels. During Monday afternoon sharp skirmishing and pretty hot artillery firing was kept up between the advance of the two armies. Our pickets held the north bank of the Rapidan, while our artillery occupied positions on the heights on this (the south) side. All day yesterday occasional firing was kept up, and to-day also at intervals heavy reports mar the stillness of the autumnal air. The casualties, so far as I have been able to learn, have been quite slight on our side, some dozen killed and some twenty-five or thirty wounded, principally artillery men. It is hard to

96

tell what will turn up here; some think we will have a general engagement, others think we will not. From all indications I am inclined to favor the former opinion. For the last six hours a heavy column of Confederate infantry and cavalry have been seen approaching the river, and it should not surprise me at all if they should cross to-night, indeed, I think it very probable; and so sure as we cross, that sure we will have a fight, unless the Yankees back down and get out of the way entirely. The enemy no doubt thinks we are weak since Longstreet[1] with his whole corps has left us, but if they engage us they will be apt to find out their mistake.

We expected a rumpus; these grand reviews by Ewell and Lee were infallible signs of a march or a battle, many of us said so then, and now we know it to be a fact.— Within the last ten days Gen. Lee, together with Gen. Ewell, has reviewed the entire army of Northern Virginia, and it is said they expressed themselves highly pleased with its discipline and condition. It would be imprudent for me to say anything about our number but the reader may rest assured that it is sufficiently large to repel any force which the enemy can bring against us. There is no doubt but our army is vastly improved since our return from Maryland, and if we should meet the enemy in battle we confidently hope for a complete triumph — nor need the people at home be surprised to hear of our engagement soon. The sun is now not more than an hour high, and at this moment the cannonading is heavier than it has been at any time during the day; the firing is incessant and betokens a bloody day coming.— who knows but it may be to-morrow? We are lying bivouacked in a pine thicket within a mile of Clark's Mountain (which some of my readers may recollect) and about one and a half miles from Raccoon Ford on the Rapidan river, some seven or eight miles below Orange Court House. It is very uncertain whether we remain here till to-morrow's sunrise or not, our movements are frequently sudden and incomprehensible, and I may add very disagreeable to boot. For instance, if we should be roused at midnight to-night, marched, quick time to the river, and then have to pitch in and wade — there would be nothing very romantic in that, especially if the Yankees should amuse themselves by throwing shells at us while we are staggering about in the water or slipping and falling on the banks. But we will not trouble ourselves about the future, self-preservation at the present is a soldier's first duty, and one which we never fail to perform.

A man was shot to-day for desertion, he belonged to the 2nd N.C., our brigade. There is no mercy shown to deserters now, so sure as they get caught, that sure will they be executed; their day of grace is past. Let me warn all good citizens against harboring men absent without leave, by so doing they are running a great risk — the law is positive.

NAT.

[Published in the *Carolina Watchman* September 28, 1863]

The writer of the following letter signed himself as "A North Carolinian."

On last Saturday two men from our Brigade and belonging to the 33d North Carolina Troops, were executed near this place for desertion. Seven others belong-

ing to our Brigade have since been tried for the same offence, five of them have
been convicted, and as their sentences have been approved by Gen. Lee, they will
be shot next Saturday. Nearly every one of them stated while upon trial that, that
they were induced to desert by the teaching of the *North Carolina Standard*. One
of them, a member of the 37th N.C.T., gave the teachings of the *Standard* as the
sole reason for his desertion. Others said they read the *Standard*, believed it to be
true, and thought they were doing their duty when they deserted.[2]

From the 4th North Carolina.
CAMP NEAR THE RAPIDAN.
Fifteen miles below Orange C. H., Va.,
September 24th, 1863.

Another week has slipped away, and contrary to all expectations, it is gone without a general battle in this section. There had been some little skirmishing, recon-
noitering, feeling round and so on, but when that is said, all is said. It is presumed
that General Lee is waiting to see what will be the result of the encounter between
Bragg and old Roxy; if that turns out favorably, I mean if what we hear turns out
to be true, I think it would be safe to bet, that the army assumes the aggressive
in less than a fortnight. But, as I have remarked before, military prognostications
are utterly useless;— to guess or conjecture about army movements is breath wasted,
so we might as well save our gas for other and more profitable purposes. Two or
three days and nights we lay in line of battle on the range of hills overlooking the
broad and fertile valley of the Rapidan; for miles along the line temporary earthworks were thrown up; underbrush and groves of timber were cut away where
they would obstruct the range of our guns; positions selected and cleared away
for batteries, and in fact every thing done that could be a benefit in any wise to
our hardy soldiers, who were hourly expecting an advance to be made by the
enemy. During the day we could see numerous Yankee cavalrymen scouting about
beyond the river, while their blue coated sentries "paced their weary round" on
the bank opposite our pickets. No firing was allowed, but in some instances friendly
salutations and jocular remarks were interchanged, as well as a little of the everlasting traffic in coffee and tobacco, swapping of Newspapers, &c. At tattoo in
the evening and reveille in the morning the rattle of innumerable drums is borne
on the breeze from yankeedom, intended no doubt to give our boys an awful
impression of their numbers, as well as a wholesome dread of their prowess, a game
at which I don't think it is likely that they will make much.

Our Generals, finding there was no great danger to be apprehended from an
advance of the enemy, have taken the troops from the earthworks and put them
in camp in woodland about half a mile to the rear of the fortifications. We have
neither drills nor dress parades, consequently we (everybody in general) have quite
an easy time; nothing to do but cook and eat our rations, (plentiful enough too,)
amuse or employ ourselves as best we can through the day, spin yarns and smoke
round our camp-fires at night, or warm our toes by them these frosty mornings;
and when we stretch ourselves on the ground at night, rolled in our blankets we
are soothed to sleep by the songs of myriads of insects chirping their own requiems,
mingled with the harsh serenade of innumerable katykids in the tree tops above

us. Everything is so calm! so tranquil! so much like the peaceful, happy nights spent in our boyhood. True, oftentimes at midnight the heavy booming of cannons jar the bracing atmosphere, but no one heeds it, save the ever-watchful sentinel, who thinks it is not a sufficient reason to justify him in disturbing our slumber, and lets us sleep on; such sweet, such refreshing sleep as only a soldier knows. And how beautiful and majestic is the queen of night as she sails in all her autumnal splendor over these battle-famed hills! Though she illumes this wreck of a once happy country with her mellow rays, yet we can imagine that she looks down with a cold pity upon the madness and folly that rules in the bosoms of a nation of people who are more brute than human.

We wonder when our insane enemies will regain their reason! But their existence is staked on our overthrow, hence, like the reckless gambler, they must play till all is either lost or won; there is no half-way ground. If we are united as a band of brothers should be, not many moons will roll over us till we shall gaze on that moon from our own cottage door, perhaps not through the vines and lattice work, but through tears of inexpressible joy and gratitude, for we will be at home and free.

NAT.

[Published in the *Carolina Watchman* October 12, 1863]

From the 4th North Carolina.
October 24th, 1863

Left camp on the Rapidan — Circuitous and exhausting marching — Obstacles at Warrenton Springs — How we cross rivers — Incidents — Cannonading some distance off — Unhealthy atmosphere near Warrenton — The enemy gone — Our return labor — Winter quarters.

On the morning of the 9th inst., as the first peep of day reddened the east, we evacuated the banks of the Rapidan, and took up the line of march westward. — Passing through the suburbs of Orange we crossed the Rapidan (forded of course) at Union Mills; thence bearing a north west we left Madison Court-House half a mile to our left; four miles further brought us to Robeson river, from the north bank of which the enemy's outposts had been driven a few hours before our arrival; we heard the firing quite distinctly, and without taking time to undress, or say much as roll up our pant legs, we crossed and pushed on briskly several miles further, hoping to get up in time to engage the enemy that night; but it was useless, he made better time than we, and was entirely out of reach, if not out of hearing before we arrived at the scene of action. This was on the night of the 10th, the darkness was most intense, and in our exhausted condition, it was impossible to go further; in two day's marching we had come about forty-five miles, and we literally fell down and slept till daylight the next morning. On Sunday the 11th, we traveled eight miles only, when for reasons best known to Gen. Lee we went into camp five miles from Culpeper on the Sperryville road; we asked no questions about it, but were glad enough to get to rest on any terms. Rations were issued, with orders to have them cooked and everything ready to leave at 3 o'clock next morning. When the time came we felt exceeding loth to get up, but it had to be done, and by sunrise we were on our way towards Warrenton. The fields were covered with a frost that looked like a minature snow, which made the air so cool that brisk walking was necessary to our comfort. About noon we came to the Hazel river, which, besides being a stout stream ordinarily, was now swollen by the late rains in the mountains. When we arrived in the broad low lands bordering the river we found two or three more brigades already congregated which with the addition of ours made several thousand men, all wondering how we were to get across; presently, however, we were relieved from the order from Gen. Rodes, or somebody else, to "doff our nether garments," no sooner said than done, and the scene which followed "beggars all description" as the novelists say on more delicate subjects. What we had been dreading all the morning turned out to be a regular frolic, and in the course of an hour all were over safely and on our way for the next river, which we passed five miles further on at Warrenton (or White Sulphur) springs. This, though not so large as the Hazel, I believe is called the Rappahannock. Here we found the enemy in pretty strong force, holding the north bank and in a bad humor besides. Their sharpshooters opened on us two miles from the river on the south side, but fell back with considerable loss as we advanced, until they got over the river where they were joined by the reserves. This was somewhat in our way, but measures were taken to clean them out immediately, which was soon done when fifteen cannons opened simultaneously on them, assisted by a heavy corps of sharpshooters. Their guns replied feebly at first but were soon silenced altogether, and fifteen minutes later we saw a blue column of yankees on their winding way over the hills beyond the river. "Forward" was shouted from one end of our line to the other. The cavalry dashed on, leaving a cloud of dust and smoke behind them, through which we groped our way to the river and crossed on the bridge partially destroyed by the enemy. On both sides of the road as we went on we saw dead and wounded men and horses, all, with a few exceptions, belonging to the enemy. The darkness was getting so thick that we could not see objects distinctly, but we could see enough to convince us that our shells and cavalry together had done no little mischief. Some of the boys were counting the dead yankees as we were jogging on a rate little short of double quick, when some one yelled out "There lies another," pointing at the same time to a dark object lying by an elm not more than eight steps from the road. "Na-rye dead," growled the blue coat. "Are you hurt!" "Yes," he replied, "I'm shot but not dead by a hornful." His wound was severe but not mortal I learned afterwards. We traveled on till eight or nine o'clock at night when we "turned in" as we have it out here. The night was right cool, and as soon as our "lodging" was deposited we went to work building fires of such things as we could find. While at this one of our fellow picked up a rail which he thought he would break over a stump and drawing away with all his might he hit another dead man. This is the way many men are scattered over many portions of northern Virginia — "unwept," no, not unwept. I will not say that for the bare mention of their names years hence will cause tears of agony to flow, — but I will say "unknelled, uncoffined, and unknown."

The next day, Tuesday 13th, we moved through Warrenton, and struck camp three miles beyond the town, without coming in contact with the enemy ourselves, though heavy cannonading was heard in front and on our right flank. Three days rations were prepared that night, and at 4 o'clock on the following morning of the 14th we were hurried up and off at a trot for two miles, when suddenly and very unexpectedly before it was quite light, the enemy's sharp shooters opened a galling fire on us. Some four or five men in our regiment were wounded, and one killed — viz: David Hunter[3] of Co. A, (the Iredell Blues) — Skirmishers were sent forward, artillery brought up, and every preparation made for battle which seemed inevitable. The musketry grew heavier every minute, and presently some half dozen brass pieces opened like surly bull dogs, making the calm and frosty atmosphere resound for miles. The fire was kept up hot during an hour and a half when it ceased entirely and our column was pushed quick time after the fleeing yankees. The force we had engaged this morning, though pretty strong, was nothing more than the enemy's rear guard — his main body was at that time retreating towards Manassas as rapidly as their heels would let them, whither our corps followed to a point eight miles from the Junction, (Manassas.) Late this evening, the 14th, Cook's and Kirkland's brigades of Hill's corps, engaged the enemy on the railroad near Bristo, six miles from Manassas, and a most desperate fight ensued, in which, I rather fear, the Confederates lost more than they gained, — let those who were present say. But the enemy had made good his escape, with the loss of some two thousand prisoners, some wagons, and a large quantity of baggage burned up on the railroad, besides a good many killed and wounded. During the 15th of this month we lay idle in a thicket of pines, while around us on almost every side was a vast forest of wagons and artillery, being very nearly the entire crop belonging to both corps, A. P. Hill and Ewell's. At intervals heavy cannonading was heard in the direction of Dumfries, sixteen miles south east of Manassas, but it occasioned no alarm in camp, and the day and night passed off quietly with the exception of a severe drenching from a thunder shower, which seems to succeed a battle or heavy discharges of artillery invariably.

On the morning of the 16th rain was falling heavily; the cedars, pines and dwarf oaks formed a labyrinth through which it was almost impossible to make our way and these dripping with water from every leaf and twig, together with the grass and mud shoe mouth deep, soon saturated our garments from head to foot in a way by no means comfortable; but we traveled on slowly in an easterly direction two miles, when we found ourselves on the Orange and Alexander railroad, down which we turned towards Richmond. We made the best of our disagreeable flight, and after following the railroad four or five miles we halted, stacked arms and proceeded to tear up the track. The very elements seemed to conspire against us; such torrents of rain as fell for two hours, and just while we were at work too, were enough to make us think another flood had broken loose upon us. By three o'clock P.M. we were done our contract, and about the same time the rain ceased falling, the clouds broke and the bright evening sun chased them far to the east where they were banked up like a huge black pall. For two or three days after this we loitered along the railroad, acting as rear guard for our working parties, working a little ourselves, and so on until we got down on the south side of the Rappahannock, where, after destroying the bridge across that stream, the work of destruction ceased, leaving the railroad a wreck from Manassas to the Rappahannock, a distance of some thirty miles. At noon on the 19th, the army of Northern Virginia was encamped on the hills between Brandy Station and the above mentioned river, and in all that vast multitude scarcely a dry thread of clothing — so incessant and terrible had been the fall of rain and hail for the preceding twelve hours. We built large fires, and by them warmed and dried ourselves as best we could till near sunset when the various divisions dispersed "to their respective places of abode" I suppose, I know nothing about any save our own, (Rodes,') which moved down in the neighborhood of Kelly's ford on the Rappahannock, five miles below the railroad bridge, where we have been picketing and putting up winter quarters. We have no idea how long we will remain here, perhaps till Christmas, but we would like to stay all winter if possible, since with our many sunny shanties we are well prepared for cold weather.

NAT.

[Published in the *Carolina Watchman* November 9, 1863]

From the 4th North Carolina.
CAMP ON THE RAPIDAN, VA.,
Nov. 11th, 1863.

A calm precedes the storm — Unwelcome as unexpected visitors — Unhealthy atmosphere — A general row — Falling back — Was somebody napping? — A panic on a small scale — Safe at last — Snow storm on the 6th — Rather coolish.

On last Saturday, the 7th inst., at 11 o'clock A.M. Mr. Rosser, corps Chaplain, preached to a large audience in our camp near Kelly's ford on the Rappahannock. At the close of the sermon notice was given that on the next day a number of persons would be baptized, some would join the church, and in the evening the sacrament would be administered, — all passed off as solemn and systematic as a quarterly meeting, so far as the announcements were concerned, and the congregation assembled; — all was quiet and calm; but the benediction was hardly pronounced when all at once, and very much to the surprise of every body a furious bombardment began at the ford, — and above and below it, not more than a mile and a half from camp. Every moment it grew heavier — shells went sparkling and hissing thro' the air in all directions, exploding above and around, scattering fragments uncomfortably near on all sides. Presently the small arms opened thick and fast, down in front; this raised the excitement higher, drums beat, horses were saddled, guns loaded, knapsacks packed, and the command resounded through the entire camp — "fall in." In less time than it takes me to write it the troops were in line and marching towards the scene of action. — From the summit of the hill on which we were encamped, we could see what was doing the whole mischief. The enemy had crossed and were advancing. There was no mistake though it hardly seemed possible. We could see a dense column of the blue coats in the low grounds this side of the river, while the hill beyond was glittering full of bayonets. Several Yankee batteries held very strong as well as advantageous positions on the opposite bluffs from which they raked us "fore and aft" for a distance of two miles or more. It was impossible to hold the place, accordingly the programme was to "fall back" to some safe position, which could not be found north of the Rapidan. The two rivers here are from ten to fifteen miles apart, and the country between them an unbroken level, or gently rolling, with the exception of Pony and Slaughter mountains, both considerable elevations, the first 3 miles southeast of Culpeper Court-house, the last about six or eight south west. On Saturday evening our troops held the enemy at bay until the most of the baggage camp equipage, &c., was moved to the rear, still some valuable clothing with other camp furniture was lost. No general engagement, as yet, had taken place along our portion of the line, and during Saturday night our forces quietly retreated to Pony mountain, mentioned above, where we formed line of battle before day on Sunday morning, raised temporary breastworks, expecting the enemy to advance rapidly, which, however, they did not do, and at 3 o'clock P.M. Sunday, we evacuated again, taking up our line of march for the hills south of the Rapidan, distant eleven miles, which we reached about 12 o'clock the same night after an exhausting march without food or rest. Not even a halt was at Raccoon ford, where our division marched across the river in close columns, and knee deep in water cold as ice itself. Meanwhile the quartermasters and commissaries, together with their wagons, cattle, &c., were scattered to the four winds. When the alarm was given on Saturday evening all struck out, pell mell for the Rapidan. No time was lost making inquiries about anybody or anything else,— nor was any time lost asking questions about roads or fords — it was a race for life or death, and by noon on Sunday, I presume every wagon belonging to the division trains was safe on the safe side of the Rapidan. The wagons and baggage were saved, so far so good; but by means of the panic, the troops, many of them, had to fast for forty-eight hours. I do not think I ever saw a set of men so sorely pinched with hunger. Our rations were left in our camp at Kelly's ford uncooked. We had not a moment's warning, no preparations were made for any sort of a move, and for these and other reasons the conviction forces itself on our minds that somebody was caught napping.

Not a man in our regiment was hurt, their escape is miraculous — each of the other regiments in our brigade suffered more or less severely. Lt. Col. Sellers of the 30th received a mortal wound, and has died since I learn — a few were killed in the 2d N.C. some wounded and about half the remainder captured,— some casualties also in the 14th. I have not learned the extent. Hoke's and Hays' brigade were hotly engaged on the left, and I am told suffered severely. The whole army of Northern Virginia now occupies the same line which it left on the 8th and 9th of October. The various brigades, so far as I know, are in their same old camps. It is rumored that the enemy is advancing, and that they calculate on giving us battle here, how true I don't pretend to say, but if such a thing is attempted hot work may be expected.

We have no quarters, nor shelter of any kind, but fortunately, are abundantly supplied with clothing, shoes and blankets; when once it is settled where we shall remain this winter, why in a week a perfect town of little shanties will spring up. The weather is exceedingly disagreeable. On Monday last we had a regular snow storm though none lay on the ground yet it has reduced the temperature of the atmosphere to the freezing point. Squalls of wind drive the smoke in our eyes and pierce our clothing to the skin, while black clouds scud across the sky spitting a little snow as they go, giving us an unpleasant foretaste of what is to come.

NAT.

[Published in the *Carolina Watchman* November 23, 1863]

From the Saltillo Boys.
CAMP ON THE RAPIDAN, SIXTEEN MILES BELOW ORANGE C. H., VA.,
November 13th, 1863.

Well, I believe I have been up this tree long enough, so venturing down to the first fork, and perceiving the coast clear, I think I shall scatter a few crumbs broadcast. — Some will, no doubt, fall in stony places, — others, perhaps, among thorns and bamboos, — peradventure the birds of the air will get a little, (let 'em have it, if they are as needy as rebel soldiers) but the greater portion, I'm forced to believe, will fall in good ground; — good, fertile ground; and if it don't produce a hundred, nor even ten fold, it will surely make the seed. I guess I had better at once paddle my canoe into the middle of the stream — to-be sure I'm down the tree and already embarked, — I say I had better get into the current as quickly as possible and keep it. — I have a bit of experience concerning the danger of fooling by the way, dabbling in politics, Union-ticks, Holden-ticks, and so on, besides sundry lesser ticks, any of which stick closer than a bad reputation; but the same remedy is equally efficacious in all cases. How's that? Smoke 'em off, smoke 'em off! that's my cure.

I presume my readers have, ere this reaches them, heard all about the late movements in this portion of the country. Our retreat from the Rappahannock, skirmishing, fasting, marching and finally, the re-establishment of our old lines South of the Rapidan. This much I will say, however, — On the eve of the 7th inst., we evacuated our shanties near Kelly's ford, and after a literal scramble during two days and nights, under all sorts of disadvantages too, our brigade landed before day on the 9th inst., in the very same camp we left on the 9th of October, when we started on this expedition. Just one month though it seems like three. We had hoped to remain in our snug quarters on the Rappahannock, but since we were ousted from them so unceremoniously, now we are indifferent about any quarters at all, and we will certainly not build any more until we have some assurance that we will get to stay in them during the winter. We are so thoroughly toughened that the ordinary changes in the weather does not affect us a particle. — On Monday last we had a regular snow storm; though none lay on the ground scarcely yet it reduced the air to the freezing point, and for two or three days and nights we suffered severely with cold, while the keen blasts of wind hurled the dust and smoke in every conceivable direction. Half blinded, half suffocated, I do not think we ever experienced a more disagreeable time. At present all is calmed down and a beautiful Indian summer spell reigns. I did intend to write a long letter, but five minutes ago we received orders to move toward Chancellorsville this evening. The enemy is trying that road to Richmond. I will send this half sheet and write more as soon as we are settled. Who will bring us a load of good things from home? Many of us are anxiously expecting Col. Chipley. We will not be hard to find.

NAT.

[Published in the *Iredell Express* December 3, 1863]

From the Saltillo Boys.
CAMP ON THE RAPIDAN, VA.,
November 25th, 1863.

My last letter was closed rather abruptly by the order to march toward Chancellorsville; but, strange to say, I begin this sitting within fifty yards of the very spot where I finished the other; under different circumstances though,—then we had no shelter save a portable, Yankee tent; now we have a very snug cabin, roomy and comfortable, with one whole gable end for a chimney and fire-place. We are encamped about an eighth of a mile in rear of the line of fortification on the Rapidan hills. Some think cigtyfications a more appropriate word than "forti," since they have been strengthened, doubled and trebled, until our works look like a continuous fort from the mouth of the Rappahannock to the Blue Ridge. If the war lasts a year or two longer we will have the Confederacy ditched loose from the abolition kingdom in the North. But you want to know how it happened that we got back here after having started on our way to some other point. I don't remember the date of my letter cut short so unceremoniously, but I had scarce time enough to bundle up my tricks after the first alarm was given, when all were off, as if on a race for life; nor was the gait slackened until we were seven miles away from this place, though precious little, if any nearer, Chancellorsville. An hour by sun in the evening (it was Friday the 13th inst.,) we halted, and after a short rest went in camp in a magnificent forest of oak and pine on the road leading from Orange C. H. to Fredericksburg. There we remained during Saturday the 14th, perfectly quiet. Not a rumor, not the report of a single gun, disturbed our peace. A more charming day never beamed in the Sunny South,—so calm, so mild and serene. Even the summer birds were tempted to try their voices, and larks and robins were turning up around us in a way that carried us in fancy back to our boyhood's days, and made us wish, when awake to the reality, that such a thing as war had never been invented. The men stretched themselves in the brown rustling leaves and slept, and dreamed of sunny days long gone by, alas! with many of us never more to return.

Soon after dark (night of the 14th,) black heavy clouds arose; glaring flashes of lightning illuminated for a moment the Western horizon—deep thunder muttered ominously, and ere we had temporary shelters constructed a perfect sluice of water fell and came near inundating our whole camp. The shower did not last more than half an hour, but that was long enough to upset all our calculations about a comfortable snooze, which we had had in anticipation. On the next morning at day-break we had another shower after the same style, but it lasted longer this time; the rain fell heavily until 7 o'clock A.M., when the clouds broke away again and the bright beams of the sun shone out cheerily. But how great the change since yesterday in the aspect of affairs around us! Instead of quiet all was bustle and hurry and confusion in camp; while on the river five or six miles away heavy discharges of cannon kept up a continual roar, filling every mind with painful apprehensions and dread forebodings. The drums throughout the camp were beating the long roll, some were drawing wet loads from their guns, some were counting their cartridges and arranging them conveniently in their boxes, new cartridges were handed out, cap boxes refilled:—others were over hauling their knapsacks in order to see what articles thy could best dispense with, and away such articles would go in the bushes,—some wringing their blankets to get as much of the water out as possible; not a few were trying their best to get the sick or lame, and went prowling round in the woods cutting walking sticks and making inquiries after the M. D.'s, and the ambulances—cooking utensils were carried up and rations half cooked thrust carelessly in haversacks. Everything and everybody was turned up side down, when the command "fall in" instantly brought "order out of chaos," and the line took up its march directly towards the cannonading. Many hearts beat violently in many manly bosoms,—not through fear, but from intense excitement and suspense natural on all such occasions. After making a quick and tiresome march to a point within sight of the river we halted, stacked arms and awaited further orders. In the course of half an hour a courier arrived bringing intelligence that the enemy had recrossed the river to their own side—that the whole uproar was the result of an attempted cavalry raid on the part of the enemy—that quiet was restored and we might return to our camps. We felt immensely relieved, and without delay returned to the camp we had left that morning. Meantime the firing had ceased, and the evening was as calm as any Sabbath we ever witnessed at home. Quite early the following morning we returned over the same road to this place; and since then fatigue parties have been at work day and night repairing and strengthening our line of breastworks. The men have erected comfortable shanties, and altogether are well prepared for winter should we get to remain here, an event very uncertain; for, though no stir was up an hour ago, nor has been during the last ten days, yet since beginning this letter we have received orders to prepare two days rations and be ready to move at a moment's notice. My luck exactly,—just as sure as I begin a letter to the *Express*, so sure do we get "marching orders," and if a certain member of the band gets a letter we are certain to march. Very discouraging, is it not? I expected that this beautiful weather would bring on a movement if not a fight, and now it seems likely to do both. But ere long we will have snow, and, rain, and then all military operations will surely cease. We will then be located in a permanent camp,—somebody will bring us boxes no matter who, whether Mr. Dillon or Mr. Chipley or any one else,—let them come, or give us cause to think that gentle hearts in Iredell, once so warm and magnanimous, have now grown cold and sordid. We don't ask sharks, shirkers or speculators to remember us, but surely the kind ladies have not forgotten that to them we owe nine tenths of the comforts we enjoy in the army. And in the melee pray don't forget

Your old friend

NAT.

[Published in the *Iredell Express* December 10, 1863]

In response to Nat's continuing pleas for something from home, the *Iredell Express* published the following:

FOR GEN. LEE'S ARMY!

Mr. C. A. Moore will be at Third Creek Station on the 5th January, 1864, to take charge of any boxes or packages, and at Salisbury on the 6th, for the same purpose. Persons having boxes, &c., are informed that four dollars will be charged for every box to pay expenses. "Nat" wants a box, and desires the Editor of the *Iredell Express* to notify his friends. We are sure "Nat" will get it, too.

From the 4th North Carolina.
CAMP ON THE RAPIDAN, VA.,
Dec. 5th, 1863.

A short campaign — Rather coolish and blue like — Early birds — Another move — "Smell a mice" — Bullets and "quarter-master hunters" — Engagement with Sharpshooters — A big hat in difficulty — A night march — In line of battle — Incidents — Yankee retreat without a fight — Our joyous return to camp, &c.

We have just been put through another campaign, the results of which, though not what they might have been, are yet more favorable than those which attended our retreat from the Rappahannock.

To give a detailed account of our recent operations would require more paper and time than I can appropriate to that purpose; but for the gratification of my numerous readers I will endeavor to give a few brief sketches and outlines, the remainder, which is of minor importance, can be supplied from imagination.

About 2 o'clock on last Friday morning, the 27th ult., we were quietly roused from our comfortable bunks and marched briskly in an easterly direction some five miles when we halted and proceeded to throw up temporary breastworks before the morning star appeared on the horizon. The ground was frozen hard, ice was spouted up in wet places, our noses blue, (at least they felt so, we couldn't see) our ears were frost-bitten, hands and feet benumbed, but none of it was taken into consideration; a battle was expected at daylight and preparations must be made for it, — I don't think I ever saw men work with such vim, and when day dawned the work was done, to be left half an hour afterwards just as we expected; well, all we could do was hope that other poor rebels (devils) might be benefited by them some day. At sunrise we again took up our line of march eastward, and after many halts we found ourselves at 10 o'clock A.M., in the vicinity of Locust Grove (I believe they call it) on the turnpike leading from Orange C. H. to Fredericksburg — and in the vicinity of yankees also, I may add; none of your peaceable sort either, for no sooner than they were apprised of our whereabouts than they began pitching minnie balls into the trees around us and sending quarter-master hunters (shells) away over us "the way Ward's ducks went." Our first corps of sharp-shooters were sent forward who were soon hotly engaged and called for reinforcements; the second corps was sent to their assistance, which, with the first, during the remainder of the day held the enemy at bay and thus prevented a general engagement, though the fire was kept up with spirit between the skirmishers until dark put a stop to it. While this was going on in front, on our left Maj. Gen. Johnson was hard pressed and beset on all sides with blue bellies. Ordinarily the old gentleman (Johnson) has his head swamped in a huge black hat, and on this occasion eyes, thus enabling the yankees to get in his rear; be this as it may the general got his eyes open in time to fight his way out. During two hours battle raged furiously; the woods in which we fought look like they had been visited by a young tornado. The enemy found they had caught a tartar and we were glad enough to let him go. I have never heard a correct account of his loss, but the blow he dealt the yankees was severe, many of their dead lay on the field unburied last Thursday morning. After the retreat of the enemy and Johnson's deliverance everything became perfectly quiet along the lines.

The troop movement Nat is referring to was the Mine Run Campaign, and Major General Edward Johnson, who was a division commander in Rodes' Second Corps, played a significant part in the engagement. A strong federal force was trying to get into the rear of the Confederates when they encountered Johnson and his men near Payne's Farm late in the afternoon. Johnson's force of 5,300 men was heavily outnumbered by a Federal corps that could call on 32,000 soldiers. However, Johnson boldly attacked over the rough, wooded landscape and blocked the Federal advance.

Nat continues:

Night had set in,—at intervals a picket gun would fire, but with that exception not a sound was heard save the monotonous rumbling of the ambulances over the uneven pike as they bore the wounded off the battle field to the hospitals in the rear. At midnight we (Ramseur's brigade) stood in the road two hundred yards in rear of the battle line; the rebels had fled to parts unknown, I had no idea where they were gone, we could hear none except the few around us and we had orders to keep very quiet — the enemy's scouts were prowling near, and at any moment a whole column of yankees might dash on us. Presently we began our march southward, parallel to the enemy's line and but a few hundred yards distant from it; I could hardly call it marching, it was more like creeping, so much caution was necessary to prevent the least possible noise. The stillness was really painful — it made us feel chilly. The men conversed in tones scarcely above a whisper or were awed into the most profound silence; no rattling of the cups or canteens was heard; the brown oak leaves lay deep and dry through the woods, but we never set foot outside of the road, and when everything rustled among the bushes on our left every eye was turned in that direction and every soldier instinctively grasped his firelock. A dim, ghost-like light was spread over the hills and fields, the effect of the dense clouds between us and the moon nearly full, and by this light we were enabled to pick our way with some degree of comfort and satisfaction. In this manner we traveled about one and a half miles, then falling in the turnpike we turned back towards Orange and on the west side of Mine Run formed line of battle at 3 o'clock Saturday morning. After arms were stacked we lay down on the rocky hillside and slept soundly until after daylight, when we were awakened by sprinkles of rain falling in our face, assisted by the firing of musketry two or three hundred yards in our front. Upon looking round we discovered the van guard of the enemy deployed on the hill side opposite, shooting into our skirmishers with considerable vengeance. The rain fell thicker and heavier and with it increased the firing between the skirmishers, who were now within two hundred yards of each other. We expected the enemy to advance with a rush, but they did not, still we did not know how soon they might and to make ourselves more secure we fell back fifty yards further, to the foot of the hill on which we had bivouaced the preceding night, and, screened by the thick underbrush in front, we proceeded to throw up earth works with all possible haste. By noon the rain ceased, the clouds broke, partially cleared away, leaving the air chill and frosty so that our frozen garments rattled like dry raw-hides. After dark our sharpshooters were relieved by fresh corps. Our boys who came in were well nigh frozen ("gone up the spout" they said) and crouching round the pitiful fires related some amusing incidents. The pickets were so near each other that they could converse with all ease, and an incessant jawing was the consequence. "An' faith you reb," said an old yankee "wouldn't you like to have a cup of hot coffee this cold morning?"— with a peculiar brogue. "Got plenty Confederate coffee," said the reb in reply, "wouldn't you like to have a chew of tobacco?" "Don't care if I do," said yank. "Well here are some of old Jeff's pills in advance"—and away would go a volley of balls that made the yank dig his nails into the ground trying to be close. Both parties were lying flat in an old field—rather an uncomfortable position in a pelting rain of five or six hours, but the slightest move was sure to draw a dozen bullets, hence it was to the interest of each that he should keep perfectly still. On another point of the line a few sheep came straggling between the pickets; a yankee shot one and calling out to a rebel opposite said, "Don't you want to go halvers on some mutton?" "Yes, I wouldn't mind it." "Come over then," and each threw down his gun and walked up to the sheep, where they had a good, jolly time over their bowie knives and mutton for an hour. Meantime the pickets on each side were peppering away at each other, careful, however, not to disturb the butchers who were working with might, chattering good humoredly and as much unconcerned as though there were neither abolitionists nor negroes in America, and when done they divided the meat fairly and honestly, each taking his half and bidding the other good-bye, with much good luck, returned to his respective "hoil" and spent the evening amusing themselves with their Enfields. (Too much hurried and mixed up to correct grammatical errors.) Saturday, Sunday, Monday and Tuesday the aspect of affairs remained unchanged. The two armies lay in sight of each other while the sharpshooters were incessantly firing between. Our troops were behind splendid breastworks and were very anxious for the enemy to advance.

Nat's words, "anxious for the enemy to advance," may sound strange, yet they are understandable. The November days were cold and freezing, and the nights were even worse. Many Southern soldiers were poorly provisioned and clothed, while their Yankee counterparts could rely on a supply of warm clothing and food. Nat has commented before about the Union supplies to be had after a battle, such as knapsacks with rations, shoes, and coats.

Nat continues:

> Our suspense was great, and situation not an enviable one by any means. A little shelling was going on both sides but nothing serious occurred. On Tuesday night, Dec. 1st, the enemy began to retreat, unknown however to us until around 3 o'clock on the next morning, when our division, with Early's also, was marched, quick time, in pursuit. Ramseur's brigade was in the van and picked up several hundred stragglers, broken down, &c., as we advanced toward Germana ford, where the yankees had barely crossed ere we arrived in sight on the south side. In their retreat they destroyed all the property belonging to citizens along the rout. I counted the smoking ruins of five different farm houses, — some of which had been costly buildings. For 12 miles scarce a rail, barn, or other outhouse was left. All or nearly all the stock and poultry in the whole country had been killed to feed the starving horde, and yet the prisoners said for lack of rations they retreated; about true I guess, since one of the prisoners offered a silver watch for a dozen of crackers, which unfortunately, could not be raised among the rebels either. People at home can form no idea of the straits to which we are sometimes reduced.
>
> When within sight of the river further pursuit was deemed inexpedient, and the whole column was turned homewards. So many glad fellows I never saw before. A bloodless victory! On Thursday morning last we arrived in the same old shanties we had left, and above the confusion in camp cheerily sang the song,
>
> "So let the wide world wag as it will,
>   I'll be gay and happy still,
> Gay and happy, gay and happy,
>   I'll be gay and happy still"
>
>   NAT.

[Published in the *Carolina Watchman* December 21, 1863]

· 14 ·

WINTER QUARTERS SOUTH
OF THE RAPIDAN

The heavy rains, muddy roads, and a shortage of rations affected both Union and Confederate armies and brought an end to any further action in the Mine Run campaign. The Federal army withdrew, and the 4th North Carolina, along with other regiments, settled into their winter quarters on the south side of the Rapidan River.

> **From the 4th North Carolina.**
> **CABINS BELOW ORANGE, VA.,**
> **Night of Jan. 13, 1864.**
>
> I have been so fortunate as to get a piece of candle, at an enormous cost this time, but that is the way we live in these war times, and feeling indebted to the readers of the "Watchman," I have concluded to spend a few leisure moments discharging that debt, by giving my friends an inkling of what is going on with us.
>
> Now that it is leap year once again, I think it just and proper that the ladies ought to be making some advances, at least so much as to "take their seats, pen in hand," occasionally, "and drop us a few lines informing us" of their welfare, their wishes and their future prospects. As it is, I don't get a letter once per month. What can be the matter? Grieving over the "anti substitute bill,"[1] no doubt, and the result is, some are settled down in a regular "pale melancholy." Well, it don't matter so much, provided they don't take a notion to settle in "pale brandy" before this muss is over. But, my dear friends, I beg you be hopeful; there are as good fish in the sea as ever been caught out, though there are not as many good men in the Confederacy as have been caught by the conscript law. We, our illustrious selves, are still alive, and kicking as vigorously as you could expect men to kick on a quarter pound of meat per day, and even that don't come as regularly as many things I have heard tell of.

At the start of the war, the *North Carolina Standard* published the following concerning a soldier's rations:

111

What a Ration Is:

Twenty ounces fresh and salt beef, or 12 ounces pork, 18 ounces soft bread or flour, or 12 ounces hard bread; 2½ ounces beans, or 3–5 ounces rice; 1⁵⁄₆ ounces sugar; 1 ounce coffee, ground; ⅛ gill vinegar; ¼ ounce candles; ⅜ ounces soap; ½ ounce salt. This answers for the subsistence of each soldier during the day, and rightly managed is a plenty; with a prudent cook the scraps can be made up into mixed dishes and nothing will be lost.[2]

Commissary sergeants could buy from farmers when the army was on the move, but Yankee destruction of farms and the slaughtering of livestock created hardships for civilians and shortages of supplies for soldiers. At the moment Nat seems to be having slim pickings.

Nat continues:

But we are flourishing, and if our fair friends would now make use of their privileges, and give us dissolving love epistles as they "orter," to help us drive away this oppressive ennui, we would get on much better. I don't doubt but many of you think "Nat" receives, weekly, delicious sheets, and long ones from his dear Je-Je-Jemi—-Oh! I can't say it, but the fact is, he has not heard from her "within the recollection of the oldest inhabitant." Am sorry it is so, but you all know how it is. The "pitching in" process, I fear, was carried too far, we shall see. This is not what I was going to say when I began, but my candle goes down prodigiously fast and I must keep writing—no time to meditate; a better time is coming, provided it is possible to get candles.

We are getting on famously; have warm, comfortable cabins, good clothing, warm bedding generally, and enough to eat to keep us from forgetting how to use our jaws, in case we should be so fortunate as to get anything which would require their services. No conjecturing about the close of the war; all have learned to consider it as something necessary, and consequently, have grown utterly callous. The men have a great deal of duty to perform. They go on picket six days out of twenty-four, on guard one day out of three, fatigue police daily. Our camp looks like a regular garrison; the cabins are alike, each sixteen feet square, with eight or nine occupants, they are built in parallel lines some two hundred yards apart, two fifty long, with the field and staff quarters at one end, and, at the other, the guard house. About three acres are enclosed in the square, which is now being cleared off for a drill ground, dress parade, &c. A hospital and church are going up. The former, I trust, may never be needed; at present we have very little sickness, though, within the last ten days, we have lost two men by death, both very suddenly; one Furchess,[3] of Co. A, died of disease of the heart, the other, Horne,[4] of Co. H, from the effects of the measles. They were buried with military honors, in which the band and a platoon of soldiers were principal actors. The church, under the direction of Mr. Anderson,[5] our chaplain, will be a complete success, energy and devotion to a single enterprise are elements of success. There is snow on the ground, and has been for the last month or nearly, though not all times covering the entire surface. As a general thing, the weather has been extremely cold, but this evening there are some indications of a thaw.

The time passes rapidly with us; we hardly know a day is begun when it is ended. The winter will soon slip away, and then spring will be upon us with its

> "Birds and flowers
> And genial showers,"

a happy season when peace reigns and we can enjoy it with youth and beauty, ay, and with some who are not so "mighty" young as you might suppose, still none the less agreeable, for that. Instead of such bliss, we expect war, disastrous, — no, we don't expect that in every sense, but bloody, terrible war. We must face the crisis next summer; and not us only, but every one throughout this scourged land. I would advise all of you to nerve yourselves for the contest. Give us what encouragement you can; bear cheerfully another year, and then, if not earlier, may Heaven grant us the reward for which we have been so long and so faithfully struggling — freedom and home with a ****.

NAT.

[Published in the *Carolina Watchman* January 25, 1864]

From the 4th North Carolina.
NIGHT OF FEB. 17th, 1864.

We left Salisbury Friday morning, the 12th instant, and arrived in camp on the Sunday following, through without accident or misconnections. On our arrival here we were greeted with cheers from all quarters; the boys seemed as much rejoiced to see us as though we had been absent a year, when to us it did not appear that we had been away a week. We found the regiment in the same quarters below Orange, which were occupied by them before our trip home, although we were told positively on the morning we left Salisbury that the Fourth had moved to Richmond or thereabouts. We took possession of our old shanties immediately, in which we found everything unmolested — except our "ration bag" which, from some cause or other, is absent without leave. And these cabins have been doing us valuable service, notwithstanding we have kitchen, parlor, dining room, bedroom and smoke house — all beneath the same roof. Snow fell all day on Monday the 15th — Tuesday morning it lay three inches deep, but the sky was clear, and when the sun arose its beams fell so mild and warm that by noon every particle of snow had disappeared; it barely remained long enough to allow the soldiers to fight half dozen minnie battles, which seems to be a favorite sport, and is certainly not so unpleasant nor unhealthy as the reality itself. Tuesday morning the atmosphere suddenly became extremely cold and a freezing, furious wind, fresh from the snow-capped mountains westward, drove everybody to his hole, there to remain until necessity forces him out or the weather becomes more favorable.

One o'clock! and I am really afraid to go to bed. I don't want to freeze into an ice peg, I can't think my time for that is come; I should be very sorry indeed if it had, not that I care a whit for myself, but then you know such an event would furnish the newspapers capital, and the fact is, I don't want my name mixed up with such phrases as "a sad occurrence," "melancholy accident," "froze to death, &c." Besides this little aversion to notoriety, I have other and more weighty reasons for my dread of the freezing process. I have made big "kalkalations" on coming events, which have truly cast their shadows before them, but the substance, the realization cannot be experienced until we see the other end of this war; at least it is so reported. And then my dear — (I might as well say it,) Jemima, would take it hard when she heard of my "going up the spout" — literally friz, because my bedfellow was an iceberg! How sad to contemplate!

I'm not right sure, but I don't think the sum and substance of "Nat" has yet made its exit from the Old North State. I feel that something is missing; I am so frequently told by others that now I half-way believe it myself. And if the truth must be told — (you will not tell anybody? 'pon honor,) well, the truth is, there is more than one shell in the 4th N.C. Band. Don't take it up in a yankee sense, and understand me to say that "inards" are left behind; I only assert what I know to be fact, and that is, somebody has stolen our hearts! I know, too, that more than one hard bargain has been made, but if they (the ladies) can stand it I am sure we can — if they are satisfied we are happy. Consoling thought! Yes! But then, laying all jokes aside, I am forced to admit (and I speak for my companions also) that during our recent visit home we spent some of the happiest hours that can crowd into our short lives. Our enjoyments at different places were of different natures, which, by the way, made the time pass more pleasantly, and after all more swiftly. Would I could have clogged the wheels of old sol's car! It should have been done soon after his disappearance below the western horizon, or a short time before his appearance above the eastern. I shall never forget those three happy nights, the first spent in Salisbury, the second in Charlotte and the third in Statesville. — Many pleasant incidents occurred which made an impression on my mind lasting as life itself. A chapter should be devoted to each, but the small hours are coming on apace — nor could I do them justice were I to attempt it. The best of order was preserved throughout, all seemed to have forgotten for the time being that such a thing as war existed on the continent. The concerts were certainly a decided hit, not only in pecuniary point of view (which was of minor importance) but in other respects also. We were enabled to form new acquaintances, some of whom were quite agreeable and attractive to say the least — young ladies and gentlemen were offered a pretext for a collision, merry evenings and social tea parties were some of the fruits, and last, but not least, we (perhaps) elevated to some degree the musical tastes among the masses. We felt proud to see so many ladies present on every occasion. It was unmistakable evidence of their good taste and judgment, and we assure them they shall never be forgotten by us; yet they deserve more than we shall ever be able to bestow.

Col. Young, of Charlotte, has our warmest thanks and best wishes. It is seldom such treats are tendered to such rough customers, still we don't think our brain is addled, nor our appetites spoiled — another glass of egg-nog, if you please, — I believe I am one behind, two for the Major since he forgot his scores; — there, we are square now — that was the contract — all right.

And the printers — I must not forget them. Their kindness has often been the subject of remark in confabe amongst ourselves. We feel under many obligations, but regret sorely the ignorance or neglect which caused us to make a serious blunder in our conduct towards them, and hope to be able to correct it, hereafter.

NAT.

[Published in the *Carolina Watchman* March 7, 1864]

John Augustus Young was appointed Lieutenant Colonel of the 4th Regiment on May 16, 1861, and resigned because of illness in March 1862. He returned to North Carolina. Colonel E. A. Osborne wrote the following about him in his "History of the 4th Regiment":

> It may be proper to say a word in regard to the absence of Lieutenant Colonel John A. Young from this battle and thereafter. He had been for some time before the war, and at its beginning, a manufacturer of woolen cloth; and had been sent home to procure clothing for the men of the regiment, which he abundantly supplied. Colonel Young was also afflicted with a distressing and incurable disease, which rendered him unfit for military service. This was a great sorrow to him, as he was a devoted patriot and naturally of a military spirit. But being assured that he could serve his country more effectively at home than in the army, he at the earnest request of Governor [Zebulon B.] Vance, as well as friends in the army and at home, resigned his commission and devoted himself to manufacturing clothing for the soldiers. This he did at much pecuniary sacrifice to himself, insomuch that at the close of the war found him almost a bankrupt in estate. He devoted himself especially in supplying the wants of the Fourth Regiment, at one time supplying every member of the regiment with a uniform and cap at his own individual cost, and his enterprise, industry and munificence contributed greatly to the comfort and welfare of North Carolina soldiers generally.[6]

From the 4th North Carolina.
MARCH 11TH, 1864.

A little difficulty — All smooth — Some uneasiness — Rain in tub fulls — The last year of the war — Rations — They see a good time — Women in camp — Not a nice thing in all cases — "Snuffers" called on.

No change has been effected in our situation or affairs since the date of my last letter. I admit that I had been a little derelict in my duties lately, but a "Watchman" just handed in reminds me of the fact, that ere this its readers are looking for another from your most obedient servant. A little difficulty, which will yet be amicably adjusted, has interfered slightly with my arrangements, and for the time being temporarily impeded my facility — rather my means of correspondence. This trouble is over now, and the excitement to the late "On to Richmond," has entirely subsided, and in its stead an unusual calm prevails. But the alarm was sufficient to have our brigade ordered out in the most disagreeable weather we have had since the winter set in, and kept out two days and nights, after all to no purpose whatever. We have the satisfaction of knowing that the late raid turned out a stupendous failure, and for the future I should not be surprised if a sharp look out should be kept for the adventurers. The result of the late operations is a standing order in our camp to "hold ourselves in readiness to move at any moment." At present our regiment is on picket at Morton's ford — to-morrow they will be relieved. And a rough time they have had. Yesterday a sluice of rain fell during the entire day, and to-day a fine mist keeps everything thoroughly saturated. We are not sorry to see this rain, not by any means. Not that we feel such deep concern in the farms and vegetables around here, but we want to see the mud so deep and the water courses so high as to render all military operations impossible; our armistice for the winter will then last a little while longer for mutual agreement. The campaign will open soon enough at best — not however before we are ready but before we are quite willing. From past experiences we can form a pretty good idea of what we may expect this summer, and, to confess the truth, we are somewhat loath to enter the arena again. Yet we hope, ah! how fondly we hope that this summer will be the last of this horrible war. I don't know why it is, but it is none the less certain for that, everybody looks forward with glowing anticipations concerning this summer's campaign. A confidence is felt which I never saw manifested before, and when the terrible ordeal comes, as come it will ere long, I don't think there is a soldier in our army but will face the danger boldfully and manfully. Last spring we were flushed and sanguine, and now the tale of last summer is easily told and in a few words. Shall it be so again? Ah! the dread, the doubt, the dim uncertainty which veils the future! Yet it is undoubtedly best for us that we cannot draw aside the curtain that hides from view the events which the future has in store for us. "Hope deferred maketh the heart sick," but let us hope on, and struggle on; the end will come, perhaps sooner than any of us imagine. We have no complaints to make. — We are blessed with good health almost universally. Our duties are light, and our rations plentiful enough, though of a coarser sort than is quite agreeable. We get barely enough meat to grease our ribs; get flour about twice per week, the balance made up in meal, sugar, coffee and molasses; on the whole, enough to keep us content and in good pork order. Some of our men have had a glorious time during the winter. Who, do you say? Those who have been at home on furlough? Yes, we had a very good time, very nice, and all that. Would like to try it over, but then we didn't have a sponsor, consequently our glory was not quite so ecstatic as it otherwise might have been. Nor our enjoyment so pure and unadulterated as it might have been with those whose better halves have been moved by the spirit, or something else, to pay a visit to the army. We have had women, more or less, larger or smaller, with us all winter. Certainly they have husbands out here, at least men who pass for husbands, and for aught I know to the contrary may indeed be "liege lords;" — and the women generally look as though the knot might have been tied in the days of "Auld lang syne," — and the "oldest inhabitant" may have a dim recollection of the happy time, I say these may be so, I don't know, but I do know that some men out here have had a jolly old time of it. Spose the feminines have had it quite as jolly; I only judge from experience and hearsay — spoiled it at last. I didn't mean to say "experience," for I'm sure I've had none, however much it may have been desired, — I meant observation and hearsay, the latter not very charitable either in all cases. There are exceptions, but, all things considered, I don't think the camp is a place at all appropriate for women. The scenes they are obliged to witness — the language they are compelled to hear is by no means calculated to make very chaste impressions on their sensitive minds. The very nature of the case prevents its being anything but damaging to morals; and to effect a change for the better (if expedient) in **** condition, habits and management of soldiers, would require such a revolution in our system out here, as to render the whole thing at once impracticable, if not impossible. Then we say that the dear women had better stay at home and grin and bear it as best they can, unless their husbands are so fortunate as to occupy a position that will enable them to board in the country temporarily, in which case we have no more to say; no objections can be urged against that plan. "Snuffers" in a late article in the *Watchman*, hit the subject forcibly, and I may add truthfully. Give us your paw "Snuffers"—guess we're on the same list—both old bachelors, with nary "old doorman" to come our here and console us and bedrabble her petti____. Finish the sentence "Snuffers," I'm caved in.

[Published in the *Carolina Watchman* March 21, 1864]

While inclement weather had been the rule, the men knew that warmer weather was coming and with it a return to active campaigning. "The campaign will open soon enough," Nat wrote, and he hoped it would be the last summer campaign of the war. "Everybody looks forward with glowing anticipations concerning this summer's campaign." Morale among the troops was high. General James Longstreet and his First Corps had returned from fighting further south, strengthening Lee's army. However, President Lincoln had appointed a new Lieutenant General to command of all the Federal forces — Ulysses S. Grant. Lee's army would face yet another new Union commander.

From the 4th North Carolina.
CABINS NEAR ORANGE, VA.,
April 7th, 1864.

April storms — Real comfort — Hopes brighter — Gov. Vance's visit — His speech — a few points given — Reviews — Enthusiastic audiences — Music &c — An agreeable change in the weather — Robin red-breasts, &c.

For several days past the weather has been so unmercifully inclement that it has been impossible to do anything with satisfaction, except smoking and telling yarns as we gather round the cozy fires. Old citizens in this section say that this is but the usual "April storm," which invariably visits this latitude between the first and middle of the month. I don't doubt it; to our own cost we have found it so for three successive springs. The first storm of this sort came on us while we were perched on Clark's mountain in April '62; the second, last spring at Fredericksburg, and the third here, below Orange; where next we can hardly say, and for my own part I'm not so intimate with the winters out here that I care much about giving them another such familiar shake at parting while my situation remains the same as it is at present. But we have no reason to complain,—indeed we are thankful that it is so well with us. Instead of freezing on picket, or in old split and demoralized tents as we did last spring, now we can sit by our snug firesides and listen with feelings aglow with real pleasure at the wind raving around the corners of our shanty, or to the sleet and raindrops incessantly clattering on our clapboard roofs. This is comfort for you, — genuine, heart-felt comfort; far exceeding anything we have experienced since the beginning of the war. Things have certainly taken a turn for the better, this fact is self-evident. Our men are well clad, better than at any former period of the war, well shod, sickness is almost unheard of, our rations are abundant but coarse, principally meal and bacon, and a spirit of contented cheerfulness and buoyant hope pervades the army truly encouraging. We are gaining ground, there is no kind of doubt about it. We hear no complaints or grumbling; desertions, with rare exceptions, are numbered among the things that were, and the encouraging news from all points of the Confederacy, and from the North also, have breathed into our soldiers a confidence not easily shaken. All seem fully convinced that the summer will tell the tale, and though the hard blows pending are dreaded, yet the men seem eager for them to begin that they may be sooner over. No one with whom I have conversed harbours in his breast a single misgiving about the result; and now, with the blessing of Providence, we can see, for the first time since the beginning of this bloody struggle, a light dawning ahead of us. My readers may think there is more fancy than fact about this assertion, but all will see for themselves ere another six months roll away, unless some unlooked for and terrible catastrophe befalls our arms.

But nothing has tended so much to inspire the troops with fresh zeal or strengthen their faith in our cause, in the loyalty of all those at home and in our intimate and early triumph as the late visit of Governor Vance and his well timed speeches. On the 26th ult. he addressed an enthusiastic audience in Daniel's, and on Monday following another in this (Ramseur's) brigade.

Zebulon Baird Vance raised a company in May 1861 in western North Carolina that was known as the "Rough and Ready Guards." It later became Company F, 14th Regiment North Carolina Troops. In August, 1861, he was elected Colonel of the 26th North Carolina Regiment and led them at the Battle of New Bern, and during the Seven Days Battle at Richmond. In 1862 he was elected the wartime governor of North Carolina. General Junius Daniel, a West Point graduate, first commanded the 14th Regiment and later the 45th Regiment.

Nat continues:

In the forenoon (Monday 28th ult.) the N.C. troops in Rodes' division, consisting of two brigades, Ramseur's and Daniel's, with the 1st and 3d N.C. regiments attached to Stewart's Virginia brigade, were mustered in an old field not far from camp where the Governor was put through a grand review in the most imposing and warlike manner imaginable. I should add that Johnson's (formerly Iverson's brigade) also belongs to this Division, but at present absent on detached service at _____ where I must not say, the news might be contraband. Well, the review closed at noon; it was said the musicians had blowed off five years of their allotted time, but no matter, the occasion demanded an effort, and we cheerfully made it. But we were not done yet; the troops under arms, together with large numbers of other commands who hoped to hear the eccentric and popular Governor speak or at least get a peek at him, — all were marched to the 30th N.C. camp, where a stand had been prepared for the occasion, and around which the immense multitude gathered in regular military order. The stand was located in a small hollow, three sides of which descend gradually to the centre, thus forming a kind of natural amphitheatre which was literally jammed with human souls from the base to the summit. Perhaps a dozen ladies were present, some on horseback and others in ambulances; but these unsuspecting and modest visitors, though thrice welcome to the audience, were, nevertheless, a serious stumbling block to the speaker when relating some of his most appropriate and best anecdotes; some of which to my certain knowledge he paraphrased, mutilated, struck out and substituted words out of regard to the sensibilities of the gentler ones who composed a small though not insignificant portion of his audience; and these few, when they belong to the upper circles, as all intelligent ladies do, always have a very nice perception of the meaning in whatever sense they may be used. The speaker knew this of course and spiced his stories accordingly, the result of which in some instances, was extremely ludicrous as the reader might well imagine. After some stirring music from the 4th N.C. and 10th Va. bands (both of which had endeavored to blow each other's horns off on review) the Governor ascended the stage midst the deafening shouts of the assembled hosts. On the platform at his side sat Gens. Ewell, Rodes, Ed. Johnson, Early, Stuart, and a score of others of lesser grade, while in the compact audience officers of every rank, without distinction of party or State, were scattered profusely. At the meeting in Daniel's brigade Lee honored the occasion with his presence, and some say A. P. Hill also. But to resume: when order was restored the speaker began, as is his custom, with some of his drolleries, very unexpected it is true to many of his hearers, but then it fixed attention and that was his aim. He said he did not know how he could make his voice reach so many: it was like the large family he once heard of, all of whom had never had the meazles, the disease always gave out before it got round. All I have to say is, if some of you get more than your share, you must divide with your less fortunate companions when you assemble around your camp-fires for a social chat. (We've done it V____.) Fellow soldiers (he continued) but, perhaps you think I have no right to say "Fellow Soldiers," since I was a soldier once myself and shirked out of it on a little furlough which you kindly gave me, and for which I'm profoundly grateful. (Guess we'll extend it one of these days.) Well, if you will not allow me to call you "fellow soldiers" I know what I can call you, and it will be all right; (then raising his voice he exclaimed) Fellow Tar Heels! (Great laughter.) Tar Heels! not misnamed either, for you always stick when the pinch comes. (Prolonged applause.) Fellow Tar Heels; I have left a herd of croakers, grumblers and growlers, and shirkers to pay a visit to the Confederacy. You are the Confederacy — you, the soldiers from whatever State, for I am happy to see many here to-day who are not Tar Heels, though your honor is none the less bright. This visit to the army of Northern Virginia has given me some real pleasure — has done me more good than anything I ever did in my life, except getting married. (Laughter.) I now face the living wall which has so long and so nobly defended our homes and our fire-sides, and proud am I to see it, after so many storms and fierce battles, yet staunch, defiant and I believe I may safely add, impregnable. He continued in this eloquent strain nearly an hour, during which the vast audience was so still, and wrapped in such close attention that we could almost hear our own hearts beat. It is impossible to describe the speech, much less the effect. But the Governor, in this sublime oratory, felt evidently somewhat like a fish out of water; so, descending from his exalted position, he continued more on the colloquial style, with occasional outbursts of genuine eloquence. He besought the soldiers to be patient, to stand firm through one more campaign, and, with God's blessing, we would have peace, as he firmly believed. He condemned desertion and deserters in the strongest possible terms. "For a conscript who had never smelt gunpowder, to desert, he thought, might be excusable, but for an old veteran who carried scars, honorable scars — for him to desert was the unpardonable sin. How inconsiderate, how criminal, to doom himself and his posterity to irretrievable disgrace! How can a true soldier feel, who has been induced by some evil-minded individual, or by the complaints and murmurings of relatives and friends, to desert his colors and his comrades in arms,— I say, how can he feel while skulking in the woods at home, dodging and hiding from a militia officer! A militia officer!"— He said there were men in N.C. who made a great deal of fuss, they considered that their right, but when the test came they were always found on the right side. They were like an old fellow down in North Carolina who once tried to evade the "Dog-tax-law." It may look a little green to some of you, but it is true, nevertheless, that we used to have a law in our parts by which dogs were taxed five dollars per head; and one day a seedy old customer went before the magistrate to make his returns. All went off smoothly; so many cattle, so many horses, some many acres of land, etc., and lastly, one dog. When all was down he turned to leave, chuckling in himself over his cuteness in fooling the magistrate out of five dollars tax for another dog which he had not given in. "Hello," says the squire to his departing friend —"you must swear to this return." "What's that you say?"—"Must swear to this." "Must swear to it, must I?" "Yes, you must swear to it." "Have to swear to it, hey!" (Feigning great surprise.) "Well since I must swear to it, just put me down another dog if you please." (A roar of laughter followed this anecdote: the reader can see the application.) "Well," continued the speaker, "I am aware that N.C. has been stigmatized as the "nest of deserters," "a harbor for traitors" and all that, and I am sorry to say that once there was a shade of truth connected with these assertions, but when the whole truth is made public it will be seen that N.C. is not more deserving of these detracting epithets than some of her sister States."

But why should I attempt to go further in giving the outlines of a speech which consumed two hours in its delivery? I began with the intention of giving only the most important points as I could call them to mind from memory, but I find that all are important alike. And the length of my letter already admonishes me that I had best wind up. With this laudable object in view I will begin by stating that the Governor concluded with a touching and eloquent appeal to the feelings of his hearers. He felt confident the end was drawing nigh — that our enemies had staked all on this summer's campaign, and that if our brave boys were only favored with success by an overruling and all-wide Providence, peace would surely follow first; that the ratification of treaties and foreign recognition and finally our triumphal march home; happy greetings, joyous meetings and bliss inexpressible, almost inconceivable awaited the soldier who is faithful to the end.

He was done, and as the speaker took his seat, three loud and prolonged cheers were given for the Governor of the Old North State, followed by lively and stirring music from the bands. This visit of our Executive and his speeches are worth a corps of troops to us. The North Carolinians feel their bosoms burn with pride when they remember what a champion they have, and how ably and powerfully he has vindicated the name and honor of our mother State and her sons.

After half an hour's intermission, during which hearty and cordial congratulations were exchanged, introductions given, music, &c., Gen. Early was called for. He responded in a few appropriate remarks, the gist of which was, the hope that our present Governor might be re-elected to serve another term. (Before this nothing had been said in anywise connected with the subject.) Rodes and Johnson responded briefly to the clamorous calls made from all quarters, after which came Gen. Ewell's turn, but the hero of Manassas, being rather disinclined, shuffled his cork leg off just in time to escape the necessity of making a harangue to his "mules,"—as the soldiers of his command are sometimes designated, and not altogether inaptly either, judging from the size of the knapsacks many of them carry and the labor they perform.

The sun was taking his last lingering peep over the Blue Ridge as we returned to camp, and since then his rays have seldom cheered us. Snow, sleet, wind and rain have been storming us day and night until we had almost given up the hope of balmy spring's return. But last evening the dark, murky clouds, as if frightened at some hideous spectre in the frigid zones, chased each other southward in a race for a more genial clime. Perhaps the abomination lately set up in Yankeeland, known as miscegenation (new name for amalgamation) had something to do with the scare in the elements; be that as it may, by the time the sun went down not a cloud was visible; instead of boisterous winds a perfect calm prevailed, and when thick darkness came on the stars seemed to hold a kind of jubilee over the vanquished and retreating storms of winter; and today the undimmed rays of the broad sun reanimate the whole face of nature. Our camp looks bright and cheerful, the soldiers are unusually merry and full of fun, while flocks of old robin red breasts trot about on the ground, occasionally stopping to turn up their white tinged eyes and ivory bills in an independent, saucy way, as much as to say as plain as words could express it "Touch me if you dare."

No signs of a move except an order to send surplus baggage to the rear, which is generally pretty good evidence of a storm brewing. Active preparations are making over the river, under Grant's directions, for the coming onslaught, which will be such a shock as has never been felt nor witnessed on this continent; it will be the dying gasp of the old government and perhaps the birth of more than a single new one.

NAT.

[Published in the *Carolina Watchman* April 18, 1864]

General Grant was well aware of the industrial might of the North and its vast reserves of soldiers. He would attack Lee in a new way. No longer would there be set battles where opposing armies would contest ground for a day or two, then withdraw for a time to rest, regroup, and rearm before coming out to fight again. Grant would use the North's industrial power and soldiery to hammer relentlessly on the Southern army. He would wage a war of attrition, never giving Lee's army a chance to rest until it was slowly worn down and forced to surrender. Against Lee's army of 65,000 men and 224 guns, Grant would field an army of 118,000 men and 316 guns. On May 4, 1864, just days after Nat wrote the following letter, Grant would cross the Rapidan River and move toward that section of Virginia known as the Wilderness.

From the 4th North Carolina.
CABINS BELOW ORANGE, VA.,
April 27th, 1864.

Still hold our position — Camp rumors — Surplus baggage sent back — Bright prospects — An appeal — Politician's logic — The conclusion — A warning — A little ballast — Health — Spring time &c., &c.

The balmy days of Spring are here and yet we occupy our quarters. We have held our position more than four months and very agreeably surprised are we to find it the case. Yet we would not be surprised to leave at any hour; indeed, we have been expecting marching orders for several days past, but up to this moment every thing remains perfectly tranquil, notwithstanding many startling rumors afloat. Nothing, however, in all the news going the rounds, is calculated to discourage the troops, — on the contrary, everything is highly animating, and the consequence is, strengthened faith and hope for the future.

All surplus baggage has been sent to Richmond; transportation for the commissary and quartermaster departments has been cut down to the very shortest limit, while each man in the ranks will be encumbered with nothing save his "armament," together with one blanket and such light articles of clothing as are indispensably necessary to decency and comfort. Under the head of "surplus baggage," a large lot of blankets, overcoats, winter clothing, tents, axes, &c., are stored away in Richmond for use again when,

"the snow gleams where the flowers have been,"

provided we are not then more comfortably quartered at home, which, from our inmost souls we hope and trust may be our good fortune. Meanwhile we must not sink into a stupor; and because our prospects are so flattering now, we must not neglect or fail to exert ourselves for our own good. It is an old adage that "Providence helps those who help themselves," and one most especially true in war. Then, instead of folding our arms and complacently waiting the result, every being in the South should be up and doing; working with our whole souls in whatever capacity becomes us, no matter how humble or insignificant; in the aggregate our labors will have a wonderful influence for good — that good the peace so earnestly desired by all good people, both North and South, that peace to be obtained only by a complete and final dissolution of the old Union, and in the independence of the Southern Confederacy. Men may talk as they please, but it is contrary to reason and to the very nature of human beings to expect peace as the result of reconstruction, or State Sovereignty, as some people seem to understand it. The idea of making North Carolina an independent kingdom (or whatever else you wish to call it) by herself, regardless of the relation she sustains to her sister States, is supremely ridiculous; and never was seriously entertained or advocated by any sane man unless he expected to build his own glory on the wreck of his State. I don't include the ignorant, short sighted persons who are for peace on any terms, regardless of the loss of national honor, and likewise regardless of future consequences. There may be some men who honesty believe that if the independence of the old North State were acknowledged, that it would bring peace to every citizen within her borders, and to every soldier in her armies; but such men hardly ever act or think for themselves — they are governed solely by the oily tongued demagogues who aspire to fortune or fame, perhaps both. Yet, this very class of men hold the balance of power, and, in order that a man may be placed in a position where he can do his country a service, it is necessary that he should attach apparent importance to the prejudices and opinions of these very men. This is but a rough and brief hint at a politician's logic, and this much I have said only to show that we are not altogether unconcerned in the political contest waging in our mother State. I have no time to argue, nor do I intend to do it; I shall only jump at the conclusion, and it is this — Grant and Lee are the individuals who must decide the fate of the candidates at the election in August next, I mean in the State of North Carolina. If we are victorious here, the great crisis will be forever past; if we sustain reverses, why then our home troubles will only be begun, and Heaven only knows when the end may come. I am rejoiced to learn that the spirit in our home people is greatly revived, and that it has been discovered, sure enough, that "we are goin' to whip 'em," — very pleasant news this; but let me remind you of the fact that two can play at this game out here. Instead of "whipping 'em," we might get licked ourselves. I say "might" — that is hardly probable, but it is best not to expect too much, then we are sure of not being disappointed. The enthusiasm of our soldiers, and also of those at home, is at such an extravagant pitch, that if we should meet with misfortune, the tumble from hope almost realized, to absolute despair, would be so great, that I fear we would hardly ever recover from its effects. Better then prepare ourselves for bad news before hand, and then hope for better. I don't think that it is at all likely that the war will hardly last more than a year longer, but no matter; it will never do to give it up, and a year hence, if we don't find it ended, let us be resolved to push ahead, cheerfully and full of courage, and the end will come some day with triumph for us — this is certain if we have faith in an over-ruling Providence. The citizens of North Carolina, besides being a law abiding people, I find are zealous in the adherence to scriptural maxims, inasmuch as they are, never lukewarm. They are either too hot or too cold, like a certain bake-over I heard of once. Perhaps I do them injustice by putting it in the superlative — At any rate, in days past a little too much coldness was manifested in certain localities, while now the thermometer has bounced up to the boiling point. Steady, friends, while I sincerely trust that nothing may occur to dampen your ardor, yet I would have you bear in mind that a cool determination will yet win the day. And if we should fail now, why, we can only try, try again.

I have no news of importance to communicate, further than a reiteration of what I have said before, and that is, you may look for stirring times in these quarters soon.—There is no use disguising the fact, the main armies of the North and South are concentrated on the banks of the Rapidan, and here will be the final tilt on a grand scale. At least the signs of the times indicate that at present. If we are blessed with success the heavy fighting will then be over. It is true, that small engagements may take place afterwards, but I feel safe in predicting a languishing death to the war.

The health of the army continues excellent, and the spirit uncommonly exuberant.

The winds and storms are over, and the warm sunshine of spring is breathing life into the fields and forests around us. We feel as though we ought to be engaged in other business, but it seems that we must content ourselves a little while longer with this monotonous and disagreeable mode of life.

NAT.

[Published in the *Carolina Watchman* May 9, 1864]

· 15 ·

SPOTSYLVANIA COURT HOUSE

While General Lee moved his forces to counter General Grant's advance, Ramseur's Brigade and other troops were left at Raccoon Ford on the Rapidan River to watch for any advance of Federal forces from that direction. Ramseur sent several groups across the river to probe for the enemy, but when none were found, he ordered all regiments to march south to rejoin the Second Corps. Grimes' 4th Regiment could only field about 325 officers and men for the coming battle.

Nat wrote the following letter between May 11 and 14. In the first part, he summarizes the fighting of May 5 through May 8.

> **From the 4th North Carolina.**
> **IN LINE OF BATTLE NEAR SPOTTSYLVANIA C.H., VA.**
> **EVE, May 11th, 1864.**
>
> Where shall I begin? That's the question. So great has been, and now is, the excitement, and so much has transpired within the last ten days, that I am utterly at a loss to know where or how to begin the record. This is the eighth day of the great battle of the Rapidan, and yet it is not over. And if we are to believe the reports of prisoners, we would suppose the heaviest has not come yet, though for the life of me, I can't imagine how the struggle is to be more sanguine or terrible than it has already been. But we are told that Grant is receiving tremendous reinforcements — where from, it is impossible for me to say — any way they may say they are coming.
>
> *Morn, May 12th.* — My letter was cut abruptly short last evening by a heavy thunder shower; a little rain fell during the night, and this morning dense clouds are sending down an incessant and very cool mist. This is the first rain or unfavorable weather of any kind since the first of the month. It is quite early, not more than 8 A.M., and while I write the thunder of a hundred cannons and the ominous rattling of thousands of muskets tell of bloody work going on in front. Already a number of wounded have been brought it, a list of which you will find appended.
>
> This is the ninth day of the battle, skirmishing began on Wednesday the 4th. —

Fighting in the Wilderness. Combat during the Battle of the Wilderness was
made difficult by what Nat described as "gentle hills interspersed with many
swamps and marshes ... underbrush and brambles so dense as to be almost
impenetrable." (David B. Scott, *A School History of the United States* [New
York: American Book, 1884]. ClipArt used by permission of the Florida Center for Instructional Technology, College of Education, University of South
Florida.)

On the 5th a fierce battle was fought by Early and Johnson on our side, in the
"Wilderness," some fifteen miles above this point. Our brigade was not engaged;
at that time we were on picket at Moreton's ford, and had been several days previously. The very air was burthened with rumors of a great battle approaching —
of the evacuation by the enemy in our front and of their crossing the river in heavy
force below us, all of which has turned out literally true, though at the time we
made due allowances for the many extravagant reports which were circulated.
Everything across the river in our front was unusually quiet; — this we regarded
as a bad sign — and sure enough, at noon Thursday, we left the river and took up
the line of march towards Chancellorsville, distant about fifteen miles. When half
way on our road we received intelligence of the battle in the "Wilderness" and of

our victory, which was reported so complete that it made us somewhat dubious. However, I ascertained, by actual observation, that the half had not been told us. Passing the battle ground of "Mine Run" and our fortifications there, on which many remarks were made, we pressed on, and at night we camped on the outskirts of the renowned Wilderness. This significant name is applied to a scope of country some ten miles square, extending from Chancellorsville upward on the plank road, and averaging some twenty to thirty miles from Orange Court House. The face of the country is broken into gentle hills, interspersed with many swamps and marshes; the soil sterile, few farms or habitations are to be seen — large timber is scarce, but the underbrush, brambles and such like, are so dense as to be almost impenetrable. For this reason very little artillery was used in the various battles, until the contested ground was transferred to this place. On the morning of the 6th, we found ourselves in the vicinity of "blue coats." Skirmishers were sent forward, who soon engaged the enemy, the troops were drawn up in line of battle and the signs generally betokened a battle. Surgeons and non-combattants were sent to the rear with orders to make ready for the reception of all who might be so unfortunate as to get wounded. Still the day passed without a fight on our portion of the line, while at other points the firing was heavy. On the day previous, Early and Johnson had driven the Yankees two miles with great slaughter. Many prisoners as well as the wounded and dead, with all the indescribable debris of the battle field, fell into our hands. On Saturday the 7th, I visited the bloody field. When within half a mile of the enemy's abandoned earthworks signs began to show where the contest was hottest, and soon I found myself standing amidst the congregation of the dead and wounded of the enemy. The few of our own men, who had been killed, were decently buried, and our wounded all cared for. Besides, our own hospitals were filled with Yankee wounded — the latter in proportion of three to one of the former; and yet, many of the enemy's wounded were lying on the field uncared for, as well as all of their dead unburied, (and so the dead remain to this day, I suppose,) and some of them partially burned to cinders by the fearful woods-fire which followed in the wake of our column. The enemy occupied trenches, out of which they did not retreat until our troops were within fifteen steps of them. Indeed, some were actually bayoneted. Finally, the enemy could not stand it any longer — no power on earth could have prevented a panic — the advance of the rebels seemed irresistible; the gaps in their ranks were closed as rapidly as they were made, and at last the enemy turned and fled in the greatest confusion, leaving their knapsacks, guns, blankets, canteens, haversacks and every conceivable sort of plunder in the trenches behind them. And from the moment they left their works, from that moment the slaughter began in earnest. I saw dead men in every imaginable posture; some with cartridges in their teeth, some with their cartridge or cap boxes, others with ramrods halfway down; and others still on their knees in the act of firing, but the large majority were killed while running for life and fell sprawling forward on their faces, or to paraphrase on each, he lay

> "_____With his face to the field
> And his feet to the foe."

The timber was literally torn into splinders — scarce a shrub escaped, and that a single soul should come out living is truly a wonder. Sickened with the many horrible sights, I left the field impressed more deeply than ever with the untold horrors of war — Bloody, terrible war!

On Sunday the 8th, the Yankees attempted to outflank us on the right — a corresponding move was made on our part, and during the entire day the two armies marched parallel and within cannon shot of each other. The course was Eastward, and at night the van of both armies was near Spottsylvania C. House, where the lines were established and remain to this day. Meantime more or less fighting has been going on every day with variable success on either, but, so far as I have been able to learn, no great advantage has been gained by either party.

The reinforcements spoken of by prisoners have arrived, I presume, and to-day a most terrible battle is raging, regardless of the pelting rain which is now falling incessant and heavily. The cannonading is hardly inferior to that at Gettysburg, while the musketry roars like a furious tornado. The great and decisive battle of this campaign is doubtless in progress now, and while I write I am so much oppressed with anxiety about the result that my hand is really nervous. This cold and constant rain has already made us exceedingly uncomfortable and to add to our unpleasant situation, shells from the enemy's batteries are hissing through the air and bursting rather near for the good of our health.

4 o'clock P.M. — The death struggle is over, for to-day, at least, and unless the tide of fortune changes to-morrow, the victory is ours. The rain has ceased — still lowering clouds hang over head, and the frightened spring birds are timidly trying to tune up their pipes. Ah! how sad their songs. Instead of joyous carrols, as is their wont, their notes are weary and plaintive, fit dirges for the thousands of dead and dying lying on the hills of Spottsylvania. The roar of battle has ceased for a while; it is said the enemy is retreating — we don't know but it is certain that our troops hold their ground at this time, though lost and won repeatedly during the day. Our loss is heavy, so it is with the enemy, it is impossible to form an estimate at present. Our wounded say the Yankees were drunk this morning — the assertion needs confirmation, any way, they showed uncommon courage. General Daniel[1] is mortally wounded. General Longstreet[2] severely. Other casualties are reported, but not confirmed.

Friday 13th — 10 o'clock, A.M. — The battle, for some reason, is not resumed. Quiet reigns this morning. Rain fell constantly last night, adding the greatest, misery to many of the wounded, who are uncomfortable enough at best. Blood! blood! It seems that everything we can lay our hands on is clotted with blood. Two-thirds of our wounded are struck in the head, neck and face — this is the result of fighting behind breastworks, and this is the first great battle since the commencement of the war, where our men were protected by artificial constructions, and it will be observed that the casualties, in the aggregate, are not near so great as they usually are. We are not apprised of any movements among the troops this morning. Possibly, the enemy may renew the attack to-day, or they may be waiting for reinforcements, expecting to fight again tomorrow, or they may be planning a retreat. It is hardly possible that General Lee indulges the remotest idea of falling back — I'm sure his troops do not.

Saturday, 14th May.—Can't make out a complete list of killed and wounded. The battle still progresses, but the enemy is certainly greatly worsted, nor should I be surprised if they retreat to-night. It has been raining terribly. P T Owens,[3] P A Heiling[4] Jacob Fraley,[5] and Serg't Otho Holtshouser,[6] Co. K, killed.—Capt. McRorie,[7] N S Brawley[8] killed, Co. A; J H Hartness,[9] Pinck Jacobs,[10] Saul Hendren,[11] killed, Co C; Peter Deal,[12] killed, Co B; Wm. Durrell's[13] left arm amputated. A great many are wounded, a complete list of which, will be given at an early date,

NAT.

[Published in the *Carolina Watchman* May 30, 1864]

The non-stop, vicious, and at times hand-to-hand fighting of May 1864 inflicted heavy casualties on both armies in men and senior commanders. With General Richard Ewell ill and almost exhausted, Lee found a replacement in General Jubal Early. Ramseur then took Early's place as commander of the division, and William Cox,[14] Colonel of the 2nd North Carolina Regiment, became Brigade Commander. Brigadier General Junius Daniel had fallen mortally wounded during the fighting at the Bloody Angle on May 12, and Grimes replaced him as Brigade Commander. James H. Wood[15] became Colonel of the 4th Regiment.

SUNDAY EVE, May 15, 1864.

[This letter follows a list of casualties from the 4th Regiment.]

Since the above report was made out, Lieut. Wm. McNeely[16] Co. A, was brought in, wounded in the right leg — not serious. He was struck while pushing the enemy who are now falling back,—perhaps massing on our right for another butchering spell. The great question now with us is, what will Grant do next? And I shouldn't be surprised if that same question bothers him no little. McNeely says it is useless to tell the people at home how men are killed and piled on each other,—men, I say the Yankees are all men except Beast Butler and perhaps a few others of the Hyena species. I have heard no estimate of our loss nor of the enemy's—theirs is certainly five times as great as ours, which figures will prove in the future, I mean it is so up to this evening, the eleventh day of battle. What the future has in store for us God only knows,—we hope an early peace.

Lieut. M. says he saw Sergt. Francis Morrison[17] this morning dead on the field. He is reported missing in the above list. Then, Sergt. Adams[18] is the only one missing from our regiment who cannot be accounted for. He was one of the sharpshooters and is supposed to be captured. J. T. Owens[19] was brought in this morning (reported killed,) mortally wounded in the head. It is hardly possible that he will survive. Jac. Fraley[20] was killed while acting gunner in a battery. Gen. Daniel is dead. Gen Ramseur was wounded in his crippled arm (the right) but still commands his brigade. Colonel Grimes commands Daniel's brigade. Rain has been falling heavily at intervals since Thursday last, and now the roads are almost impassable; still men go cherily plodding through the mud nearly up to their knees. Our troops are in excellent spirits notwithstanding their unparalleled hardships. To-day the enemy is moving back,— perhaps massing on our right, but no matter, if they will fight they will have a satisfaction of it.

NAT.

[Published in the *Carolina Watchman* June 6, 1864]

Ramseur's Brigade held a position just to the left of the Bloody Angle. Colonel E. A. Osborne, writing of the performance of the Brigade that day, recalled:

The fate of the army was at stake. Ramseur, with his Brigade, led the charge, and in the face of the most murderous fire drove back the foe and restored the broken line.... Ramseur, on his fiery steed, looked like an angel of war. Grimes, too, was on his horse, the very picture of coolness, grim determination and undaunted courage, while Wood and the other officers and men moved into the horrible conflict like men of iron and steel. The enemy, flushed with their temporary success, stood their ground with persistence and stubborn firmness, and poured into our ranks a destructive fire. But onward moved our lion-hearted men, closing up their rapidly thinning ranks, and pouring a continuous storm of leaden hail into the enemy's ranks, as he slowly, but stubbornly retired, until he reached the line of works, from which he was driven at the very point of the bayonet. The pits at the breastworks were filled with water from recent rains; many dead and wounded from both sides were lying in the pits when we reached them. The water was red with human gore. The bodies of the dead were dragged out, and the men took shelter in their places, which they held for the balance of the day. The writer received a painful contusion from a ball that passed through a heavy canteen of water which he carried, and which no doubt saved his life. After recovering from the temporary shock, he resumed his place in the line of battle, where he remained the rest of the day. After the battle General Rodes thanked the brigade in person, saying they deserved the thanks of the country, and that they had saved Ewell's Corps. General Early also made a similar statement in regard to this occasion.

This was one of the most prolonged and stubbornly contested engagements of the war. It began about halfpast five in the morning and lasted till near two o'clock the next morning.[21]

· 16 ·

INTO THE SHENANDOAH VALLEY

Nat's closing line in his last letter would prove prophetic: "If they will fight they will have a satisfaction of it." Military movements would prevent him from writing again until August 24.

The two armies would skirmish and maneuver for the remainder of May. Then, on June 3, within twelve miles of Richmond, Grant attacked Lee's formidable lines at Cold Harbor. Within thirty minutes the field was littered with over 7,000 dead Union soldiers. It was another defeat for Grant, who had engaged Lee four times — the Wilderness, Spotsylvania Court House, North Anna River, and now Cold Harbor — each with the same result.

Now Grant moved toward Petersburg. Five railroads converged there — the Southside, Petersburg & Weldon, Norfolk & Petersburg, City Point, and Richmond & Petersburg. If he could take Petersburg, Richmond would be cut off from supplies and forced into surrender.

By mid–June, Lee and the Army of Northern Virginia were under siege. In an attempt to relieve the pressure on his outnumbered soldiers, Lee detached 13,000 men from his force and sent them to the Shenandoah Valley under the command of General Jubal Early. The Valley had to be held because its farms supplied Lee's army. Without this vital resource, the army at Petersburg would be starved into submission.

Early was assigned four things to accomplish: drive the Union army out of the Valley, protect the farms and supply routes, threaten Washington, and, if possible, free the Confederate prisoners held at Point Lookout, Maryland. There were 17,000 soldiers there — needed regiments for Lee's beleaguered army if they could be freed. Lee hoped that Early's movements would force Grant to detach some of his besieging soldiers to counter Early.

Nat's regiment was part of the force that moved towards the Valley. On

July 4, Early's men captured Harpers Ferry and a number of Union soldiers. James Steele recalled the day: "They had prepared for a gala day by having a big feast, but we finished the day by eating it."[1]

On July 5, the army crossed the Potomac River at nearby Shepherdstown, and marched towards Frederick, Maryland, reaching it by July 9. Resistance had been light, but that would soon change. General Lew Wallace, who would gain fame after the war as the author of *Ben Hur,* was at Baltimore and soon learned of the approaching Confederate army. On his own he ordered his small force of 3,000 soldiers to advance to the Monocracy River. There he was reinforced by cavalry and soldiers, bringing his total to 6,500 against Early's 13,000.

The July 9 Battle on the Monocracy was sharp, decisive, and bloody. Wallace's force lost almost 1,900 in killed, wounded, captured, and missing, while Early's losses were between 600 and 700. Wallace was driven back, but, more importantly, Early's advance on Washington had been held up one day. On July 10, the Confederate army marched into Rockville, Maryland, and the Seventh Street Pike, which led straight into Washington, was reached on the 11th. Capture of the nation's capital was within his grasp.

However, General Grant, learning of the grave situation developing at Washington, ordered General Meade to build up the defenses there, and reinforcements arrived on the same day as General Early. Wallace's fight on the Monocracy had proven critical. Twenty thousand Union soldiers now manned the forts surrounding Washington.

July was fiercely hot; heat drained the men. The hard marching and fighting had nearly exhausted them. They had come several hundred miles. They had fought General Hunter in the Valley and driven him out; they had fought at Harpers Ferry; two days previously, they had engaged General Wallace. Hot, dry weather and the lack of rain which raised dust clouds when they marched had taken its toll. Still Early attacked on July 12.

Fort Stevens was the target. Heavy skirmishing broke out around the fort, and artillery fire was exchanged. Abraham Lincoln came out from the White House to view the fighting, and when Union officer Oliver Wendell Holmes saw the President standing in a dangerous position, he yelled at him, "Get down, you fool!" As the day wore on, Early realized that the forces opposing him were too strongly entrenched, and during the night, he began a withdrawal. When the Union soldiers looked out from their forts on the morning of July 13, the Confederates were gone. Early retreated back into Virginia, crossing the Blue Ridge at Snicker's Gap and the Shenandoah River at Snicker's Ford.

On July 18, 1864, a pursuing enemy force came through Snicker's Gap. Several brigades waded the Shenandoah and were on the south side while a larger force of Union troops remained on the north shore to cover their movements. James Steele described the moment:

> Here one of the most exciting scenes of the war occurred. The enemy formed line of battle and started to advance on us, and our force started to meet them and about half way between the two lines was a stone fence, both lines made a break for the fence, but as our line had the advantage of down grade they saw we would get there first, they made a hasty retreat across the ford. Our men poured a heavy volley into them and they lost many men and three regimental flags on the field and many prisoners.[2]

Colonel James H. Wood, who was in command of the 4th Regiment, was killed in the fighting at Snicker's Gap. He was buried in the yard of a local citizen, who gave the soldiers his consent. Command of the regiment passed to Captain S. A. Kelly.[3] Almost one week later, on July 24, Early's small army defeated a Federal force at the Second Battle of Kernstown.

General Grant now decided to remove the threat of Early's force and take control of the Shenandoah Valley once and for all. He dispatched General Philip Sheridan to take command of the 40,000 soldiers there and engage Early's small army of 13,000 soldiers and cavalry and crush it.

During the month of August the brigade was constantly on the move, and Nat's letter begins with a comment on that.

FROM THE 4TH NORTH CAROLINA.
CHARLESTOWN, VA., Aug. 24, 1864.

Military movements have kept me from writing sooner, and now I have barely time to send a note. I would like to write full particulars of our operations, and will certainly do so at an early day, but for the present a few lines must suffice. I am anxious to let my good readers know that I am still jogging round on "terra firma," and that everything has worked to my heart's entire satisfaction. Am sorry that I have so long been forced to keep silent, simply because I have not been "at the front," and letters from any other quarter would surely be insipid and irksome. Henceforth I trust no obstacle will be in my way, and at every opportunity to mail I shall endeavor to send the latest news, even though very short it be.

For the last ten days we have been marching and fighting almost incessantly. The enemy was started at Strasburg on the 17th inst., and up to this time they have kept up a perfect run down the valley, once in a while turning to fight a little, but never slacking the retrograde movement. And now they lie in line of battle two miles east of this town and six from Harper's Ferry, having "crawfished" about 50 miles. On their retreat they have committed many depredations. Some dwellings were burnt, and many barns with large quantities of grain, forage, &c., were consumed. They pressed all the bacon and beef, and killed all the hogs sheep, cattle, poultry, &c., along their line of march, whether needed or not. If needed, they would take them along; if not, they were left lying where they were shot. In the many skirmishes along the march, a few Confederates were killed, very few — not one in our regiment, and but few wounded. Geo. Roe, Co. I[4] is, I fear, mortally wounded. Andy Thorpe, Co. H,[5] has his left arm broken. McHargue,[6] Co. H, also received a slight wound, and Geo. Suggs,[7] Co. K, received a very painful wound in the knee. None but sharpshooters were engaged. Our corps is faring sumptuously. We get fine new flour and beef of the best quality in abundance, to say nothing of the "roast'neers" and apples, no small item. I never saw men more gay and cheerful; they evidently have the utmost confidence in Early, who is renowned for his caution and unexpected flank movements, and more for his incessant marching. This Corps has marched hardly less than 1500 miles since the opening of this campaign, yet the men are hearty generally well clothed and shod, and so much soiled that the as-es-or would be perfectly justified in putting them down as real estate. Sickness and desertion are two words knocked out of our vocabulary. Possibly, once in a month a man may take "French leave" of the army around Richmond, but it is certain that none leaves the Valley. I find it here like at other places down South; everybody thinks this is the last year of the war — the yankees themselves think so, and I'm sure all fondly hope it is. Who wouldn't prefer camp meeting to a campaign!

NAT.

[Published in the *Carolina Watchman* September 5, 1864]

FROM THE 4TH NORTH CAROLINA.
CAMP NEAR BUNKER'S HILL, VA.,
September 1, 1864.

About 8 o'clock on the morning of the 25th ult., we left Charlestown, and after an oppressive march of some ten miles, in scorching heat, and suffocating dust, we came suddenly on a stumbling block on the Baltimore and Ohio Rail Road, four miles from Shephardstown, Va. "Bluecoats" were, apparently, abundant in those parts, and they stoutly resisted our advance. But "Jubal" didn't seem to consider matters very serious. In the coolest manner possible the troops were brought up in battle line, batteries placed in position, skirmishers sent forward and at noon the fight began in earnest. After an hour's vigorous shelling and skirmishing the enemy fell back in disorder, leaving their dead and wounded and also a considerable lot of prisoners in our hands. We were pushed in pursuit at once, and not until we landed in Shephardstown was I allowed time enough to stop and take a gravel about the size of a partridge egg out of my shoe. In town we had five minutes breathing spell, when again we were marched rapidly one mile down the river, where we formed another "streak of fight" and scoured the wood's to the water's edge; found no yankees (no live ones at least) south of the Potomac at this point, and at sunset we lay down for a little rest. Eight o'clock at night found us again moving back toward Shephardstown, which is half mile from the river and three miles above the ford where troops generally cross here. Passing through the town with stirring music, at 9 o'clock that night, we were greeted with shouts and yells from all quarters;—even the ladies seemed to have lost all control of themselves and went dancing and clapping their hands and waving handkerchiefs as if an universal matrimonial day (or night) had been proclaimed. Such a joyous welcome is worth six months service at any time. Keeping the road to Martinsburg at midnight we "turned in" three miles from Charlestown. Notwithstanding the men were very tired, yet the arms were scarcely stacked when squads were seen striking out in every direction foraging while a portion of those who remained went to work cooking rations, in all probability, for another expedition tomorrow similar to the one we have had to-dad. At break of day the next morning the foragers returned, many of them earlier, some later, with their companions relating their marvelous adventures, hair-breath escapes, &c. Many didn't get further than the apple orchard, others found a cornfield and "oodles" of roast-neers; some happened, by the merest accident in the world, to stumble into a spring house where it was evident milk and butter were to be had for less than schedule prices;—a few bee hives, sheepskins, duck heads, and such like trifling articles might be found half concealed somewhere in the neighborhood of camp; how they got there is a mystery that has puzzled graver and bolder heads than mine.

Since the affair at Shephardstown things have been comparatively quiet, that is, as quiet as it ever gets in the Valley, by which we mean a march or a "scrimmage" almost every day, but short and easy marches and light fights. The enemy's forces, I believe, at various points above Harper's Ferry, consists entirely of cavalry, for whom our boys have the most supreme contempt. Citizens in Shephardstown told us the Yankee forces there, on the 25th ult., amounted to 8,000, yet they hardly stood for a showing. The same kind of fight occurred at Smithfield (six miles below Bunker Hill) on last Monday, and yesterday again our division had a running fight with them from Darksville to some place beyond Martinsburg, in which the enemy lost more than usual in men and horses. Besides these we captured a considerable quantity of Quartermaster and Commissary stores in and around Martinsburg, such as boots, shoes, clothing, pork, crackers, &c. An unopened yankee mail was also captured,—nothing of importance, however, was found. Two or three of the letters are enclosed;—if they are fit for publication, extracts, at least will appear. They are fair samples of all yankee letters.

We have no complaints to make. The best of health prevails—plenty to eat and jolly times generally. The weather continues fine, the mornings are cool, almost frosty, but the days are oppressively warm, especially when we are on a march.

NAT.

[Published in the *Carolina Watchman* September 12, 1864]

FROM THE 4TH NORTH CAROLINA.
ON PICKET NORTH OF WINCHESTER, VA.,
Sept. 14, 1864.

It seems that the "weather clerk" has forgotten himself, or has made some mistake by sending us chill autumn before the proper time. Indeed such cold, blustery gales as we have had during yesterday, last night and to-day remind us more of winter than anything else. At these licks we will have frost in less than a fort-night, and what is worse our prospects are rendered more disagreeable when we remember that we are not at all prepared for cold weather. It is hardly to be expected that our clothes and shoes partake of the nature of those worn by the children of Israel in the Wilderness; their garments never waxed old, but somehow ours do, and rents, patches and frizzles are exhibited accordingly. I doubt very much whether our nearest and dearest friends would recognize us, or if they did their business would doubtless be to transfer us to the soap and candle factory.

We have had two days of rest and quiet undisturbed. An uncommon thing with us, and unaccountable to boot. Previous to the two days just past we had rain eight or ten days in succession, and, finally, on Sunday last the juicy spell closed with a furious hail storm, the whole of which, as well as many soaking showers before it, we had to take patiently as we were marching along the road. The hail stones were, on an average, about the size of large bullets, and when the storm ceased the ground was very nearly covered. I have heard of no injury done except a right serious pelting of several thousands of soldiers, and they, I am sure, were thankful for the luxury, ice. We have been in many skirmishes recently but so far not a man in our regiment has been killed or wounded since the affair at Charlestown on the 21st ult.; we were engaged in a hot skirmish at Dulheld Sta-tion, (I believe that is the name) on the Baltimore and Ohio Railroad between Harper's Ferry and Martinsburg.

Duffield's Station (which Nat calls "Dulheld Station" in his letter of Sept. 14, 1864) was a depot and warehouse made of rough siding. In peacetime, grain and other plantation products were shipped from there. During the war sup-plies to support the Federal troops in the Shenandoah Valley were shipped to and deposited there. Mosby's Rangers raided the station on June 29, 1864. (*With Sheridan in the Shenandoah Valley in 1864: Leaves from a Special Artist's Sketch-book and Diary, James A. Taylor, 1839–1901.* Used by permission of The West-ern Reserve Historical Society, Cleveland, Ohio.)

At that time Capt. Hofflin,[8] (of Salisbury, N.C.) was in command of our regiment, and while leading his men across a knoll exposed to the enemy's fire his horse was killed under him by a shell. In the fall the Captain's foot was considerably bruised, otherwise he sustained no injury what ever.

I believe every Confederate soldier in the Valley is glad that his lot is cast in Early's Corps. We have made many hard marches, and have been engaged in many skirmishes, yet our mode of life is perfect happiness compared to the dreadful inactivity around Petersburg. While the soldiers there have spent days and weeks, I might say months in those trenches, scorched with a burning sun, suffering for lack of good water, scarce of palatable rations, exposed every hour to sharpshooters, and worse than all their suspense, their awful dread of another explosion;[9] while that has been their condition, we have been skirmishing a little, or marching, (which is the life of an army) or luxuriating in the shade, feasting on the finest fruit or other unmentionable luxuries for which this Valley is famous. This is soldiering in the summer of 1864. How thankful we should be that it is so well with us! We cannot even guess, hardly imagine what Gen. Early's plans may be. By incessant marching and countermarching we have been made familiar with every by-road and hog path in the lower valley. Sometimes we think we will have a general engagement surely, when perhaps the next hour will find us traveling from the enemy at such a break neck gait that one would suppose the old scratch himself was after us. And when we imagine ourselves entirely out of danger, all at once, to our utter amazement, a few shells come screeching over us, a line of battle is formed, guns loaded and a charge with demonized yells is made on the Yankee cavalry which is trying to get in our rear. The blue coats are generally **** and sent scampering in all directions, through the woods and fields, and an hour after dark we go into camp somewhere near the scene of action. The next day the very same game is played over. This is the way we get on in the valley. When one party is ready and shows fight, the others skedaddled out of reach of danger. Our **** of everlasting maneuvering is kept up over an area of some fifty miles in diameter. It is darkly hinted by the knowing ones that Sheridan and Early are shirking duty and trying to keep out of the war in this interesting game of base they have up between Strasburg and the Potomac. So far their success pleases us extremely well, and I trust I may be pardoned for expressing the hope that their playful mood may last indefinitely. The prevailing impression, however, is that we will be expected to hold the valley until winter sets in earnest, what will become of then, or to what point we shall go is a question unanswerable at present.

The best of health is universal, and the spirit of the army is uncommonly buoyant, notwithstanding the reverses sustained by our arms in other quarters. We are faring sumptuously, and perhaps that more than anything else is our reason for liking the valley so well.

NAT.

[Published in the *Carolina Watchman* September 26, 1864]

James Steele remembered those August days when he and Nat and the brigade were on the march:

The Brigade under the command of Colonel Cox was kept constantly on the move around Berryville, Newton, Middletown, Strasburg, Kernerstown and Bunkerhill. Sometimes tearing up railroad tracks, skirmishing, and sometimes resting. At one time we crossed the Potomac going as far as Hagerstown, then returning to Bunkerhill and to Winchester, then back to Strasburg and to Harper's Ferry. The troops liked to be on the move, even if it did make a skirmish. At Steven's Depot and Berryville there was a lot of fighting with varying results, sometimes advancing, sometimes retreating.[10]

Nat described the movements of Early and Sheridan as a game of base, but on September 19, at Winchester, the game became serious. Sheridan attacked with 35,000 men in what is called the Third Battle of Winchester. James Steele described the battle:

The Brigade was early in line. Three brigades in line, Grimes on the right, Cox in the center and Cook on the left. Our command was on the left of the Winchester and Martinsburg road. We soon engaged the enemy who came near our position, but after a short encounter they gave way, and Cox drove them through the open field and Grimes pressed them through the woods, Cook supporting our left. At this point General Rodes was killed, and the men drove everything before them, capturing many prisoners who were hidden in a ditch. The Brigade moved to the crest of the hill where Grimes had formed his line. Here General Evans' line was driven back leaving our left exposed. A battery was sent to our relief, and the enemy was checked at this point. About five o'clock we fell back in good order as the enemy had passed our left and threatened our rear. Line of battle was formed on the crest of the hill, from which we advanced again driving the enemy but being out-flanked we had to retire again, and now the whole army was in retreat. Our division held the enemy in check till the greater part of our men had withdrawn, then retreated in column some distance, then formed line of battle and protected our artillery until night. We then continued our retreat to Fisher's Hill about 15 miles. This was the first time the army of Northern Virginia had been defeated. In fact we never thought of being defeated before. The Band always acted as hospital helps, assisting the surgeons, etc.[11]

The battle had lasted almost nine hours, and Early's army suffered a disaster. Over one-third was gone. Of his men in the infantry and artillery, 3,600 were either killed, wounded, or missing, and his cavalry has suffered losses of about 1,000 men. Another hard blow was the loss of another gallant commander. Shrapnel struck General Rodes in the head as he was leading his division forward. He tumbled from the saddle and died in a few minutes.

As usual during the battle band members were bearing litters and helping the surgeons. James Steele recalled an incident:

Just then one of our cavalry men rode up and told all of the non-combatants to "lookout for themselves, the Yankee Cavalrymen were in town." Charles Heyer and myself picked up our horns and books and started down through the old burned depot, he being in front came to the door three feet above the ground and after climbing down found a fence all around the door ten feet high and he made a comical jump with his big base horn, but could not reach the top of the fence by three feet. I stood in the door and said, 'Charlie, come here and I will help you up again,' which I did, and as we started down the pike just then a lady said to us (who were non-combatants) 'men don't run.' I said, 'Nat, I can't stand that,' and stopped and picked up a gun off the ground and was fixing to lead it. Nat looked at me and said, 'Lum, come on, don't make a fool of yourself, what can you do by yourself?' I told him I would rather make a fool of myself than be considered running. We got out without being captured.[12]

EARLY'S ARMY.
Lost in the Woods not a thousand miles from Strasburg, Va.

Orders from headquarters respecting certain letters — Contraband news — Feel laced up — Return of "Refugees" — Condition of the army.

What next, I wonder? Visions of bayonets, guard houses, bucking sticks and gags quiver menacingly in the distance; and for what? All because a poor, wayward "worm in the dust" has been so indiscreet as to let the truth eke out once — just once, and the people got it. Well, I don't believe I'll follow the example set by Polly Woggs, who, when asked by Josh to be his wife, "got so mad she wouldn't say nothing" (guess she knew that silence always means "yes") — I do not intend to be altogether silent, notwithstanding the threatening order recently issued by the War Department: — I have ever been very cautious in my correspondence, and up to this hour I am not aware of ever having written anything that could, in any wise, be prejudiced to our cause, but in future letters I shall more than ever, look carefully to my phraseology. I take it for granted that the reader has already seen the stringent order to which I refer, prohibiting, under severe penalties, army correspondence for the press within one month subsequent to the affair treated of. Now this smacks of "muzzling the press" and clogging our "quills," but to all honest, faithful and earnest well-wishers-of-the South it will appear at once just and proper, and is just the thing that should have been done long ago. I know it will bear hard upon the thousands at home who are always on the qui vice for latest news relative to military operations, perhaps solely to carpe at, find fault and condemn: but when we remember that by suppression of such information, we deprive the enemy (both internal and external) of much valuable foothold, surely no good man will complain. This order does not forbid the publication of casualties in battle, nor of anything that can be of real interest to the wives, daughters, sisters and — expectants in the South, whose hearts are kept in painful suspense by reason of the frequent and bloody battles fought during this campaign, and we assure them that every effort will be made to relieve their minds of that agony, that anxiety which all feel for those who, perhaps, are dearer to them than life itself.

But in spite of every effort to appear otherwise, I feel cramped; in fancy I can hear the clank of something exceedingly unpleasant, — there is a clog rattling after me, and an oppressive sensation steals over me if I were laced up in an iron jacket. Accustomed to unbounded freedom in my correspondence, though having never abused that freedom to my knowledge, yet I am now constantly looking around lest I tread where the crust is thin and thus unconsciously bring trouble on myself. The reader can easily understand the state of affairs, and for any imperfections in any letters hereafter make due allowance. A weak hobby, with a sore back, but will answer the purpose admirably.

Since my last was written nothing of unusual interest has transpired. Our loss at Strasburg (or, more properly, Fisher's Hill) was not near so great as was at first reported. No one in the 4th N.C. regiment was killed, nor any severely wounded,— none about whom we are positively certain. A great many from the various brigades composing the "Army in the Valley" reported missing, or prisoners, have recently rejoined their respective commands. Some were actually prisoners in the hands of the enemy and were lucky enough to make their escape, while many others fled for safety to the mountains, where they rambled during a fortnight amongst the rugged precipices and dark coves of the Blue Ridge before an opportunity to escape presented itself. Numbers of these "mountain refugees" have found their way into camp within the past few days, each of whom has a miraculous and oftimes an amusing story to tell. The return of so many we supposed killed or captured has had a wonderful effect on the spirits of our men generally, and now something like hope and confidence is felt where a week ago a good deal distrust and dissatisfaction was shown. I have often been surprised to see the rapidity with which soldiers recover their wonted cheerfulness after what might be considered rather trying reverses, but this time I have heard many express their astonishment at the sudden and agreeable turn affairs have taken.

My report of the casualties at Winchester is correct. (I presume it has been published ere this.) — One of our prisoners, (Gries Shives[13] of Davie county, N.C.) was captured there and held a prisoner from Monday the 19th ultimo, to Wednesday night following, when he effected his escape by disguising himself as a yankee, and a few days since landed safely in our camp. He says the enemy has 35 prisoners, unhurt, from our regiment. Among the number he mentions Lieutenants Kelly,[14] Davidson[15] and Warren.[16] He knows nothing concerning Lt. Wiseman.[17] The list of privates and non-commissioned officers is about the same as already given.

We are still getting on very well. Have been provided with clothing in abundance, paid off and shoes furnished.

The weather is getting colder, and last night we had frequent blasts of snow and sleet. We are really glad to see winter coming; we hope to have some rest then, and until that time we expect nothing but marches, hardships and suffering.

NAT.

NEW MARKET, VA., Oct. 10th, '64.

[Published in the *Carolina Watchman* October 24, 1864]

After Winchester, Early's army retreated to Fisher's Hill, where, on September 22, Sheridan attacked again. The fight began about four in the afternoon, and Sheridan's forces outflanked and overran the outnumbered Confederates. The battle turned into a rout, and only darkness saved Early's army. Over 1,200 men were lost here, shrinking his army even further.

James Steele described the movements of the army band after the Battle of Fisher's Hill:

> We returned to Strasburg and then to New Market, fighting most of the way. We marched to Port Republic and Weer's Cave, where the Band, with two guides, explored that wonderful cave with its large halls, brooks, hills and curiosities. In the hall called the Ballroom we played many pieces of music, among which was "Sweet Home," "Vacant Chair," and others, anything sounded solemn but especially these pieces alluded to. The Rev. A.D. Betts, chaplain of the 2nd Regiment enjoyed the music, but tears were streaming down his cheeks. He was a grand man. We then marched to Waynesboro, Mt. Sidney, Harrisburg and then back to New Market, where we were always among friends. The 4th Band always stopped at Dr. Neffs, who always had something good for us to eat. He with his three daughters, Misses Eliza, Kate, and Amanda, ennobled themselves in our estimation. They were all that was good, noble, true, and loving, like all of the good people of the valley, full of hospitality and kindness; though overrun by both armies, first one and then the other, they would always divide with us. Sheridan boasted of destroying everything eatable, "that even a crow in flying over would have to carry his rations with him."[18]

The fatal blow for the Southern army in the Valley fell on October 19, 1864, at Cedar Creek. The Union army held a strong position on the north side of the creek. Having defeated Early twice in one month and holding numerical superiority over him, the Federal officers and men gave no thought to the idea that Early would take the offensive.

James Steele described the moment:

> On the 18th of October, 1864, our army was encamped at Fisher's Hill, the enemy were encamped on the hill near Cedar Creek. General Ramseur and Gordon crossed the Shenandoah river south of Strasburg, climbed the Massanutten mountain, from its summit located the enemy's camp, picket posts, and planned a surprise attack. After night the army being stripped of all canteens, tin cups, or anything that would rattle marched past the picket line very quietly just before day, but some one stepped on a rail and it broke with a loud crash, the men fell to the ground and the picket fired over them, then a charge was made and the pickets were captured, and the charge up the hill and into the Yankee Camp, and the surprise was complete. Some were cooking, some sleeping, some were running out of their tents on all fours.
> Six thousand prisoners and many pieces of artillery and baggage were captured.[19]

General Sheridan was not with the army. He was in Winchester, and the sounds of the morning battle could be plainly heard. Quickly mounting his horse, he galloped toward Cedar Creek twenty miles away. Soon he encountered fleeing Union soldiers. When he rode onto the battlefield, it was if an electric current passed through the Union soldiers. The Commander had arrived! Order was restored.

Around 4:00 that afternoon Sheridan launched a massive counterattack. Early's stunning victory of the morning was snatched away as his army crumbled under the onslaught. Nat's comments on the battle of October 19 are at the end of this letter:

> ### Lists of Casualties in the 4th N.C.S. Troops, in the battle near Strasburg, VA., on the 19th of October, 1864.
>
> Co. A. Killed: None. Wounded: Lieut. John A. Stikeleather,[20] color bearer, head severe, not dangerous, now with us. Missing: Lt. Wm. R. NcNeely,[21] reported killed; S. N. Barnes[22] and J. H. Cohen,[23] the last said to be prisoner, unhurt.
>
> Co. B. Killed, None. Wounded: P. A. Seaford,[24] slight, prisoner. Missing: Serg. H. Miller,[25] J. W. Gullett,[26] T. S. Lyerly,[27] W. R. Moore.[28]
>
> Co. C. None. Wounded: Serg't. J. C. Turner,[29] A. S. Mills,[30] H. L. Lollar,[31] G. A. Reid,[32] Joseph Christie,[33] each slightly, but now doing duty with us. Missing: J. L. Wilson.[34]
>
> Co. D. Killed. None. Wounded: Jas. Burner,[35] slight. Missing: J. Lane[36]
>
> Co. E. Killed. None. Wounded: L. Ed Tripp,[37] leg slight; G. Toraber,[38] side severe; J. N. Hawkins,[39] foot severe. Missing: L. Latham,[40] J. W. King[41] and B. S. Swindle.[42]
>
> Co. F. Killed. None. Wounded: B. Rodes[43] and B. Woodard.[44]
>
> Co. G. Killed. None. Wounded: A. Athan,[45] T. M. Waller,[46] slight, both now on duty. Missing: None.
>
> Co. H. Killed. None. Wounded: J. Reingo,[47] slight. Missing: None.
>
> Co. I. Killed: John Stephens.[48] Wounded: None. Missing. None.
>
> Co. K. Killed. None. Wounded: B. Mathis,[49] musician, right arm, flesh; Serg't. W. C. Fraley,[50] slight; C. Holtshouser,[51] right hand slight. Missing: A. Friedhelm.[52]
>
> Total — Killed, 1 — Wounded, 10 — Missing, 16.

Upon the whole our loss in killed and wounded is not very severe; but the "missing list" is unusually large. Most of them, however, fled to the mountains and doubtless the greater portion of them will yet turn up all right. Many of those who were missing at first (not those now reported) have already come in.

The entire army regrets the loss of Gen. Ramseur. He was mortally wounded and left in the enemy's hands. To-day we hear, upon what seems to be good authority, that he is dead. He was renowned throughout the army in the Valley for his dashing, invincible courage as well as for his kind and gentlemanly deportment. — We can ill afford to spare such officers.

At Cedar Creek General Stephen Dodson Ramseur and his men were all that stood firm between an orderly withdrawal and a complete rout of Early's forces. Ramseur held a low stone wall, and on his right, Union artillery were firing into them. Still he and his men stood their ground, returning fire into the ranks of Sheridan's attacking soldiers, but it was only a matter of time. As he directed his men, his horse was shot from under him. A soldier brought him a second mount; within minutes it, too, was shot down. As he mounted yet a third animal, a minié ball struck him in the right side, penetrating both lungs, and he fell mortally wounded.

Nat continues:

It would hardly be prudent for me to give any of the particulars concerning this affair at present. But I trust I shall be doing nothing wrong by stating that the 19th of October, 1864, was one of the most eventful days, and filled with the most remarkable incidents that have ever transpired in any one day since first breaking out of this terrible revolution. The morning dawned on us inspired with victory the most complete and decisive; — the evening shades gathered on our army broken, dispirited, and _____ but I feel too sad; — and it might be unwise to say more. All things, they say, "happens for the best," and I have no reason for saying that this will prove an exception to the rule. If the truth were told my reader would be satisfied that, in the aggregate, our gains are greater than our losses, and with this, for the present, we must be content.

NAT.

New Market, Va., Oct. 24, 1864.

[Published in the *Carolina Watchman* November 7, 1864]

From the 4th North Carolina.
CAMP NEAR NEW MARKET, VA.,

A trip down the Valley — Rather cool — What for — Our prospect — What we live for — Outward and inward, with good advice — Something about boxes — Hartshorn, &c., &c.

Owing to the bad weather and constant marching, I have been hindered from writing as frequently as I should like to have done; but it is the old saw "better late than never," and trusting that my readers may think so too, I shall proceed at once to give such items as are likely to be of some interest.

On the morning of the 10th inst., our whole army, largely reinforced and in pretty good trim, generally, was brought out from their camps in the vicinity of New Market and marched down the Valley. On the evening of the 11th, we" jumped" the yankees in the neighborhood of New Town, eight miles this side of Winchester. Sharpshooters were thrown out, and that night and day following were spent skirmishing along the lines, at some points hot and heavy. We thought surely a general engagement would come off Saturday; every preparation was made for it; and occasionally through the day things looked decided squally. The pickets were incessantly popping away at each other, but on the main line of battle no excitement whatever occurred — except once. About two o'clock in the afternoon a tremendous yell was raised on the extreme left of the line. "Ah, there it is," said some — "That's a charge" — "Didn't I tell you the yankees would endeavor to turn our left flank again" — "Guess they will find an obstacle this time" — "Just listen!" "Boys it's getting closer!"—and a greasy fellow whose hat I thought was then rising —"What does it mean?"—wondered half a dozen at a time as the shouting evidently came nearer—"Strange there is not much firing;" such and many like them were the remarks made by the men around me,—each standing with mouths agape and eyes strained trying to see something as yet invisible. Presently we saw about half a brigade of hatless men tearing through the thickets at a furious gait, some two hundred yards in rear of the line of battle and coming up parallel with it, and just ahead of them we discovered as they emerged from the woods into a large open field—What? Not a rabbit I'm sure else the chase would not have lasted so long, but a fox, a red fox, and one of the largest of his species. Quick as thought hundreds more joined in the chase, yelling and hooting like mad man,—heading, flanking, first on the right then on the left until finally poor Reynard found further effort useless and accordingly "caved in." He was captured without receiving the slightest injury, and is now kept as a pet in one of the brigades in this division. Altogether it was the most exciting chase I ever witnessed. Soon after dark we began a "crawfish movement" (not a military way of expressing it,) but then even the little folks will know what I mean—and it is highly important they should know all these things, since it is highly probable they or the darkies will have to wind up this war. Well, we crawfished, or in other words we advanced backwards, leaving only our pickets on the line. About 8 o'clock at night the full moon peeped over the snow capped Blue Ridge and poured over us such a flood of bright, mellow light that our columns could be seen a mile moving briskly on the pike, dense and black like a huge serpent dragging his unwieldy body over the hills and plains, while a line of the enemy's cavalry, like specters in the dim distance, pressed our skirmishers in the rear rather too close for comfort. But continuous and accurate firing by the rear guard enabled them to hold off the prowling enemy until the army proper was out of danger, and at 11 o'clock we found ourselves in old camps on Fisher's Hill, safe and sound, having marched fourteen miles in less than five hours. Apart from the necessity of getting out of danger and reaching a safe position we were compelled to march rapidly to keep from freezing. The wind from the snow covered mountains seemed to pierce the very marrow, while with all the blankets and handkerchiefs we could get muffled about our ears and noses we could hardly retain those useful as well as ornamental appendages. I never saw the moon's rays come down with such undimmed lustre. Under other circumstances this would have been very agreeable, but on this occasion it was really annoying. Our movement might have been discovered by the enemy, as well as our exact situation; we expected an attack at any moment, and when at last we reached Fisher's Hill in safety is it any wonder that we should feel immediately relieved!

Before it was quite light on the morning of the 13th, we set out again, though the blast from the snowy regions was keener and colder than ever. By 9 A.M., furious storms of snow were dashed mercilessly in our faces, but all unmindful of it the troops marched as lightly, and evinced a spirit as gay and cheerful as though nothing but a gentle breeze from the forests,

"Linger with the hectic flush of autumn"

impeded their progress. At intervals during the day a single beam of sunshine would gleam through the heaving mass of black, lowering clouds, but the next moment it was shut out again, and this freezing atmosphere would be darkened with the dense showers of snow. At night we pitched camp in the neighborhood of Edenburg — just imagine a camp in a snow storm — I can't describe it — or if I could you could not then form an idea of the way we slayed timber and built fires; or how our fingers and toes ached — or how blue our noses got — nor how we lay down, pulled the blankets over our head and — let it snow.

On the next morning (Monday the 14th) the bugle aroused us before we got our nap out, — and, what is worse, spoiled a most delicious dream besides. My dear reader might have heard a good deal of growling, and perhaps a little "cussin" and threats as to how we'd sleep until we got ready to get up when the war is ended, and such like but it was no use; we found it advisable to make the best of a bad bargin and therefore "snumered" — Arose, shook the snow off our heads and blankets, bundled up and set out with as much independence and perfect nonchalance we intended to show on the morning of our wedding day. That night we rejoiced to find ourselves stretched on the same luxurious straw we left on the morning of the 10th; as much as to say the troops reoccupied their old camps and quarters around New Market. We were absent five days on three days rations, short enough at best, Heaven knows — marched eighty five miles, skirmished one day and night, and what have we gained? It is said that Gen. Early did not intend to fight his only object being to ascertain the strength and position of the enemy. This we accomplished without a battle and returned to his base. Very well we know now that the Yankees hold Winchester with a strong force, and are erecting winter quarters there. Very likely their outposts during the winter will be on the hills north of Cedar Creek, near Strasburg, while their main army will be quartered near New Town and Winchester, and supplied by Railroad from Harpers Ferry to the latter town which is being rebuilt for that purpose. We may conclude then that the fighting in the Valley is virtually ended for the winter. What is going to be done with us? Ay, that is one of the mysteries. Nothing, however, can surprise us — not even if we were ordered to Mobile, or to reinforce Price in Kansas; in fact it wouldn't be a matter of wonder if we were specially detailed to plant torpedoes around Salisbury to prevent Kirk's intended raid on the old factory. But laying jokes aside we do hope, sincerely hope, that we may soon get into winter quarters. We will not be choice about the locality, anywhere between Fort Delaware and Galveston will do. We are completely run down trying to keep out of the smoke, if beauty causes this attention I would advise any of my fair readers who are anxious to make a good match to come out here — sure they can be suited, even the most fastidious. Our eyes are red (many drap of whiskey though) our cheeks look like canvass hams, our whiskers crisped, hair frizzled, and hands, well, just imagine an alligators claw. Yet notwithstanding all these draw-backs (very trifling they are too) our hearts are still as sensitive as ever, as warm and if possible more fully capable of appreciating the worth of a woman as well as the intensity and constancy of her devotion.

I intended to close this communication with the paragraph above, but there is a little more I want to say. I'm told it is half an hour till mail time. But indeed I have the shivers so badly that I can hardly follow the lines — or even keep respect-fully between them. Rain patters down on my little tent cold, dreary, pitiless. Nothing but a column of smoke rises where our fire ought to be — no hopes of thawing there. Well, I'll "turn in," i.e. get under the blankets as soon as I get through with this — may be I can, in that way retain the spark of vitality still flick-ering in this battered frame. But if we do have the luck of getting into winter quarters near Staunton, or any where else some distance from Richmond — will those agents sent out by Dr. Warren, with packages, boxes, &c., for soldiers, come to our portion of the army, wherever we may be? If we can get luxuries from the old North State this winter (and that is about two-thirds of all we live for now,) — if packages, I say, can be sent to this regiment, in the care of a trust-worthy agent, I do hope I have friends among my readers who will remember me in this the time of my great calamity. If you do I will make all sorts of promises, that is one half my business, you know. And the other half is to — O, no! no! — dear me! — it isn't to break ham I'm sure! — Give me the Hartshorn!

NAT.

[Published in the *Carolina Watchman* December 5, 1864]

From the Fourth North Carolina.
CAMP NEAR NEW MARKET, VA.,
December 12, 1864.

A Tight Squeeze — Snowed Shut — Straw, a remedy for several ills flesh is heir to — An unexpected change of base — The way Soldiers take pleasure excursions on the Cars — Time around Petersburg, &c.

A "Watchman" fresh from the press reminds me of my promise to friends at home to "write more frequently," and I suppose it is my duty to "take my seat, pen in hand, to inform you" that we still have our heads out of the snow, — but it is somewhat like Scroggins going to heaven — "mit a tam tight squeeze." At noon on Friday last (9th instant) we pulled up stakes and moved camp about a quarter of a mile. This was done from necessity; — for a fortnight before we had been toting our wood, like pack mules, an incredible distance, and to be more convenient to this needful article at this season, we pitched in a forest of substan-tial oak and hickory, much to the annoyance of the proprietor, a close-fisted old gentleman who lives not far about, and who, I fear, is going to fret himself crazy, if not to death, if we don't soon leave these diggings entirely. Well, by 2 P.M., on the 9th, as stated above, our different positions in the new camp were assigned to us, when we at once proceeded to work cutting timber for a temporary shanty, notwithstanding the rumor still floated round that we would not remain there longer than a week, or ten days at farthest; and this rumor, coming as it did from official sources, deterred many from making preparations whatever for the snow storm which was evidently brewing. But your humble servant, together with the others attached to his noisy squad, were determined to take Time by the forelock and "live while we did live;" — upon the whole a wise conclusion, and our adopted motto for the balance of our lives let the consequences be what they may. Whilst some of our party were working faithfully and vigorously at our "dens," as they are called in the army, others were sent for straw, with which they returned just as the shades of night were gathering thick and oppressively calm,—so calm and profoundly quiet that in spite of our efforts to appear cheerful we could not banish a feeling similar to awe, and an indefinable dread that was evidently creeping over the whole party. Now, this straw, no doubt, puzzles some of my readers— What in the name of common sense could we want with it? True, it is not equal to feathers, not quite so elastic nor so comfortable, but it answers amazingly well for a substitute, and I would earnestly recommend it to any of my readers who may be pestered with nightmares, or who may be compelled to spend the first half the night restless and sleepless;—a bed of straw is also said to be good for the toothache, and in desperate cases of love-sickness it was never known to fail,— indeed it is a most admirable remedy for that distressing disease if commenced in time and administered faithfully. I merely give these highly important recipes on hearsay, not having had occasion to test them in the cases specified I cannot say positively.

Night put a stop to active operations, and with it came a blinding snow storm. Upon consultation it was concluded that we would fare better without a tent than with one, and instead of stretching them up, as we usually do when foul weather threatens, we spread them as a counterpane on our blankets. We had no time to lose getting in bed—the job was exceedingly unpleasant at best, and on taking a last peep into the gloom before drawing the covering over our heads we saw the flakes coming down so thick and fast that it was almost impossible to see a man ten steps. We slept soundly until midnight, when we awoke and found ourselves nearly smothered to death. We were obliged to have fresh air, and all made a rush for the bed clothes which were jerked off of our heads at once, letting about two and a half bushels of snow roll in about our necks and shoulders.—Ugh! It makes me shudder to think about it. Just imagine a comfortable snooze broken up in that manner, and then let us know how you would like soldiering in the Valley during the winter. Perhaps there are some persons who could have lain in that situation until the break of day, but it is certain we could not. It was a bitter pill to get up in snow half knee deep and build a fire, but we were obliged to do it or freeze. The night was terribly long—we began to think it would never end.— Paul when he was shipwrecked never wished more urgently or wistfully for day than we did, and when the dull gray morning did at last break, it revealed to us a world covered seven or eight inches deep with snow.

PETERSBURG, Va., Dec. 27.

Well, this is decidedly an unexpected change of base. I have no possible chance to mail the foregoing part of this letter up to within the last few days, and not exactly wishing to lose my labor I have decided to send all together. Though the first is rather old, yet I trust it will not be entirely without interest. On the night of the 13th instant, we received orders to move at daylight the next morning, and, as usual, all hands proceeded to prepare for the hard task; meanwhile guessing and wondering where we were bound for was the sole topic of conversation. Not the least light, however, could we get on the subject, and on the morning following; after wading thro' snow six inches deep for a distance of a mile and a half to reach the pike, we were agreeably surprised to see the head of the column turn up towards Staunton. The early part of the way intensely cold, and the limestone pike was hard and slick as a frozen mill pond. Towards evening the air grew milder, and the ice thawed sufficiently to form a kind of mush through which we trudged vigorously with the most extreme difficulty, and at night struck camp near Mount Crawford, having traveled six miles from our starting point. The reader can imagine our condition; but tired and broken down as we were, our first duty was to prepare for a cold night, which we did by raking the snow from the spots where we expected to lie, and building large fires on them. The night, after all, was spent more comfortably than many might suppose, and on the next morning (15th,) we were bright and early for the tramp, and that evening, at 3 o'clock, we found ourselves at Staunton, forty here miles from New Market. — By 10 o'clock at night we were jammed aboard the cars like so many market hogs, forty and fifty in a box, half frozen, and particularly out of humor in general. For my part I think it would have been but clever had some of the managers divided the whiskey instead of drinking too much themselves, and then by their negligence and mismanagement keep two brigades standing in snow eight and ten hours waiting to be put aboard the train.

Without any serious accident we landed near Petersburg on the eve of the 16th, and went into camp. The 17th and 18th we "rested our weary bones," and on the 19th went to work putting up winter quarter in earnest. Our camp is located four miles from the city and in a healthy atmosphere, that is, out of reach of the shells which frequently pay their unwelcome visits over this way. I mention this little circumstance merely for the relief of those at home who may feel some anxiety with respect to the comfort of relatives and friends in our division. Since our arrival here we have been on one very disagreeable trip to the lines near Drury's Bluff, which consumed two days and nights; all is over now, though, and we are quietly enjoying our winter shanties.

Unless something very serious turns up we expect to remain in this vicinity during the winter. Everything is quiet on the lines unless I except the customary cannonading which is kept up day and night incessantly. Upon the whole, we are well pleased with our change, and ere long we hope to hear from friends at home, who have not entirely forgotten the use of various tools as well as the pen.

NAT.

[Published in the *Carolina Watchman* January 4, 1865]

· 17 ·

PETERSBURG, VIRGINIA

Life in the Trenches near Petersburg.

I always had a very great curiosity to see the trenches at Petersburg.—I had heard so much said concerning them—such extravagance, almost impossible accounts, and incredible stories, that I was determined to see for myself, and accordingly, on the 3d inst., set out with that objective in view. After crossing "Pocahontas Bridge," on the Northern suburbs of the city, I turned directly to the left on the City Point railroad down which I walked about three quarters of a mile, and after crossing a fine iron bridge, struck the "covered way" as it is called here, which means simply a ditch sufficiently deep to protect persons from the enemy's shots. From the western terminus of this ditch to the trenches proper the distance is something near three fourths of a mile,—it is from three to eight feet wide, and, the banks included, from seven to nine feet deep,—there is no "covering" at all. This constitutes the main thoroughfare through which the men belonging to Ransom's brigade go to and from the city. On nearing the lines I discovered many similar ditches intersecting the main one and thence running in every conceivable direction. It is no wonder I got lost;—a man might as well attempt to explore the Mammoth cave alone and without light,—but by the most indefatigable exertions, and by making all possible inquiries of every one I met, I found at last the headquarters of the 49th N.C. Reg't,—and thence, in company with a competent guide (Lt. Jas. Sherrill[1]). I continued my observations and explorations with a greater degree of satisfaction. The men I found all burrowed in the earth like so many ground rats,—from four to six in a hole, which is called a "bomb-proof"; because, in the first place, it is sunken several feet beneath the surface, and in the second place it is covered with logs and earth varying from six to the feet in thickness. Still, these "Bomb-proofs" are not altogether a safe retreat;—it is no very uncommon thing for heavy mortar shells to penetrate to the interior—an accident which never fails to cause a general getting out, you may well imagine. The fact is, the men have discovered recently that they are safer in the trenches than in their holes during a shelling spree, which occurs perhaps once in twenty-four hours, sometimes in day-light, sometimes at night and lasts one or two hours at a time. There is always a lookout kept, and warning givin when there is any danger; and the men have become as exploit dodging in the

149

trenches and around the "traverses" that it is seldom any one is hurt. In daylight the shells may be seen distinctly from the time they leave the enemy's mortars until they explode inside our works, and at night their fiery tails, comet like, indicate their course. The range is entirely too short to admit of the use of artillery; consequently nothing but mortars are used; and, like everything else, they are so far beneath the surface, in a kind of pit, as to be entirely out of sight. — no one could know where they are were it not for the cloud of white smoke produced by a discharge, which always betrays their exact locality. Before leaving that part of the subject, however, I should state that the holes in which the men live are small, and so low that a boy ten years old could scarcely stand erect; — they are dark and damp and in many instances smoked thoroughly black by the little handful of stone coal and old field pine, their only hope of fuel. It is really surprising that such universal good health prevails; — I did not see a single sick man, notwithstanding their exceedingly disagreeable mode of life. One of the greatest inconveniences to which they are subject is the horrible mud when it rains or during a thaw. A ditch leads from every domicile to others, and also to the main trench, the bottom of which, in wet weather, is filled with a mud six inches deep. — yet no man dare attempt to shun it by going over a bank: so sure as he risks it he is shot at, — in this way many have been killed by unnecessarily exposing themselves. Really the lines of the two armies are not more than two hundred yards apart at the farthest, and in some places the distance is not half so great. The pickets, of course, are much nearer, scarcely fifty yards separate them, yet there they have lain for the past three or four months, and how much longer they may remain we cannot tell. The Yankees live like our men beneath the surface of the earth — it is rare that one shows his head about the breastworks. You might stand on a mound in the centre of that wreck of earth (for such it is in reality) and imagine that no living soul dwelt within five miles of you, while in truth the very earth beneath and around you is full of living soldiers numbered by hundreds and thousands.

I might say a great deal with reference to the defences, but it might be imprudent — I will only add that so far as I am able to judge I believe them to be impregnable. The men I found cheerful and lively, more so that I could be under the circumstances, unless like them, I had served a six months' apprenticeship, and then, besides, had the unlimited quantities of good things from home which they are luxuriating. I confess to a feeling of squeamishness once or twice when a ponderous mortar shell would light near enough to give one the headache; and, once I was chilled slightly when Capt. H. A. Chambers[2] and I mounted a small bank to take just one peep at the — "Pats" — I was really fidgetty, and actually could not suppress a desire to see what was going on over there, — it may have been a weakness bordering, perhaps, on a peculiar feminine trait, but so it was. — We ventured our heads up barely a second, and the moment after we stepped back in the ditch a minnie ball cut the dirt immediately above. — Well, it is hardly necessary for me to state that I didn't suffer my curiosity to get the better of prudence a second time.

In the 49th N.C.T. I met many old friends and associates, among whom I may mention Wm. Morrison,[3] Thos. Watts,[4] Jos. Beard,[5] Capt. Jno. Crawford,[6] Lt. Clay Sharpe,[7] J. I. Woodside,[8] Lt. Bailey,[9] Capt. Conner,[10] and many others, all of whom are doing amazingly well when the situation is considered. Fortunately, on the day I spent in the trenches the ground was frozen and towards evening snow fell, through which I felt my way to camp where I landed safely at 9 P.M., thankful that the time is not yet come when it may be necessary for me to make my home under the ground.

NAT.

[Published in the *Iredell Express* February 9, 1865]

James Steele remembered their time in camp near Petersburg:

We enjoyed this camp with good quarters which we built of logs, with stick and mud chimneys. Telling jokes and playing pranks for pastime. Each house contained a mess, (a mess was 6 or 8 who lived together and ate together and were partners for the winter.) If one mess would go to bed too soon, some one would climb to the top of the chimney and drop in a pod of red pepper and lay a board over the chimney and hide. Presently the boys would begin to cough. When they could stand the pepper smoke no longer they would break out of the house and hunt the perpetrator and if they could find him they would initiate him with a paddle, which would mean a spanking on a large scale.[11]

He also mentioned that the band played for the Merritt family who were near their camp. "Nat Raymer hesitated to go in because his pants were worn out, but he slipped in and took a seat. A dance started, some of the ladies asked him why he did not dance, and he said: 'Please excuse me, but I have very stern reasons for not dancing.'"[12]

On April 2, the Confederate lines began to give way before the attacking Federals.

James Steele recalled the moments:

We started our retreat up the Appomattox river. Before the Band left Petersburg we could see both armies fighting in our rear through an open field and as we had no officer to look to for orders we had to look out for ourselves, so we crossed a bridge over the Appomattox river in the northwest corner of the city and began our part of the retreat up the Appomattox river. I was seldom on the sick list, but our surgeon gave me a permit to ride in an ambulance, but I could not find one. I found a good horse so near starved that it had been abandoned, so I tried to ride him, but when he tried to step over the branch his knee gave way and let me down over his head in the branch. So I had to abandon him, too, then I concluded to dispose of everything that I could spare, left off my patent leather knapsack (the best one I ever had) took up my blanket and rolled it up. My whole regalia was changed so that I did not know when I had everything. I was tired and sleepy and when night came on I stopped and lay down by a fire that some other stragglers had made, went to sleep but before day the rear guard came along and woke us all up and told us the Yankees were coming. I got up half asleep, overlooked my horn and went on about a mile and a half before I missed it. I then went back and found it by chance.[13]

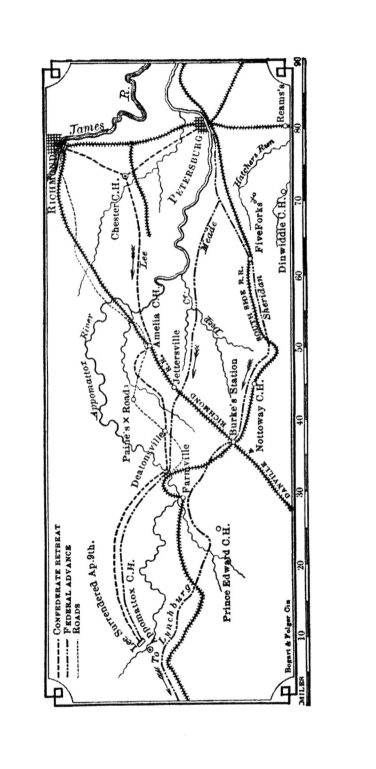

On April 7, General Grimes' three brigades rushed to the support of General Mahone, whose lines were giving way under the Federal attack near Farmville. Grimes' men charged the enemy and drove them off. General Lee went to Grimes and his men personally complimented the men for their gallantry. Weary and hungry, the men marched all day on April 8; those who could not keep up fell exhausted. That night Grimes and his men camped close to a small stream, but heavy artillery fire roused them at 9 o'clock. Grimes ordered them to move out, and by daylight on April 9, Sunday, they were moving through the silent streets of Appomattox Court House.

Here the Army of Northern Virginia fought their last battle. Grimes' exhausted, hungry, and outnumbered veterans attacked the Federal troops at the crossroads and drove them back half a mile. The road to Lynchburg was now open for the escape of the army's wagons. Grimes sent word back of his success, but the reply was not what he expected. He was ordered to fall back. The army had been surrendered.

Opposite: **This map shows the route taken by Nat and other members of the 4th Regiment as they retreated from the Federal attack on April 2, 1865, until the final surrender at Appomattox Court House on April 9, 1865. (W. H. DePuy,** *People's Cyclopedia of Universal Knowledge,* **Vol. 1 [New York: Phillips & Hunt, 1881]. Map used by permission of the Florida Center for Instructional Technology, College of Education, University of South Florida.)**

· 18 ·

HOME TO IREDELL COUNTY

It was over.

The commanders met; they signed the surrender documents; and although General Joseph Johnston would surrender all Confederate forces to General William Sherman in North Carolina later in April, for the Army of Northern Virginia the war ended at Appomattox Court House.

That ending had to be one of the strangest for any civil war in the history of the world. No recriminations; no prison camps for the defeated; just, it's over — pack up — everyone go home.

The Fourth Regiment was on the right of the brigade at Appomattox on the 9th of April, 1865, and was the first in the brigade to stack arms. When this was done, General Grimes called them to "attention" for the last time and had them file past him in order the he might shake hands with each man, and as he did so, with streaming eyes and faltering voice, he said, "Go home, boys, and act like men, as you have always done during the war."[1]

James Steele recalled the last days:

After General Lee surrendered on the 9th of April, two days were spent in getting our paroles and getting ready to start home. On the night of the 11th, our Band serenaded General Lee for the last time. After playing three or four pieces he came out of his tent and complimented the music and thanked us for it, and said, "I hope you will get home safely and find your friends well." He did not shake hands with us, but bade us good-bye, and went back in his tent.

On Wednesday the 12th, we were up early and started for home on foot. Nat Raymer who had been the war correspondent of the home papers during the war, and myself who had been room mates and bed fellows during the war planned that we would make the trip home together, and take the most direct route we could find. We would have to depend on the country for a living as we had neither rations nor money, but we found the same hospitality for which Virginia was noted, still existed. On our way home we crossed Dan river a few miles above Danville and came through Leaksville, N.C., and spent the night at Mocksville.

154

The war was over and I was back home, and everything we had was gone. I began at once to cast about for something to do to get a new start in life, but I could find nothing to do but stay at home and plow to pay my board.[2]

James Columbus Steele lived in Statesville the remainder of his life. He became a manufacturer of bricks, and in 1889, he designed and built improved brick making machinery, which was the start of his company. Over a century later, J. C. Steele & Sons is the largest producer of heavy clay products machinery in the nation. James Steele died in 1921.

After he returned home, Nat wrote the following around 1871.[3]

> The four years of war, together with its prime cause and final result, are now things of history. I need not make any comments here. My private opinion is of little consequence anyway, the same which may be said of any southern man at this time. I will only remark that in so far as the grand result of the war is concerned (the abolition of slavery,) I would not have it otherwise on any consideration. I am truly thankful that it is so, but my opinions concerning the righteousness or unrighteousness of the war will ever remain the same. To say that the South had no right to rebel and form a government of their own, is to say that the old colonies had no right to rebel against England. But this is enough in black and white. So far as I am concerned, I am thoroughly subjugated if not altogether harmonized. I mean to spend the remainder of my life in peace, unless some unforeseen event transpires which shall forcibly break this resolution. I was connected with the old Southern army under Gen. Lee for four years, in the capacity of Musician in the 4th Regimental Band. I kept a journal complete, which may be read in other books. By the helping of Providence my life and health were spared, and on the 9th of Apr. 1865 I was in Lee's surrender at Appomattox Court House, Virginia. In two weeks, I walked home (to my father's house in southwestern Iredell N.C.) — accompanied in my journey by J. C. Steele alone, (i.e. No others were in our squad; the soldiers generally, after receiving their paroles, traveled homewards, in squads, by the nearest rout.) During the summer of 1865, I made a hand on my father's farm, or about his mill, or wherever my labor was necessary — every man's work being required to provide against threatening starvation.
>
> Married the 20th of September 1865, by the Rev. W. B. Pressly, Mr. J. N. Raymer to Elizabeth Brady, youngest daughter of the late George Brady.
>
> So this marks a new epoch in my history, and turns the current of my life in a new direction! But I have just now begun to live for some purpose, and for the future must shape my life accordingly.

(Nat's great-granddaughter Lois Carter described his new wife as "very skilled in the skills of the housewife of her time. Her bread was made with 'starter.' It was a homemade yeast. A bit was pinched off and saved, let rise for the next batch. Each time a bit was saved for the next baking. Very skilled in cooking, canning, even drying fruits and vegetables for winter. She carded wool, spun thread, wove the cloth and made Nat's wedding suit and had it ready for him when he came home from the Civil War.")

Nat continues:

> During the winter of 65–'66, I taught school near my father's — some two miles from the W.N.C.R.R.[4] bridge across the Catawba. I boarded at my father's where my wife resided temporarily; — so also did my brother-in-law, J. W. Mitchel, who was married to my sister Sarah on the 25th of Sept. '65. (My sister was a widow, having been first married to Thos. L. Stevenson[5] who was killed below Richmond the second year of the war.) —
>
> Throughout the summer of '66, I assisted on my father's farm, sold and delivered lumber etc. According to the rule for Cause and Effect, it is usual to expect, after marriage, a slight multiplying, replenishing, etc. — Therefore Lulu Octavia, daughter of Nat and Lizzie Raymer was born Aug. 1st, 1866. There now!
>
> About the first of Oct. 1866, I moved to York Institute,[6] Alexander County, N.C., where in co-partnership with Col. Geo. Flowers, I taught school during a five months session.

In November 1866, Nat's residence was entered and a number of clothing articles were stolen. He filed the following search warrant with a Justice of the Peace:

> Form for Search Warrant.
> State of N. Carolina
> Alexander County.
>
> To any lawful officers to execute and return as the law directs. Whereas: J. N. Raymer complains on oath before me, that on or about the night of the 31st of Nov. 1866, he had stolen from his premises certain articles of clothing, male and female wearing apparel, bedclothing, &c. and that he has reason to believe, and does believe that some or all of these articles are concealed about the premises of one John Rogers or John Boyle, freedmen, in

Lulu Octavia Raymer. Nat's first child, she was born in Iredell County on August 1, 1866, and was around 30 years old when this picture was taken. She was a schoolteacher. On July 17, 1896, she married Warren Edward Bailey in Cherokee County, Texas. They were the parents of Nat's granddaughter, Frances Delphine Bailey, born on March 25, 1898. Lulu died in Rusk, Texas, on July 5, 1900, reportedly from a tubal pregnancy. (Property of McClain Family. Used by permission.)

said county. These are therefore to command you to go upon and search the premises aforesaid, and if any of the articles are found, bring them and the person in
whose possession found before me, or some other Justice of the Peace, to answer
the charge, and be dealt with as the law directs Herein fail not. Given under my
hand and seal, Jan. 12, 1867 —

A. C. McIntosh J.P (seal)

(And on the back-folded across of the rules is this endorsement) — viz.

State
Vs,
John Rogers &
John Boyle
Freedmen,

Search Warrant.
I certify the foregoing to be a true copy.

Nat. Raymer.
Jan. 24 '67[7]

Nat continues with his memoir:

The winter was unusually severe, which in connexion with a loose regulation
allowing students to pay for only the time present, cause our school to fail in remu-
nerating us as well as we had anticipated. But so far as I am concerned, I consider
my self fully compensated in the lectures and diplomas received from Prof. Brantley York,[8] on grammar. I am really glad that it has so happened. In my estima-
tion his grammar[9] is certainly far superior to any other that I have ever seen and
if merit is any evidence of future success and popularity, this work of the "Blind
Preacher" will someday, not far distant, either, become the standard text-book with
all appreciative teachers throughout the country. A thorough understanding is all
that is necessary,

On the 1st day of January 1866, I leased a small plantation in Iredell (said plantation belonging to my wife) to Jos. A. Fleming, for three years. Early in the spring
of '67, I bought out his lease, and on the 26th of March 1867 we moved from York
Institute to this plantation (above mentioned) lying near Island ford road, about 8
miles west of Statesville. The plantation contained only 65 acres, all of which is
woodland, with the exception of some 7 acres partially cleared by Fleming. The soil
is better than most of the land in western Iredell. At the time moved to it, there was
a small dwelling house of logs, 18 x 20 a story and a half high, — with roof of a Negro-
cabin attachment which served as a kitchen. A small lot around the house was
enclosed by a rail fence, — outside grounds such a mess of logs, treetops, logs ****
and so forth, as to render it almost impossible to reach the dwelling house at ****.
During the summer of 1867 I taught school at Elgin Academy, near Milas Brady's
residence, also I taught a flourishing school there during the winter of '67 & '68.
In the summer of '67, I had my lumber house built by Jos. Stikeleather.

Edward Mitchel, son of Nat and Lizzie Raymer, was born May 24th 1868, in
Nat Raymer's house 8½ miles S. W. of Statesville, N.C. Baptized by the Rev. Wm.
Faucett, in Shiloh Church.

A copy of the warrant Nat signed to have a search conducted to find his family's stolen property. (Warrant property of McClain family. Used by permission.)

Through the summer of 1868 I worked on my farm getting help wherever I could clearing new grounds, burning logs, brush, etc. around my dwelling. In the fall of '68 I bought the wall of an old house from Mrs. Mag [or May] Brady, which I moved to my own premises, erected, and fitted it up for a school house some 150 yards east of north from my dwelling, and through the winter of '68 & '69 I taught one of the most pleasant schools I ever had. In the spring of '69, I attempted a summer school in the same building. The school was thriving finely, but the great freshet[10] of June 14, 1869 (the same that swept my father's mills) broke in to every body's arrangements, and the school was suspended. Meantime, I had planted a corn crop of some 40 acres good fresh upland, and to the crop I devoted my whole attention often closing my school. I had found by experience that the crop and school at the same time were too much for me, and that I was breaking down under the pressure. I had my ground pre-pared, and the crop cultivated in the best possible manner, but after all made nearly a failure, not making more than 200 bushels of corn in all. This was owing to the unprecedented drouth which set in immediately after the freshet; and continued with just no relief for three months. As a matter of course **** crops were failures, almost universal, and subsequently dis-tressing times followed. How-ever, during the summer of 1869, I had a nice new school house built — by Phillip Fry and Jno. Wyckoff. The new school house we located about 60 yards east of the old one, and in it had a very large school throughout the win-ter of '69 & 70, closing with a grand exhibition on the first day.

Mrs. Sallie Brady (mother-in-law) moved to my house on the 12th day of April 1870.

Cora Fidelia, daughter of Nat and Lizzie Raymer was born Aug. 3rd, 1871 in the same house in which her brother Edward Mitchel was born. Baptized by the Rev. _____ in Concord Church.

Cora Fidelia Raymer, Nat's third child, was about 35 years old when this picture was taken. No occupation was listed for her in the census records. Cora married James C. Tompkins on January 17, 1897, in Cherokee County, Texas. They were the parents of Nat's grandson, James Fairis Tompkins, who was born July 6, 1898 and died November 15, 1960. He did not have children. Cora died March 27, 1949. James C. died Novem-ber 13, 1933. (Property of Susan E. L. Lake. Used by permission.)

Nat is listed in the U.S. Census of 1860 as teaching in the state's common schools, but after he returned to Iredell County in 1865, he established several schools of his own. These were called subscription schools. The schools would last as long as the parents could afford to send their children to them. If times were hard or the children were needed to help out on the farm, Nat would have to close his school. This appears to be the pattern of his life up through the early 1880s — teaching in a public school or in one of his own.

The *Statesville Landmark* of April 22, 1881, contained this short write-up indicating that perhaps Nat sought new ways to add to his livelihood:

The Entertainment at Troutman's.
Correspondence of *The Landmark*.
TROUTMAN, N.C. April 19, '81.

The entertainment which came off at this place last Friday night proved to be (under the management of Mr. Nat Raymer) a perfect success. Notwithstanding the threatening aspect of the weather, the hall was filled to its utmost capacity, and everyone seemed to be pleased, judging from the frequent burst of hearty applause. For the treat we are under obligations to each and all of those who took part in the *exercises*, and we hope that ere long we may have the pleasure of another like it.

CITIZENS.

It would be interesting to know the type of entertainment. It could have been a performance of any kind — music, drama, readings. The use of the word exercises might suggest a performance by his students.

In 1882, Nat did something quite principled, but also something unusual for the times: He was involved with a school that taught African Americans. The *Statesville Landmark* carried the following article in the September 22, 1882, edition:

The Colored Normal School
Reported for *The Landmark*.

The normal school for the colored people of Iredell county, under the management of the Rev. W. B. Pressly, superintendent, assisted by the Rev. D. R. Stokes, colored, and Mr. J. Nat. Raymer, teachers, was opened in the court house in this place on last Monday.

Twenty-eight names are on the roll — thirteen males and fifteen females. The pupils have been punctual in attendance, and are making considerable progress. They feel much encouraged by the interest shown by the good citizens of the town and vicinity, some of whom are frequently present as spectators.

One of the chief points of attraction in this school is the model class from the colored graded school, under the management of the Rev. Mr. Rives, colored, assisted by Miss Annie Walker, a graduate of Scotia Female Seminary. This lady is an accomplished scholar, and does certainly understand her business.

A pleasant relief from the monotony of the daily exercises, is the excellent music thrown in at intervals.

The school is preparing a literary and musical entertainment for next Friday night, Sept. 29th. The particulars will be given by circular next week.

It appears from the article that the citizens of Statesville were, for the most part, supportive of all those involved with the school. Brantley York recorded in his autobiography information on a black school in nearby Salisbury in which the teachers received different treatment.

There are great many colored people in town at this time, and three churches had been erected by them, or rather for them, viz: Baptist, Presbyterian, and Methodist. But the Methodist, either by accident or incendiary, had just been burned, hence the reason for holding their services in the Court House. The Baptist colored people used their house both as a church and as a school-room. As a school-room it was well furnished with maps, charts, and other apparatus. Two well-educated ladies from the North taught the school, and because they taught the colored people the people of Salisbury did not associate with them, hence they were seldom seen at church, except the colored. They were efficient, industrious teachers, instructing the children by day and the adults by night."[11]

It is an interesting comparison — a former Confederate soldier teaching African American children in one town and two Northern ladies in another. In one town the work was acceptable, and in the other it apparently was not, perhaps because of where the teachers came from. The war had been over for seventeen years, but many still bore ill feelings toward the North.

Sometime during the postwar period Nat's wife developed a lump in her breast. According to his great-granddaughter Edith McClain Moss, "Nat had not been able to make enough money teaching to pay for the surgery, so he went to his father, Moses Raymer, for help. He told his dad that if he would give him the money to pay for the operation, he would take that as his share of the inheritance and never ask for anything else. This was done, and Elizabeth had the surgery done and recovered to live to a ripe old age."

Still, even though he never made a great deal of money through teaching, Nat was a firm believer in funding public education, as this June 23, 1882, letter to the *Statesville Landmark* reveals:

A Suggestion.

Each candidate for legislative honors, throughout our entire State, should be required to commit himself, one way or the other, on three questions, viz:

1st. For or against an increase of the tax for the benefit of public schools.

2nd, For or against a complete revolution in the present method of keeping up public roads; and

3rd. For or against a dog tax.

Either of these questions, is, to-day, of more vital importance to every North Carolinian than prohibition, which is certainly dead, if 118,000 majority will kill anything.

J. NAT. RAYMER.

In the summer of 1882, Nat put the following advertisement in the *Statesville Landmark*. It would be published over several months. This particular one is from the *Landmark* of February 16, 1883. There is no information in the Raymer family records on why Nat put his farm up for sale or if he even sold it.

LAND BUYERS, HO!

I will sell the whole or a part of the plantation upon which I reside, seven miles S. W. of Statesville on the Railroad.

For particulars address

J. NAT. RAYMER.
Rock Cut, Iredell Co., N.C.
August 13, 1882.

In the April 13, 1883, edition of the *Landmark*, citizens were distressed to read the following:

Stricken With Paralysis.

We learn with regret that on Sunday, 1st inst., J. Nat. Raymer, Esq., of Shiloh township, was stricken with paralysis, involving seriously his whole left side and distorting his features. Drs. B. H. Yount and J. F. Long are attending Mr. Raymer, and his improvement under their treatment has been such as to warrant the hope of a complete recovery.

Just one week later, the April 20, 1883, edition of the *Landmark* reported on Nat's condition:

Mr. J. Nat Raymer, of Shiloh, who was stricken with paralysis on the 1st, was in town Wednesday. His features are again natural, but he walks with difficulty, his left side being yet partially paralyzed. Mr. Raymer's physicians ascribe his paralysis to the excessive indulgence in tobacco, and have ordered him to discontinue the use of it altogether — an injunction to which he has yielded perfect obedience.

Whatever physical difficulties he was experiencing seem to have improved by the summer. On July 7, 1883, the following lines appeared in the Personal Column of the *Statesville Landmark*:

Mr. J. Nat. Raymer, of this county, left last Monday for Pleasant Plains, Independence county, Arkansas, where he has an engagement to teach a school. He is a most excellent teacher, thorough, accurate and painstaking, and his removal, although but temporary, is a detriment to the educational interests of this county.

For reasons unknown to his descendants, Nat decided to move to Arkansas, though the article indicates it is only temporary. Nor is there any evidence that his family accompanied him. As a teacher and former Confederate soldier, he certainly had respect in the community, but he could not have been very prosperous if he had to seek financial assistance from his father for Elizabeth's surgery. Possibly memories of his prewar days there might have drawn him back. Brantley York had been teaching and preaching in Arkansas in the late 1870s. Since both men were educators, Nat might have had contact with him and been encouraged to go. Or it may have been as simple as no jobs available in North Carolina, but one available in Arkansas.

For whatever reason, Nat left North Carolina in July 1883.

· 19 ·

RETURN TO ARKANSAS

There is no mention that Nat's wife and children went with him to Arkansas, nor do his descendants in Texas have any record of his time there. The July article seems to indicate that he had taken a job for a period of time and would return. What is known of his time there is contained in two letters he wrote to the home newspaper.

On July 20, 1883, the *Landmark* published this letter from Nat, under the title "How Arkansas Strikes an Iredell Man."

After a travel by rail of nearly one thousand miles I arrived in this place on last Saturday, safe and sound, but terribly begrimed with dust and coal smoke, as might be expected in so long a journey in such hot weather. But I am resting now, and luxuriating in one of the most lovely sections of the country to be found on earth. These are the table lands separating the low grounds on the White and Little Red rivers; gently undulating, but in many places, for miles, barely sufficient to carry away the water that falls in copious showers during the summer season. The soil here is not so extravagantly fertile as it is near the rivers, where a bale and a half of cotton to the acre is an average crop; but even here it is as good as the best creek bottom lands in North Carolina. There are no gullies, old fields, or impoverished land to be seen. There is no prairie; but, where not cleared by man, the virgin forest stands unbroken, and, apparently impenetrable; sometimes, for many miles, covered with a dense underbrush consisting almost entirely of sumach. The country is sparsely settled, and game of all kinds, common to this portion of America, is still moderately abundant. Except in cultivated fields, the surface of the earth is everywhere covered with grass half knee high, often much higher. It matters not how dense the timber may be, the grass grows all the same. Consequently, as a stock country, it would be hard to find one superior to this.

On these highlands are many never failing springs and small streams, affording an abundant supply of water. Wells are generally about twenty-five feet deep, the water excellent; and, as a matter of course, good health follows.

Wheat does tolerably well, making eight to fifteen bushels per acre. Corn is in silk and tassel, and going through a field is like squeezing through a cane brake by twilight. This year, owing to the late, cold spring, the fruit crop is a partial failure, an event of rare occurrence. Usually, a great deal more fruit is raised then is saved.

Grapes, walnuts, hickorynuts, wild fruits and berries of all kinds grow in the greatest profusion.

Now, as to society: This will compare favorably with that anywhere. None are immensely wealthy, none are poverty-stricken; neither is there any sham-aristocracy, but all seem to be on a level, socially. I haven't heard an oath since I've been here; no whiskey is to be had — in fact, nobody seems to want any. No locks are seen on cribs, smoke houses, milk houses or anywhere else worth naming; and clothes out of the wash hang to the open air until dry, even if two or three days and nights are necessary — and all, no doubt, because there is not one "pusson of color" within nine miles of this place.

J. NAT. RAYMER.

Pleasant Plains, Independence Co.,

Ark., July 9th, 1883.

On December 21, 1883, the *Statesville Landmark* carried Nat's letter about revival meetings in Arkansas.

Jacob Nathaniel Raymer. Probably taken in the late 1870s or early 1880s when he was living in Iredell County. (Property of McClain family. Used by permission.)

Protracted Meeting in Arkansas.

Probably there is not another spot on the earth's surface, equal in extent with the State of Arkansas, in which, during the fall of 1883, so many "protracted" religious meetings have been and are still in progress. The exercises, in a great majority, are pretty much the same. In the main, the make-up of the meetings themselves and their peculiarities are said to be so identical throughout the State; so, a brief description of one will serve to give a general idea of all. Surely there must be some exceptions, but I am persuaded that such are few, and widely scattered.

On the night of the 14th inst. I attended one of these meetings, distant from this point about half a mile. I must confess that my motives were not altogether devotional; in fact there is not much about them to inspire devotional feelings;

but the loud singing and general uproar, which, at the distance of half a mile, had lulled to me sleep every night for more than a week, had excited my curiosity to such a pitch that I went, I saw, and I *fell back*. In a charming grove was located a rude log building about twenty-four by thirty feet, called a church. It was already filled with the "salt of the earth," but, like an omnibus, there was room found for one more. On the book board were two tin lamps, one of which, it is surmised, was brought by the foolish virgins, since it has no oil; but the other was all right. There were present eight preachers, or "parsons" as they are called in this country, but I didn't know, until later, that they were all loaded. It doesn't cost much, nor require any great amount of mental labor to make a "parson" of this caliber. There must be a factory somewhere west of the "father of waters" where they are turned out as rapidly as an awkward hand can mould bullets. As a rule, they are deplorably illiterate, consequently our mother tongue is most wretchedly butchered. True, most of them can read after a fashion, but it is not done intelligently. Few of them comprehend what they read, and fewer still understand the preacher who says: "My breethring and sistern; you have heerd of the mighty hostes of satan; yes sir, ah! and we warn you to flee unto the mountings, ah! and drink of the pure fountings thar prepared, ah!" Something after this fashion I heard a discourse on the text:—"The kingdom of heaven is like unto a merchant man seeking goodly *apparel*, who, when he had found one *peril* of great price, &c.," and the sermon that followed would have made a good companion to the celebrated "whang-doodle" sermon that went the rounds of the press a few years ago. "Yes, sir," preceded each phrase and clause, oftentimes each alternate word, and a prolonged "ah!" followed it. The speaker soon worked himself up to the boiling point, and the last half of the sermon was given in thirds of the musical scale, to which a bass could have been improvised easily. He frothed at the mouth but would not stop long enough to spit. He would bob his head behind the bookboard, all the while keeping his exhortation going in a spasmodic gurgle, while he would bark and spit, scraping his No. 10 brogan about on the pulpit floor as he resumed an erect posture. At times he would have his hands clasped at the back of his head, and then he would look for all the world as he if were going for a flea between his shoulders. Then again he would be gesticulating wildly in front, and one of these front gestures happened to knock the only light (one of the tin lamps) about ten feet out in the floor, upon which our situation was, instantly, like unto that of a blind man. The battle ceased raging for a spell, and I have no doubt the "Old Boy" was glad enough to have a truce; it had been going ill with him for more than an hour. By and by, a match was found; so was the lamp; a light was struck, and hostilities re-opened. But his resources were exhausted, and the first speaker collapsed suddenly, rallying, however, sufficiently to call for mourners, after which he stepped down and proceeded to shake hands with those in the "amen corner," the dear sistern more especially; whereupon some half dozen men, with stentorian lungs, began singing as if their very lives depended on it, particularly upon the higher notes, which they would bring out with a kind of screeching yawp that no word in the English language will exactly describe.

Meanwhile another gun was unlimbered and brought to bear upon the "devil's stronghold," as they were pleased to term it. This one did not go into the pulpit at all, but shifted his position about on the floor, something a swivel howitzer, so that he could have an enfilading fire on every seat. He may have been a "granger" also, as there were bits of fodder and hay sticking in his hair and whiskers and on his coat, which was of the frockcoat pattern, and well supplied with buttons where they could be of no possible use. His ammunition was fresh and it seemed on the brink of spontaneous combustion. He had a good deal to say about the "anteluvian world," and while yelling at the top of his voice, he would charge around the room, pounding his breethring and sistren on the back, and altogether raising such an unearthly row, that your correspondent felt compelled to plug his ears with his fingers and beat a hasty retreat at the first opportunity. It was the nearly 10 o'clock, and the custom is (as I learned afterwards) to keep up the cannonade until a very late hour, provided there was a sufficient number of "parsons" present.

The meeting had now been going on for more than a week, with a very slim attendance through the day, but at night the house was filled. Learning that services were appointed for 11 o'clock on Saturday, at that hour I repaired to the church, and there found assembled the majority of the eight preachers — no other males — and some sad-eyed females, who might have been grief-stricken over the destruction amongst their chickens; at all events, they didn't have that happy, saucy look which is said to convert them into one of the dangerous "beggarly elements." While waiting for the congregation to appear, I sauntered to the spring, which, by the way, is the finest I have seen in the State. After an absence of nearly an hour, I returned to find the number present had not increased by the addition of a single soul. The parsons had formed themselves into a kind of knife-swapping association, in which each had the best, and of course, each thought he ought to have some boot. I did not see any trades consummated; indeed, it is a matter of grave doubt whether there was a nickel in the whole crowd. Time was dull, and I thought they could get along without me — which they did. On the next day the drag net was cast, but no fish taken, except two by certificate; there is not much raw material to work on, aside from your humble servant.

As education, like leaven, permeates the masses, this style of preaching becomes more and more unpopular; and eventually, it will be forced to take the trail of the poor Indian and move toward the setting sun.

J. NAT. RAYMER.   Pleasant Plains, Ark.

· 20 ·

GONE TO TEXAS

Family records in Texas indicate that Nat came there from North Carolina, and not Arkansas. He is also reported to have made a journey to Texas alone, and while there scouted out the West Texas territory and the city of Dallas.

He returned to North Carolina resolved to move yet again. Probably in the spring or early summer of 1884, Nat and his son Edward loaded two wagons with the family's belongings and drove them to Texas. His destination was Field Store, near Hempstead, where the family would set up housekeeping.

When everything was ready, he notified Elizabeth, Lulu, and Cora to come by train. Nat was a member of the Mt. Moriah Masonic Lodge No. 82 in Iredell County. He was initiated on February 10, 1871, passed April 14, 1871, and was raised on May 26, 1871. Before his family journeyed westward, he had contacted Masonic Lodges in cities along the train's route. As the train stopped at a particular station, a local Mason would meet the train and take the family to his home for the night. In the morning he would take them back and see them safely aboard the next train. In this fashion the family reached their new home in Texas.

A few months after reaching Texas, Nat affiliated on October 18, 1884, with the Pleasant Hill Masonic Lodge No. 380 at Field Store. He continued his membership there until July 20, 1889. He later affiliated with the Euclid Masonic Lodge No. 45 in Rusk, Texas, on June 3, 1893, and was a member until June 5, 1897.

Nat went back to his profession of teaching. He presented his qualifications to the Board of Examiners for Waller County and was duly licensed to teach in August 1884.

Very little is known of Nat's time in Texas. He would continue teaching school, and the 1900 United States Census listed him as a farmer. His son Ed was living with him and also farming. Sorrow would touch his later years. His oldest child, Lulu Octavia Raymer Bailey, died July 5, 1900, in Rusk, Texas. Her husband died on July 24, 1905. They were the parents of his granddaughter, Frances Delphine Bailey, who was born March 25, 1898, in Rusk. Cora and her husband, J. C. Tompkins, were the parents of Nat's grandson, James Fairis Tompkins.

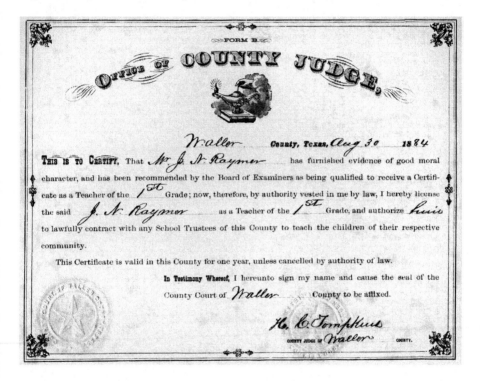

Nat's Texas teaching certificate, which licenses him as a "Teacher of the 1st Grade." This does not refer to a grade level to teach, but to a level of teacher skill and ability, much like a Class A certificate today would refer to a top-rated teacher. The majority of schools at this time were one-room schools with multi-grade levels. With this certificate he could seek employment with any school district in Waller County. His daughter Lulu was also a teacher in Cherokee County, and on September 7, 1896, she signed a contract with the Board of Trustees of the Salem School District to teach for four months, at a salary of $34.37½ per month. At the bottom of her contract is an explanation of certificate ranks: "Note.—Salaries allowed by law. 1st Grade certificates, not exceeding $75 per month. 2nd Grade certificates, not exceeding $60 per month. 3rd Grade certificates, not exceeding $40 per month." Lulu's contract was for a 2nd Grade certificate. (Property of McClain Family. Used by permission.)

Back of Nat's Teaching Certificate. At the end of each teaching period, Nat would present his certificate for renewal for the following year. The 1885 and 1886 renewals are for Waller County, and in 1887, the renewal was for Grimes County. The certificate had been folded many times and is held together with circular stickers. (Property of McClain Family. Used by permission.)

Frances Delphine McClain, Nat's granddaughter, was approximately 17 years old when this picture was taken. The locket she is wearing remains in possession of the McClain family. Delphine was born March 25, 1898, at Rusk, Cherokee County, Texas. She was orphaned at age 7 when her father died in July 1905, and raised by her Aunt Cora, J. C. Tompkins, and Nat and Elizabeth Raymer. She married Elbert Russell McClain on July 9, 1916, and died November 7, 1962, at Huntsville, Waller County, Texas. She and her husband were the parents of seven children. Delphine almost died of a tubal pregnancy, which required emergency surgery. (Property of McClain Family. Used by permission.)

The March 28, 1900, edition of the *Statesville Landmark* carried an obituary of Nat's brother Charles Augustus Raymer, who had died suddenly of a heart attack in his 51st year. His sister, Mrs. Margaret E. Raymer Puntch, who had come to Texas in January 1889 as a widow with children, died September 29, 1905, in Jacksonville, Texas.

Nat was ill the last few years of his life, and the family hired a male nurse to look after him and stay with him until his death. It was during this time that the journal he had kept for so many years disappeared, perhaps either given by Nat to the man who cared for him or taken by this individual in payment for his time.

On August 20, 1909, Jacob Nathaniel Raymer, Company C, 4th Regiment North Carolina Troops, answered the last roll call and was buried in the cemetery at Athens, Texas.

Jacob Nathaniel Raymer. A photographer identified as Miss Puntch, who had a studio in Jacksonville, Texas, took this photograph of Nat in the early 1900s. He would have been in his late 60s. (Property of McClain Family. Used by permission.)

After Nat's death in 1909, Elizabeth lived with her son Edward, but family records do not indicate if she lived with him or he with her. Edward died in 1911, leaving her to depend on family members for assistance. In 1913, she applied for a Texas Confederate widow's pension. At the time, she stated she was not receiving any money or means of support amounting to $300 per year and did not receive a Confederate pension from North Carolina or any other state. The application contains detailed questions, and affidavits were taken of Texas citizens who swore to the fact that she was a citizen of Texas and of North Carolinians who attested to the fact that Nat was indeed a

Nat's gravesite, Athens City Cemetery, Athens, Texas. According to family records, Nat's son Edward marked his grave with a cairn or iron ore rocks, which were stolen over the years for use on other gravesites. In time, all that remained to mark the grave was a stub sticking out of the ground. In 2001, Nat's great-granddaughters, Lois McClain Carter and Edith McClain Moss, applied to the United States Department of Veterans Affairs in Washington, D.C., for a new stone marker, pictured here. Photograph by Thomas O. Wylie, LaRue, Texas. (Property of McClain Family. Used by permission.)

Confederate veteran. One of the North Carolinians was Nat's old friend and fellow-soldier, James Columbus Steele.

Here is Elizabeth Raymer's application for a Confederate widow's pension, transcribed from the holdings of the Texas State Archives:

For Use of Widows of Soldiers Who are in Indigent Circumstances

THE STATE OF TEXAS
County of Cherokee

I, Mrs. Elizabeth Raymer, do hereby make application to the Commissioner of Pensions for a pension, to be granted me under the Act passed by the Thirty-first Legislature of the State of Texas, and approved March 26, A.D. 1909, on he following grounds:

Elizabeth Raymer appears somewhat frail. The photograph was probably taken in Waller County, Texas, in the late 1920s or early 1930s, not long before her death in 1933. She is not wearing a wedding band, and Edith McClain Moss has commented, "She may never have had one due to modest circumstances of school teachers in that period, as demonstrated by the pay scale shown under Nat's teaching certificate." (Property of McClain Family. Used by permission.)

I am the widow of Jacob Nathaniel Raymer, deceased, who departed this life on the 20th of August, A.D. 1909, in the county of Henderson, in the State of Texas.

I have not remarried since the death of my said husband, and I do solemnly swear that I was never divorced from my said husband, and that I never voluntarily abandoned him during his life, but remained his true, faithful and lawful wife up to the date of his death. I was married to him on the 20 day of Sept, A.D. 1865 in the county of Iredell, in the State of North Carolina.

My husband, the said Jacob Nathaniel Raymer, enlisted and served in the military service of the Confederate States during the war between the States of the United States, and that he did not desert the Confederate Service. I have been a resident of the State of Texas since prior to Jan 1, 1900 and I have been continuously since a citizen of the State of Texas. I do further state that I do not receive from any source whatever money or other means of support amounting in value to the sum of three hundred dollars per annum, nor do I own in my own right, nor does any one hold in trust for my benefit or use, estate or property, either real, personal or mixed, either in fee or for life, of the assessed value of over two thousand dollars; nor do I receive any aid or pension from any other State, or from the United States, or from any other source, and I do further state that the answers given to the following questions are true:

• What is your age? <u>68 years</u>
• Where were you born? <u>Iredell Co. North Carolina</u>

- How long have you resided in the State of Texas? <u>Since 1885</u>
- How long have you resided in the county of your present residence? And what is your postoffice address? <u>Thirty five years, Rusk Texas</u>
- What was your husband's full name? <u>Jacob Nathaniel Raymer</u>
- When and where were you married? <u>Sept 20, 1865 — Iredell Co. N.C.</u>
- What was the date of his death? <u>August 20 1909</u>
- In what State was your husband's command originally organized? <u>N.C.</u>
- How long did your husband serve? If known to you, give date of enlistment and discharge. <u>4 years — May 1861 to Apr 1865</u>
- What was the name or letter of the company, or name or number of the battalion, regiment or battery of artillery in which your husband served? If he was transferred from one branch of service to another, give time of transfer, description of command and time of service. <u>No answer recorded</u>
- Name the branch of service in which your husband served, whether infantry, cavalry, artillery or the navy, or if commissioned as an officer by the President, his rank and line of duty, or if detailed for special service, under the law of conscription, the nature of such service, and time of service. <u>Infantry</u>
- Have you transferred to others any property of any kind for the purpose of becoming a beneficiary under this law? <u>No</u>

Wherefore your petitioner prays that her application for a pension be approved and such other proceedings be had in the premises as are required by law.

(Signature of Applicant) *Elizabeth Raymer*

Sworn to and subscribed before me, this 7th day of July, A.D. 1913.

C. F. Gibson

County Judge Cherokee County, Texas

AFFIDAVIT OF WITNESSES

[Note. — There must be at least two credible witnesses.]

THE STATE OF TEXAS

County of Cherokee

Before me C.F. Gibson, County Judge of Cherokee County, State of Texas, on this day personally appeared T. J. Clay & G. M. Eddins, who are personally known to be credible citizens, who, being by me duly sworn, on oath state that they personally know that Mrs. Elizabeth Raymer, applicant for a pension as the widow of J.N. Raymer deceased, is in truth and fact the widow of J. N. Raymer deceased; that they personally know that she has not remarried since the death of her husband, for whose service in the army she claims a pension, and that they have no interest in this claim.

(Signature of Witness) <u>T. J. Clay</u>
(Signature of Witness) <u>G. M. Eddins</u>

Sworn to and subscribed before me, this 7th day of July, A.D. 1913.

C. F. Gibson

County Judge Cherokee County, Texas

AFFIDAVIT OF WITNESSES

[Note.— There must be at least two credible witnesses.]
THE STATE OF TEXAS
County of Cherokee
Before me C.F. Gibson, County Judge of Cherokee County, State of Texas, on this day personally appeared T. J. Clay & G. M. Eddins, who are personally known to be credible citizens, who, being by me duly sworn, on oath state that they personally know the above-named applicant for a pension, and that they personally know that the said Mrs. Elizabeth Raymer has been a bona fide resident citizen of the State of Texas since prior to Jan 1, 1900 and that they have no interest in this claim.
(Signature of Witness) T. J. Clay
(Signature of Witness) G. M. Eddins

Sworn to and subscribed before me, this 7th day of July, A.D. 1913.

C. F. Gibson
County Judge Cherokee County, Texas

CERTIFICATE OF STATE AND COUNTY ASSESSOR.

I, P. B. Musselwhite, State and County Assessor in the County of Cherokee, State of Texas, do hereby certify that Mrs. Elizabeth Raymer, whose name is signed to the foregoing application for a pension, under the Act of the Thirty-first Legislature, approved March 26, A.D. 1909, is charged on the land and personal property rolls of the said county, in her name, or the name of a trustee, with estate, real, personal and mixed, at the assessed value of not any dollars.
Given under my hand, this 5 day of August, A.D. 1913.

P. B. Musselwhite
State and County Assessor

INTERROGATORIES TO WITNESSES IN PENSION CLAIMS

EX PARTE
Mrs. Elizabeth Raymer
Applicant for Confederate Pension.

The Honorable County Judge of Cherokee County, Texas, will please take notice that, five days after the service hereof, applicant herein will apply to the County Court of said County and State for a commission to take the depositions of P.C. Carlton and J. C. Steele who reside in the County of Iredell in the State of N.C. in answer to the following interrogatories and such cross-interrogatories as may be propounded by the County Judge of said County which will be read in evidence upon hearing the applicant's claim for pension in behalf of applicant; said testimony is material and indispensable to applicant in furnishing the required proof of claim for a pension under the Act of March 26, 1909, the application for which is now pending before the Honorable County Judge, and the facts necessary and required to be proven under the provisions of said act, the applicant believes cannot be proven by any witness residing in the County of Cherokee and State of Texas, of which _____ is a bona fide resident.

Elizabeth Raymer
(Applicant)

Direct Interrogatories to be Propounded to the Witnesses.
P. C. Carlton and J. C. Steele.

INT. 1. What is your name? Age? Place of residence and postoffice address?

INT. 2. Do you personally know, or did you at any time know Jacob Nathaniel Raymer, whose widow is an applicant for pension under the Act of March 26, 1909?

INT. 3. How long had you known the said J. N. Raymer and where and when did you first know him?

INT. 4. Do you personally know that the said J. N. Raymer enlisted in the services of the Confederacy, and performed the duties of a soldier or a sailor?

INT. 5. Do you personally know in what company and regiment the said J. N. Raymer enlisted and served in the Confederate army? When? Where? And the time of service? If you personally knew and so have stated that he enlisted and served in the Confederate navy, then state: When? Where? And how long he served?

INT. 6. Do you personally know that J. N. Raymer was commissioned as an officer directly by the President of the Confederate States? What was his rank and line of duty?

INT. 7. Do you further know if J. N. Raymer was, under the provisions of the conscript law, detailed for any kind of special service in the field, shops, armories, etc., of the Confederacy? What was the nature of his service, and how long did he serve?

CROSS INTERROGATORIES
To be Propounded to P. C. Carlton and J. C. Steele

CROSS INTERROGATORY 1. If, in answer to the foregoing direct interrogatories, you have stated that you personally know or did know said J. N. Raymer and that you know that he enlisted in the service of the Confederacy and performed the duties of a soldier or sailor, and having named the company and regiment, or special service in which J. N. Raymer so enlisted and served, then please state fully what is your source of such knowledge? And state whether or not you know or at any time you knew of any other soldier or sailor by the name of J. N. Raymer serving in the same company or regiment, or special service in which you say the said J. N. Raymer enlisted, if you have stated that said J. N. Raymer enlisted and served in the navy of the Confederacy, then state whether or not you know any other soldier or sailor of the same name as said J. N. Raymer applicant serving in the same command, or the special service to which he was assigned?

If you say that you so know of other soldiers or sailors of the same name of J. N. Raymer then can you and how do you identify and locate the one from the other or others?

CROSS INT. 2. Are you positively certain that said J. N. Raymer is the identical person serving as testified by you?

CROSS INT. 3. Do you know whether or not the said J. N. Raymer served honorably from the date of his enlistment until the close of the late Civil War between the States, or until he was discharged from said company and regiment, or the special service to which he had been assigned?

CROSS INT. 4. Do you whether or not the said J. N. Raymer deserted his command, or voluntarily abandoned his post of duty or the service during said war?

THE STATE OF TEXAS,

County of Cherokee

I, C. F. Gibson, County Judge of said County, in said State, do hereby waive copy of interrogatories, notice, time and issuance of commission, and it is hereby agreed that the answers to the hereinabove direct and cross interrogatories of the said herein named witness may be attached hereto.

C. F. Gibson
County Judge Cherokee County, Texas
Elizabeth Raymer
(Applicant)

DEPOSITION IN PENSION CLAIMS, WITH CAPTIONS AND CERTIFICATES.

EX PARTE

In re Mrs. Elizabeth Raymer

Applicant for Confederate Pension.

Answers and depositions of (1)* Capt. P. C. Carlton and J. C. Steele

to the accompanying interrogatories (2)

propounded to them in the above entitled cause taken before (3) J. A. Hartness Clerk Superior Court in accordance with the accompanying (7)

To the first interrogatory the said Captain P. [Pinkney] C. Carlton.

Witness answers I was Captain of Company A — 7 Regiment of N.C. Troops and know that J. Nat Raymer was a member of Co. C, 4 Regiment of N.C. Troops and that he remained in service to the end of war and was paroled at Appomattox April 9, 1865.

J. C. Steele says that he was personally acquainted with J. Nat Raymer and that he says he was enlisted at Statesville, N.C. in Capt. Andrew's Company which was afterward Co. C, 4 Regiment N.C. troops and that I served with him through the war of 4 years and slept with him and was paroled with him at Appomattox Apr. 9 —1865 at the surrender of Gen. Lee.

Capt. P. C. Carlton and J. C. Steele both live in Statesville, N.C.

J. A. Hartness who takes this deposition is Clerk Superior Court of Iredell County N.C. at Statesville.

Subscribed and sworn to before me, this 12th day of July, 1913.

J. A. Hartness
Clerk Superior Court

*The numbers in parentheses refer to page numbers in the original document.

THE STATE OF North Carolina
County of Iredell
I, J. A. Hartness, Clerk of Superior Court, do hereby certify that Capt. P. C. Carlton and J. C. Steele are personally known to me to be credible citizens of said County and State, and that the foregoing answers of Capt. P. C. Carlton and J. C. Steele, the witnesses before named, and whose names appear as signed to the foregoing deposition, were made before me and were sworn to and subscribed before me, by said witnesses.

Given under my hand and official seal, this 12th day of July, 1913.

J. A. Hartness
Clerk Superior Court

Transcribed from the Holdings of the Texas State Archives.

BOND

This BOND must be sworn to by the owner of the original warrant, and also signed by the owner and two sureties before it will be approved and duplicate warrant issued.

THE STATE OF TEXAS,
County of Cherokee

Before me, the undersigned authority, on this day personally appeared Mrs. E. Raymer, who, after being by me duly sworn on oath, says that she is the true owner of Confederate Pension Warrant No. 6166 for the sum of SIXTEEN and No/100 Dollars, drawn by the Comptroller of the State of Texas, on NOV 30, 1916, in favor of Mrs. E. Raymer, and that the same is in fact lost or destroyed, or has not been received.

Elizabeth Raymer
Owner of the Warrant.

Sworn to and subscribed before me this the 26 day of December, 1916.

C. F. Gibson
Co. Judge for Cherokee Co., Texas.

THE STATE OF TEXAS
County of Cherokee
KNOW ALL MEN BY THESE PRESENTS, That we, Mrs. E. Raymer, as principal, and J. B. Copeland and B. C. Copeland, as sureties, are held and bound unto JAS E. FERGUSON, Governor of the State of Texas, and his successors in office, in the sum of THIRTY-TWO and No/100 Dollars, for the payment of which sum, well and truly to be made, we do bind ourselves, our heirs, executors and administrators, jointly and severally.

Whereas, the above named principal has filed with the Comptroller her affidavit, stating that she is the true owner of said Confederate Pension warrant, drawn by the Comptroller of the State of Texas, on the date shown in the above

This photograph of Elizabeth Raymer was taken in Cherokee County, Texas, sometime in the second decade of the 20th century. During this time she had applied to the State of Texas for a Confederate widow's pension. (Property of McClain Family. Used by permission.)

affidavit, in favor of said payee, and that the same is in fact lost or destroyed; and

Whereas, duplicate of said Confederate Pension warrant, in favor of the original payee will be issued.

Now, therefore, the condition of the above obligation is such that the owner of said warrant will hold the State harmless and return to the Comptroller, upon demand being made therefore, such duplicate or copies, or the amount of money named therein, together with all costs that may accrue against the State, on collecting the same.

Given under our hands, this 26 day
of Dec, A.D. 1916

Elizabeth Raymer
Principal.
J.B. Copeland
Surety.
B. C. Copeland
Surety.

County Cherokee
Number 22346
Address R. F. D.
City or Town — Rusk, Texas

As Elizabeth grew older, she went to live with her daughter Cora and son-in-law, J.C. Tompkins. The 1930 United States Census for Texas lists Cora and Elizabeth as living together, but J. C. Tompkins is not listed. Family records do not indicate where he was, but he is reported to have died in an automobile accident in November 1933, a few months after Elizabeth passed. He was the person, however, who filled out the following mortuary warrant, transcribed from the Holdings of the Texas State Archives

APPLICATION FOR
MORTUARY WARRANT

THE STATE OF TEXAS
County of Waller

I, J. C. Tompkins do hereby certify that I am the person to whom is entrusted the paying of the accounts and indebtedness of the late Elizabeth Raymer, who was a pensioner of the State of Texas, and whose file number was 22346, and whose original county was Cherokee.

The said pensioner Elizabeth Raymer, died on the 7 day of July, 1933, in the town of _____ County of Waller, Texas.

The pensioner died in the home of J. C. Tompkins who was related to the pensioner as Mother-in-law.

That the warrant, which application is hereby made for, shall be applied to paying all or part of the funeral expenses incurred by the said pensioner

I further certify that the warrant for the current quarter has not been cashed by the pensioner, to the best of my knowledge and belief.

I am related to the pensioner as Son in law that my postoffice address is Route #1 Hempstead Texas

Signed J. C. Tompkins

Sworn to before me this 16 day of July, 1933

    Tom B Cuny

Notary Public in and for Waller County State of Texas

CERTIFICATE OF UNDERTAKER

I, Tom B. Cuny, do certify that I am undertaker in the town of Hempstead, County of Waller, State of Texas, that I had charge of the body of Elizabeth Raymer, who died in the town of _____, County of Waller, State of Texas, on the 7 day of July 1933. That said body was prepared for burial by me on the 7 day of July 1933, and that I am of the opinion that warrant herein applied for should be issued to the said J. C. Tompkins who makes the foregoing application.

Signed Tom B. Cuny

CERTIFICATE OF PHYSICIAN

I, F. K. Laurentz, MD, do certify that I am a practicing physician, and that I attended Mrs. Elizabeth Raymer in her last illness, and am of the opinion that her ailments were arterio-sclerisis — myocardio aortic and mitral regurgitation.

I further certify that I am of the opinion that the Mortuary Warrant above requested should be issued in the name of the aforementioned applicant, in accordance with Act passed by the Thirty-eighth Legislature and approved March 2, 1923.

Signed F. K. Laurentz, MD
Physician's Address Hempstead, TX

APPENDIX:
"AN ARKANSAS FROLIC"

"I do not profess to be a poet and only make rhymes sometimes when I am not otherwise engaged," Nat wrote in 1857. How many poems he may have written during his lifetime is unknown. Seven that he composed between 1857 and 1862 remain in his personal papers, in addition to some poetic inclusions in his letters. In his description of an Arkansas hoedown, Nat demonstrates his rhyming skill, as the poem generally follows a rhyme scheme of A-A-B-C-C-B.

Nat's letters, poems, and some surviving diary entries show his talent for writing, and one might wonder why he didn't pursue writing as a career after the war, perhaps in journalism. His great-great-granddaughter Nancy Moss Miller offers her thoughts: "I imagine that writing as a profession wasn't well regarded in those days. Nat's father was a businessman, and as such probably thought his son was being frivolous."

The following poem might not have advanced Nat's arguments against this charge, but it captures Nat's sense of fun.

"An Arkansas Frolic"
[circa 1857]
(descriptive of an Arkansas hoedown)

1.
Hail, mighty muse! Return once more,
And reign where thou hast reigned before —
In my unsettled brain.
Be valiant too, with all thy might,
A song for sport I wish to write.
Then O! return again.

2.

What, here so soon! I did not dream
You e'er would come without a theme,
    Something fresh and hearty; —
    A lad, a lass, a noisy row —
    Or — what, O yes, I have it now —
        An Arkansas party.

3.

One balmy evening just at night
I went to see a wondrous sight, —
    And there I almost died.
    I will tell it as I know it,
    And describe it as I saw it —
        Then for yourselves decide.

4.

A jovial crowd had gathered then,
Of ladies fair and gallant men —
    At least 'twas so I thought,
    And each at the other glancing
    Roguish look which spoke of dancing —
        Or "will you dance or not?"

5.

With rapid beats soft bosoms swelled
And sunk again, — and beauty held
    Possession there, supreme.
    And stifled sighs, and choking sobs
    Were heard, while with swift rising throbs
        Beat tender hearts in time.

6.

Next music's lively swell arose,
And roused them from that short repose,
    In which they seemed to rest; —
    Then quick as thought each active lad
    Rushed for a partner, good or bad —
        Took worse if not the best.

7.

The dance commenced, — with measured steps
At first, but soon the coupled sets
    Became dissatisfied
    With the music slow and sluggish —
    Wanted something "quick and der'lish" —
        Their wish was gratified.

8.

The music swelled with rapid pace,
The dancers whirled with easy grace
    In rousing revelry:
With easy grace I said,—yes all
But one, a gawk, both slim and tall,
    Who blundered dreadfully.

9.

He leaped about with gestures wild,
And shook the earth methought a mile,
    In all directions round.
I trembled o'er with dread alarm,
Away I feared he'd flung his arm,
    And never more be found.

10.

A fate still worse seemed drawing near,
Which might sink each heart in fear
    And moisten every cheek;
For all who saw him said they thought
His supple legs would surely lock,
    And break his precious neck.

11.

Yet happened not so sad a fate,
And now I hope advice he'll take,
    Nor think it very long,
Never try such capers over,
If you do you will discover
    You're sadly in the wrong.

12.

But I must stop this digression,
For I know 'tis growing irksome
    To those who read this song,
But hold—ere I close let me tell
About his lass the lively belle
    Of that vivacious throng.

13.

But why begin a task so hard?
'Twould take a witty Scottish bard
    To praise Miss Loretta.
(Of course this name is fictitious,
Yet 'twill do,—I can't do justice
    To so rare a beauty.)

14.

Strange indeed so fair a creature —
One with love in every feature,
Should dance with such a beau.
But who'll dispute a woman's right!
'Tis vain, succumb, and shout with might
"For me there's hope I know!"

15.

Her glossy hair in heavy braids,
And black as mid-night sable shades
Fell on her shoulders, thick,
And 'neath a brow as white as snow,
Her hazel eyes with beauty's glow,
Glanced in succession quick.

16.

Her cheeks, like a fresh opened rose,
Were red as crimson, but who knows
From which — nature or paint!
And her lips though slightly pouting,
Yet to kiss were very tempting —
But to kiss was to faint.

17.

Her soft, upheaving bosom swelled
With tender beauty, — though partly veiled
With transparent muslin,
Which was, methought, unfolded there,
To prove a sly bewitching snare
To entice a victim.

18.

And on that voluptuous bust
Shone bright jewels, a sacred trust,
(Though doubtless, worn before)
And given her, when she in faith
With him, *alone*, would *"keep them safe,"*
I dare to tell no more.

19.

Her slender waist, her ankles small,
Her wrists begirt with golden foil,
A bachelor would tempt; —
But I must quit this description
Unfinished, — through strict completion
I do now attempt.

20.

But right or wrong it was too much,
To see her partner give her such
Tremendous shakes and jerks,
And in my heart I thought I'd send
A challenge to that female friend —
To shoot and fight with dirks.

21.

In silence thought I stood and gazed
On that sweet form so roughly used,
And tripped at very whirl. —
But I was soon amazed to learn
That she, like all the ladies, seemed
To like it very well.

22.

All were fired with mirth and pleasure,
All possessed a precious treasure —
A *heart* to give away.
I offered mine at set of sun,
It was received and one
In turn was given me that day.

23.

'Twas Christmas eve, and twilight there,
Which bade us all for night prepare,
And plunge into the fun,
Which should be ours all that night,
And if we would but manage right, —
Until tomorrow noon.

24.

Scarcely had rose the green of night
When wine and eggnog bubbling bright
In crystal vases shone; —
And lips, which ere the morn touched mine,
Lightly supped that sparkling wine —
'Twas for *their health alone.*

25.

But, ere midnight spread o'er those plains,
The wine they drank inflamed their brains —
Enough to make them gay; —
Still those designing looks were glanced,
And still with fiery zeal they danced
Until the dawn of day.

26.

Midst dust and smoke and slipper stroke,
'Twas thus their leader spoke —
"Hands round," methought he said,
Or, "swing your partners gentlemen,"
"Balance!" "A cross!" "Three shuffles!" Then,
"Return and promenade."

27.

Thus passed the night, long remembered
By me, though such nights unnumbered
In my short life should crowd,
Ah! few balmy summers shall roll
Around till one, a virtuous soul,
Shall be my happy bride.

28.

Unlike ten thousand men, alas!
Who live an humble henpecked mass
Of sinews, flesh and bones, —
I will live a life of pleasure,
Eat and drink, and sleep by measure,
Till time appointed comes.

29.

O, Yes! That party — I must close
What I've begun while genius glows,
And prompts, within, to write,
Many reels were run, and hearts
That knew not grief, felt cupid's darts,
While dancing there that night.

30.

At last a pond'rous Shanghai crowed
While spread a gloom throughout the crowd.
Too well we knew the sign —
Day was coming, like a cloud
Borne on the wind midst thunder loud,
And swift as lightning.

31.

Silently, night's dark shadows fled,
And with them went our mirth, — instead
Of which was drowsiness.
Then followed a hasty parting,
For all longed to be "anapping"
At home in loneliness.

32.
Ere noon, are closed those hazel eyes,
While beauty's self in slumber lies,
And dreams that all is well,—
But, first—that braid, that golden foil,
Those scallops, ruffles, garments, all
In grand confusion fell!!!
(nuff sed.)

CHAPTER NOTES

Introduction

1. Jacob Nathaniel Raymer, private papers.

2. Raymer family Bible.

3. Raymer, private papers.

4. Raymer, private papers.

5. Raymer, private papers.

6. Raymer, private papers.

7. Bilious fever is an archaic term for a fever caused by a liver disorder. It is accompanied by chills, fever, and vomiting.

8. Raymer, private papers.

9. Raymer, private papers.

10. Raymer, private papers.

11. Letter published in the *Carolina Watchman* (Salisbury, NC), April 13, 1863.

12. Letter published in the *Carolina Watchman*, May 25, 1863.

13. Letter published in the *Carolina Watchman*, April 13, 1863.

14. Letter published in the *Carolina Watchman*, May 25, 1863.

15. Letter published in the *Carolina Watchman*, October 6, 1862.

16. Letter published in the *Carolina Watchman*, April 28, 1863.

17. W.N. Watt, *Iredell County Soldiers in the Civil War* (Taylorsville, NC: W.N. Watt, 1995).

Chapter 1

1. Absalom Knox Simonton was a resident of Iredell County and was 26 years old when he enlisted. He was appointed Captain in May 1861 and led Company A (Iredell Blues). He was promoted to Major on May 1, 1862. Thirty days later he was killed during the Battle of Seven Pines, May 31, 1862. From R. Lee Hadden, *The Bloody Fourth: The Roster of the Fourth North Carolina Regiment CSA, 1861–1865* (unpublished manuscript).

2. Francis M. Y. McNeely lived in Rowan County and enlisted at age 21. He was appointed captain of Company K (Rowan Rifle Guard) in May 1861. He resigned his commission in June 1862 because of pneumonia and a hernia; he was given light duties and retained his commission but did not return to his Company. When Union general Stoneman's troops entered Salisbury, North Carolina, in April 1865, they found McNeely at the arsenal. In an exchange of gunfire, he shot and killed two Union soldiers before being shot and killed himself. From Hadden, *Bloody Fourth*.

3. William Frohoch Kelly resided in Davie County and was 29 at the time of his enlistment. He was appointed Captain in May 1861 and commanded Company G (Davie Sweepstakes). Frustrated that two officers of lesser rank were promoted over him to Major and Lieutenant Colonel, Kelly resigned his commission in February 1863. From Hadden, *Bloody Fourth*.

4. David Miller Carter lived in Moore County and was 31 when he enlisted. He was appointed Captain in May 1861 and commanded Company E (Southern Guards). At the Battle of Seven Pines, May

31, 1862, he was wounded in the right arm and shoulder, disabling him from further service in the field. He resigned the following December but was later named Judge Advocate of the General Court Martial for the remainder of the war. From Hadden, *Bloody Fourth.*

5. John Barr Andrews was 24 and living in Iredell County when he organized a volunteer company in 1861 that later became Company C (Saltillo Boys). At the Battle of Gaines' Mill, June 27, 1862, he was wounded in the right hand and shoulder as he was drawing his sword. Infection set in, then typhoid fever, and he died on July 22, 1862. He is buried in the Fourth Creek Presbyterian Church Cemetery in Iredell County. From Hadden, *Bloody Fourth.*

6. James H. Wood was a Rowan County resident and enlisted at age 21. He was appointed Captain in May 1861 and commanded Company B (Scotch Ireland Grays). He was wounded at the Battle of Seven Pines, Virginia, May 31, 1862, or at the Battle of Gaines' Mill, June 27, 1862, and later returned to service with the regiment. From Hadden, *Bloody Fourth.*

7. A John Z. Dalton, who resigned early in the war, is mentioned by Edwin Augustus Osborne in his "History of the Fourth Regiment," which appears in Volume 1 of Walter Clark, ed., *Histories of the Several Regiments from North Carolina in the Great War, 1861–'65, Written by Members of the Respective Commands* (Goldsboro, NC: Nash Brothers Book and Job Printers, for the State of North Carolina, 1901; reprint, Wendell, NC: Broadfoot's Bookmark, 1982). No other mention of a Dalton could be located in any information on the 4th Regiment.

8. William T. Marsh was a resident of Beaufort County and enlisted at age 30. He was appointed Captain in May 1861 and commanded Company I (Pamlico Riflemen). From Hadden, *Bloody Fourth.*

9. Colonel Charles Courtenay Tew commanded the 2nd Regiment North Carolina State Troops. At the Battle of Sharpsburg, September 17, 1862, he was killed.

10. George Burgwyn Anderson was a West Point graduate and was 30 years old when he was appointed Colonel, 4th Regiment, N.C.T., before it was formally organized. Later, he was promoted to Brigadier General and led his brigade, consisting of four North Carolina regiments, into the Battle of Sharpsburg, September 17, 1862. From Hadden, *Bloody Fourth.*

11. John Augustus Young was appointed Lieutenant Colonel in May 1861, but illness forced him to resign his commission March 22, 1862. From Hadden, *Bloody Fourth.*

12. Bryan Grimes was Major and later Colonel of the 4th during the Battle of Sharpsburg. From Hadden, *Bloody Fourth.*

13. Laura Elizabeth Lee, *Forget-Me-Nots of the Civil War, A Romance, Containing Reminiscences and Original Letters of Two Confederate Soldiers* (St. Louis, MO: A. H. Fleming Printing, 1909), pp. 37–38.

14. No information available on Private James A. Sprinkle. Possibly a misspelling for Private James E. Springle, Iredell County, of Company A, who died near Manassas on August 6, 1861. From Hadden, *Bloody Fourth.*

15. Letter from "Chap.," published in *The Landmark* (Statesville, NC), November 23, 1883.

16. Col. George W. Chipley, 1810–1890, was a wealthy, prominent citizen in Iredell County. He is buried there in the Snow Creek United Methodist Church Cemetery.

17. James Columbus Steele, *Sketches of the Civil War, Especially of Companies A, C and H, from Iredell County, N.C. and the 4th N.C. Regimental Band* (Statesville, NC: Brady Printing, 1921), p. 21.

18. Edwin Augustus Osborne, "The Fourth N.C. Regiment, Col. E. A. Osborne's Sketch of It," *Daily Charlotte Observer* (Charlotte, NC), May 31, 1896.

19. Osborne, "Fourth N.C. Regiment."

20. Steele, *Sketches,* p. 22.

21. Steele, *Sketches,* p. 22.

Chapter 2

1. Alexander Hunter, "A High Private's Account of the Battle of Sharpsburg,"

Southern Society Historical Papers, Vol. X, Richmond, Va., Oct. and Nov. 1882. Microform Collection, Joyner Library, East Carolina University.

2. Lt. John C. Gorman, of the 2nd Regiment North Carolina Troops, in a letter to the Raleigh *Spirit of the Age*, published on October 6, 1862.

3. Steele, "Sketches."

4. Captain Marsh died from his wounds on September 24, 1862. From Hadden, *Bloody Fourth.*

5. Captain Osborne survived his wounding, but was captured at Shepherdstown, Virginia (now West Virginia), just across the Potomac River. He was exchanged in December 1862. From Hadden, *Bloody Fourth.*

7. 2nd Lt. Franklin Harrison Weaver was the last unwounded officer of the 4th and was killed holding the regimental colors in the Sunken Road, better known as "Bloody Lane." The whole of Anderson's Brigade defended this infamous spot. From Hadden, *Bloody Fourth.*

8. Ashbel S. Fraley died of typhoid fever. From Hadden, *Bloody Fourth.*

Chapter 3

1. The railroad that Nat described was the Winchester & Potomac Railroad, which was 32 miles long. The line ran through Charlestown to Harpers Ferry, where it converged with the Baltimore & Ohio Railroad.

2. Published in the *North Carolina Standard* (Raleigh, NC), February 24, 1863.

Chapter 5

1. Charles Heyer, Company K, was detailed for duty with the regimental band in the fall of 1861. He was promoted to Musician and permanently transferred to the Regimental Band on February 11, 1863. Heyer played the bass horn. He was one of the band members paroled at Appomattox Court House, Virginia, April 9, 1865. From Hadden, *Bloody Fourth.*

2. The Asylum for the Insane came into

being largely through the efforts of Dorothea Lynde Dix, who came to North Carolina in 1848. Through her efforts a bill was passed in the North Carolina General Assembly on December 30, 1848, establishing the institution and providing $7,000 for construction. The institution was later renamed Dorothea Dix Hospital.

3. In 1853, Dr. Edward C. Fisher of Virginia, who was experienced and trained in the care of the mentally ill, was appointed superintendent of the institution.

4. The Spotswood Hotel was located at the southwest corner of 8th and Main streets in Richmond. The *Richmond Dispatch* of December 26, 1870, announced the destruction of the building by fire on Christmas Day.

Chapter 7

1. In 1863, Wilderness Tavern, located in Spotsylvania County, VA, was a busy crossroads. A general store, blacksmith shop, and tavern were among the buildings there. On May 2, during the Battle of Chancellorsville, it served as a Confederate field hospital site. Over 3,000 wounded and dying soldiers were treated in the buildings and in tents nearby. It was here, near Wilderness Church, that Nat's conversation with the dying soldier took place. It was here also that the wounded Stonewall Jackson was brought to have his left arm amputated.

2. Ramseur's Brigade lost 789 men at Chancellorsville—151 killed, 530 wounded, and 108 missing. The 4th Regiment lost 47 killed, 155 wounded, and 58 missing, a total of 260.

3. Nat has written the wrong name; it was Stephen Ramseur's Brigade.

4. Nat's statement was correct. The reluctant soldiers had fought bravely the day before and had taken many casualties. Still they would not move.

Chapter 8

1. General John B. Gordon was a brigade commander in General Jubal Early's

Division. The brigade was comprised of the 13th, 26th, 31st, 38th, 60th, and 61st Georgia regiments.

2. Polkweed (also spelled pokeweed) was one of the plants discovered by the early settlers. Although the plant and its berries are poisonous, a person familiar with the plant can pick young shoots and boil them to eliminate the poison. It resembles spinach when cooked. Dock is an edible weed sometimes used for table greens and in folk medicine.

Chapter 9

1. An excerpt from Gorman's writings quoted by A.W. Mangum, "Memorial Sketch of William R. Gorman," in S. D. Pool, ed., *Our Living and Our Dead; Devoted to North Carolina — Her Past, Her Present, and Her Future* (Raleigh, NC: North Carolina Branch Southern Historical Society, 1874–), Volume II, March to August, 1875, pp. 20–21.

2. Gorman, quoted by Mangum.

Chapter 11

1. The initial "E." was an error, either Nat's or the typesetter's. The name was James C. Steele.

2. Moses B. Mayhew was 27 years old and a resident of Iredell County when he enlisted on July 11, 1862. He was killed at Gettysburg, July 1, 1863. From Hadden, *Bloody Fourth*.

3. Robert M. Brawley, an Iredell County resident, enlisted in Brunswick County on May 29, 1861. He was 32. He was wounded in the thigh at the Battle of Seven Pines and killed at Gettysburg, July 1, 1863. From Hadden, *Bloody Fourth*.

4. Eli Day was 24 years old when he enlisted on February 26, 1862. He was wounded in the thigh during the fighting at Gettysburg and taken prisoner. He was sent to Davids Island in New York Harbor and exchanged in August 1863. He rejoined his company around January 1, 1864, and was again taken prisoner during the battle at Spotsylvania Court House in May 1864. He

was held captive at Point Lookout, Maryland, and later Elmira, New York, beginning on July 6, 1864. Day died a prisoner at Elmira on April 21, 1865, after the surrender of General Lee on April 9. From Hadden, *Bloody Fourth*.

5. Jacob W. Massey, Iredell County resident, was 21 years old when he enlisted on June 10, 1861. At Gettysburg, July 3, 1863, he was severely wounded in the left leg, which was later amputated. Massey died a prisoner of war in a hospital at Gettysburg, September 2, 1863. From Hadden, *Bloody Fourth*.

6. M. T. Clark was 27 years old when he enlisted on February 26, 1862. He had both legs broken at Gettysburg and died from his wounds. From Hadden, *Bloody Fourth*.

7. James A. Coan was 19 years old when he enlisted on March 21, 1861. He survived the Battle of Gettysburg but was captured at Petersburg on April 3, 1865. He was released from Hart's Island, New York Harbor, in June 1865, after taking the Oath of Allegiance. From Hadden, *Bloody Fourth*.

8. Possibly Martin Snow, a resident of Iredell County, who was 24 years old when he enlisted on April 30, 1861. He was captured at Fredericksburg on May 3, 1863. Confined at Washington, D.C., he was sent to City Point, Virginia, for exchange on May 13, 1863. Snow was killed at Snicker's Gap, Virginia, July 18, 1864, and later reburied in Hebron Cemetery, Winchester, Virginia. From Hadden, *Bloody Fourth*.

9. Francis M. Morrison, a resident of Iredell County, was 21 years old when he enlisted on June 27, 1861. He survived the Battle of Gettysburg but was killed at the Battle of Spotsylvania Court House, Virginia, May 12, 1864. From Hadden, *Bloody Fourth*.

10. Jesse F. Stancil, a Rowan County resident, was 27 years old at the time of his enlistment. He was wounded at the Battle of Chancellorsville, Virginia, May 3, 1863, and received slight wounds at Gettysburg. He was wounded in the chest at Snicker's Gap, July 18, 1864. He was later paroled at Salisbury, NC, on May 19, 1865. From Hadden, *Bloody Fourth*.

11. John M. Sides, a resident of Rowan County, was 26 years old when he enlisted on June 3, 1861. He was wounded in the left leg at Gettysburg, July 1, 1863. He then served in noncombatant roles and was retired to the Invalid Corps on January 10, 1865. He received his parole at Salisbury, North Carolina, on May 10, 1865. From Hadden, *Bloody Fourth.*

12. William Rainey was transferred from the 8th Regiment North Carolina Troops to the 4th Regiment N.C.T., November 7, 1862. He was wounded by friendly fire at the Battle of Gettysburg, but survived. He was captured during the fighting at the Wilderness, Virginia, May 12, 1864. He was confined as a prisoner of war at Point Lookout, Maryland, and later at Elmira, New York. He was freed from Elmira on June 12, 1865, after taking the Oath of Allegiance. From Hadden, *Bloody Fourth.*

13. Thomas S. Lyerly, a Rowan County resident, was 20 years old when he enlisted on June 19, 1861. He was captured near Fredericksburg, Virginia, May 3, 1863, and held at Washington, D.C. Exchanged, he returned to his company in time for the Battle of Gettysburg, where he was wounded. He was captured again at Strasburg, Virginia, October 19, 1864, and held a prisoner at Point Lookout, Maryland. He was released in the spring of 1865. From Hadden, *Bloody Fourth.*

14. William Marshall Chipley, an Iredell County resident, was 19 years old when he enlisted on June 7, 1861. He was captured at the Battle of Chancellorsville, May 3, 1863. Released the very next day, he went with his company to Gettysburg, where he was killed. From Hadden, *Bloody Fourth.*

15. Albert M. White, a resident of Iredell County, was 24 years old when he enlisted on June 7, 1861. He sustained a shoulder wound in the fighting at Gettysburg. White was paroled at Appomattox Court House, Virginia, April 9, 1865. From Hadden, *Bloody Fourth.*

16. No information.

17. Martin L. Arthurs was 20 years old when he enlisted on February 26, 1862. He

was wounded in the chest at the Battle of Gettysburg. He was captured at Burkeville, Virginia, on April 6, 1865, and held at Newport News, Virginia, until June 30, 1865. From Louis H. Manarin and Weymouth T. Jordan, Jr., comps., *North Carolina Troops, 1861–1865: A Roster* (Raleigh, NC: Division of Archives and History, Department of Cultural Resources, 1966–), Vol. 4, p. 36.

18. H. Lewis Lollar, an Iredell County resident, was 24 years of age when he enlisted on February 26, 1862. Lollar was captured at Boonsboro, Maryland, September 15, 1862, just two days before the Battle of Sharpsburg. He was held prisoner at Fort Delaware, Delaware, until exchanged November 10, 1862. Lollar sustained facial wounds at the Battle of Gettysburg. He was paroled at Appomattox Court House, Virginia, April 9, 1865. From Hadden, *Bloody Fourth.*

19. William Dobson, a resident of Iredell County, was 19 years old when he enlisted on June 7, 1861. He was wounded and captured during the Battle of Gettysburg. He was held at several prisons: Fort McHenry and Point Lookout, Maryland, and Fort Delaware, Delaware. Dobson was released April 19, 1864, after taking the Oath of Allegiance. From Hadden, *Bloody Fourth.*

20. Constantine S. Sharp, a resident of Iredell County, was 18 years old when he enlisted on February 26, 1862. He was first wounded at the Battle of Sharpsburg, Maryland, September 17, 1862. At Gettysburg, July 1–3, 1863, he was wounded in the leg and captured. He was held first at Fort Delaware, Delaware, and then at Point Lookout, Maryland. Sharp was paroled at Point Lookout on February 18, 1865. From Hadden, *Bloody Fourth.*

21. Charles L. Johnston, a resident of Iredell County, was 30 years old when he enlisted on February 26, 1862. He was wounded and captured during the fighting in Maryland in September 1862. He was shortly paroled and was wounded and captured again during the Battle of Gettysburg. He was sent to hospitals in Cham-

bersburg and Harrisburg, Pennsylvania, and then confined at Fort Delaware, Delaware, for the remainder of the war. He was paroled June 19, 1865, after taking the Oath of Allegiance. From Hadden, *Bloody Fourth*.

22. James H. Harkness (Nat misspelled the name) was living in Iredell County when he enlisted as a Private at age 27 in June 1861. He was wounded in the leg at Gettysburg and taken prisoner. After his wounds were treated, he was sent to Davids Island in New York Harbor. Paroled in August 1863, Harkness rejoined his company later in 1863. He was killed at the Battle of Spotsylvania Court House, May 12, 1864. From Manarin and Jordan, *North Carolina Troops*, Volume 4, p. 41.

23. John M. Rickert, a resident of Iredell County, was 21 years when he enlisted on June 7, 1861. He was wounded at the Battle of Chancellorsville, May 3, 1863, and again at Gettysburg, where he was wounded in the leg. He returned to Company C in the fall of 1863, and was paroled at Appomattox Court House, April 9, 1865. From Hadden, *Bloody Fourth*.

24. William H. Gurley, a resident of Wayne County, was 28 years old when he enlisted, May 7, 1861. He sustained a wound in his left leg at Gettysburg and was captured. He remained hospitalized at Gettysburg until October 1863, when he was sent to Baltimore, Maryland. He was exchanged later in the year and was retired from service because of his wounds in February 1865. From Hadden, *Bloody Fourth*.

25. No information.

26. Andrew Sauls, a resident of Wayne County, was 32 years of age when he enlisted on April 2, 1861. He was wounded in the right arm and captured at Gettysburg. He was held prisoner at Fort Delaware, Delaware, where he contracted small pox and died on October 28, 1863. From Hadden, *Bloody Fourth*.

27. No information.

28. James D. Litchfield, a resident of Hyde County, was 18 years old when he enlisted on April 28, 1863. He was killed in action at Gettysburg. From Hadden, *Bloody Fourth*.

29. William F. Beal was 25 years old when he enlisted on April 22, 1863. He sustained a head wound at Gettysburg and was captured. Beal spent the remainder of the war as a prisoner at Fort Delaware, Delaware, until he took the Oath of Allegiance and was released June 19, 1865. From Hadden, *Bloody Fourth*.

30. William B. Nolly, a native of Wilson County, was 18 years old and farming when he enlisted on June 28, 1861. He was killed at Gettysburg, July 1, 1863. From Hadden, *Bloody Fourth*.

31. Thomas E. Thompson, a resident of Wilson County, was 22 years old when he enlisted. He was wounded at Fredericksburg, Virginia, December 13, 1862. He was wounded in the knee at Gettysburg. Thompson resigned his commission August 20, 1864, because of heart problems. From Hadden, *Bloody Fourth*.

32. George H. Cunningham, a resident of Davie County, was 22 years old when he enlisted on June 14, 1861. He was killed at the battle of Gettysburg. From Hadden, *Bloody Fourth*.

33. William Clary, a resident of Davie County, enlisted August 9, 1861. He was wounded in both legs at Gettysburg and captured. He was confined first at Fort Delaware, Delaware, and later at Point Lookout, Maryland. He was received for exchange in October 1864 and paroled at Appomattox Court House April 9, 1865. From Hadden, *Bloody Fourth*.

34. John B. Stockton, a resident of Iredell County, was 18 years old when he enlisted on March 1, 1862. He was captured at the Battle of Sharpsburg, September 17, 1862, and held a prisoner at Fort Delaware, Delaware, until he was exchanged November 10, 1862. He was killed at Gettysburg on July 1, 1863. From Hadden, *Bloody Fourth*.

35. Burgess A. Campbell, a resident of Iredell County, was 18 years old when he enlisted on March 1, 1862. He was killed at Gettysburg, July 3, 1863. From Hadden, *Bloody Fourth*.

36. John Farr, of Iredell County, was 27 years old when he enlisted on March 1, 1862. He was wounded slightly at Gettys-

burg and again at Cold Harbor on June 3, 1864. Farr survived the war and was paroled at Appomattox Court House, April 9, 1865. From Hadden, *Bloody Fourth*.

37. Otho Holshouser was 25 years old when he enlisted in July 1861. He was captured September 17, 1862, the day of the Battle of Sharpsburg. He was held prisoner at Fort Delaware, Delaware, and exchanged in November 1862. He sustained wounds in the left elbow during the Battle of Gettysburg and was killed during the fighting at Spotsylvania Court House, Virginia, May 10–11, 1864. From Manarin and Jordan, *North Carolina Troops*, Vol. 4, p. 108.

38. Hugh Hall was 31 years old when he enlisted in April 1861. Sometime during the Battle of Gettysburg he deserted to the Union side. From Manarin and Jordan, *North Carolina Troops*, Vol. 4, p. 18.

39. No information.

40. No information.

41. Alfred F. Goodman was 23 years old and living in Iredell County when he enlisted in June 1861. Wounded and captured at Gettysburg, he was held a prisoner of war first at Fort Delaware, Delaware, then at Point Lookout, Maryland, until paroled in February 1865. From Manarin and Jordan, *North Carolina Troops*, Vol. 4, p. 40.

42. James C. Norton, a resident of Iredell County, was 24 years old when he enlisted on June 7, 1861. The 12th Illinois Cavalry captured him while raiding the rear of General Lee's army in May 1863, but he was paroled later that month. Norton was captured at Gettysburg and later confined at Fort Delaware, Delaware, then transferred to Point Lookout, Maryland. He was paroled at Point Lookout on January 17, 1865. From Hadden, *Bloody Fourth*.

43. Michael Hennessey was 26 years old and residing in Rowan County when he enlisted in July 1861. He deserted to the Union during the Battle of Gettysburg and was held prisoner for the remainder of the war at Fort Delaware, Delaware. He was released in May 1865. From Manarin and Jordan, *North Carolina Troops*, Vol. 4, pp. 107–108.

Chapter 12

1. Either Nat skipped a word or two here or the typesetter left words out.

2. According to Manarin and Jordan, Marcus L. Hall was not killed but wounded and captured at or near Front Royal, Virginia, on or about July 23, 1863. He was held prisoner at Point Lookout, Maryland, until paroled for exchange on March 6, 1864. He was captured a second time at Petersburg, Virginia, on April 2, 1865, when the Union army began the final assault on the city. He was sent to a prison camp at Hart's Island, New York Harbor, and was released June 19, 1865. From Manarin and Jordan, *North Carolina Troops*, Vol. 4, p. 114.

3. The commissary sergeant was responsible for feeding his company. His job required that he maintain a sufficient amount of rations, not let them run short, and make certain each soldier got his fair share. Some commissary sergeants did a better job than others.

4. Brigadier General George Dole's Brigade was part of General Rodes' Division and consisted of the 4th, 12th, 21st, and 44th Georgia regiments.

Chapter 13

1. General James Longstreet and a large portion of his corps had been dispatched to Georgia to bolster the Army of Tennessee under the command of General Braxton Bragg.

2. Letter published in the *Carolina Watchman*, October 12, 1863.

3. David C. Hunter was a resident of Iredell County and was 23 years old when he enlisted as a Private in May 1861. He rose to the rank of Sergeant and was killed at Warrenton, Virginia, on October 14, 1863. From Manarin and Jordan, *North Carolina Troops*, Vol. 4, p. 19.

Chapter 14

1. Prior to the passage of the anti-substitute bill, any man in the South could pay

someone to take his place in the army. He would stay home and his substitute would go off to war — sometimes to be killed or wounded. As the war dragged on, the South's supply of able men dwindled. Passage of the bill meant a man could no longer pay someone else to do his military service. According to Nat, the women would be grieving because there would be fewer men on the home front.

2. Published in the *North Carolina Standard* (Raleigh, NC), June 8, 1861.

3. No information.

4. No information.

5. Chaplain Robert B. Anderson was appointed on December 3, 1863, and resigned in June 1864 for health reasons. From Manarin and Jordan, *North Carolina Troops*, Vol. 4, p. 11.

6. Osborne quoted in Clark, ed., *Histories*, Volume 1, pp. 241–242.

Chapter 15

1. Brigadier General Junius Daniel was shot in the abdomen while leading his brigade at the Bloody Angle. He died the next day, May 13, 1864.

2. Ironically, General James Longstreet and General Stonewall Jackson were both shot down in the Wilderness, just one year apart. Both had been fired on by their own troops, and both were with a mounted party when they were mistaken for the enemy.

3. Nat may have written the wrong initial. Manarin and Jordan, *North Carolina Troops*, Vol. 4, p. 111, lists a J. T. Owens of Company K, who was killed at Spotsylvania. He was 36 at the time of his enlistment in July 1863.

4. Philip A. Heilig was a resident of Rowan County and was 19 years old when he enlisted as a Private in June 1861. He was captured at the Battle of Sharpsburg, September 17, 1862, held a prisoner of war at Fort Delaware, Delaware, and later exchanged in November 1862. He was killed at Spotsylvania Court House, May 12, 1864. From Manarin and Jordan, *North Carolina Troops*, Vol. 4, p. 107.

5. Jacob L. Fraley was a resident of Rowan County and was 30 years old when he enlisted as a Private in May 1861. He was killed at Spotsylvania Court House, May 12, 1864. From Hadden, *Bloody Fourth*.

6. Colonel Edwin Augustus Osborne wrote the following on p. 278 of his "History of the Fourth Regiment": "During the skirmish on the 11th of May, 1864, near Spotsylvania Court House, Sergeant Holshouser, of Company K, was sitting with his back against a good sized tree, our part of the line not being then engaged, when a cannonball struck the other side of the tree, killing him instantly by the shock."

7. William F. McRorie was a resident of Iredell County and was 18 years old when he enlisted in April 1861. He rose through the ranks and was promoted to Captain May 3, 1863. He was wounded at the Battle of Seven Pines, May 31, 1862, and at Chancellorsville, May 3, 1863. He was killed at Spotsylvania Court House on May 12, 1864. From Hadden, *Bloody Fourth*.

8. Neil Singleton Brawley was a resident of Iredell County and was 28 years old when he enlisted as a Private in July 1862. He was killed at the Battle of the Wilderness, May 6, 1864. From Manarin and Jordan, *North Carolina Troops*, Vol. 4, p. 15.

9. See note 22, chapter 11.

10. Pink Jacobs was a resident of Iredell County and was 22 years old when he enlisted as a Private in August 1862. He was killed at Spotsylvania Court House. From Manarin and Jordan, *North Carolina Troops*, Vol. 4, p. 42.

11. Solomon Hendren was a resident of Iredell County and was 18 years old when he enlisted as a Private in February 1863. He was in the Battle of Chancellorsville and killed at Spotsylvania Court House on May 12, 1864. From Manarin and Jordan, *North Carolina Troops*, Vol. 4, p. 41.

12. Peter Deal enlisted as a Private in Rowan County in September 1863. He was killed at Spotsylvania Court House on May 12, 1864. From Manarin and Jordan, *North Carolina Troops*, Vol. 4, p. 29.

13. William M. Durell enlisted as a Private in May 1861, at the age of 18. He was

wounded at Spotsylvania Court House on May 12, 1864, and retired to the Invalid Corps. From Manarin and Jordan, *North Carolina Troops*, Vol. 4, p. 106.

14. William Ruffin Cox was appointed Major of the 2nd Regiment North Carolina Troops in May 1861. He had attained the rank of Colonel just prior to the Battle of Chancellorsville, where he sustained wounds. After the Battle of Spotsylvania Court House he was promoted to Brigadier General and assigned command of a brigade. From Manarin and Jordan, *North Carolina Troops*, Vol. 3, p. 379.

15. James H. Wood was promoted to Lieutenant Colonel a few months after the Battle of Sharpsburg, and to Colonel after the Battle of Spotsylvania Court House. From Manarin and Jordan, *North Carolina Troops*, Vol. 4, p. 9.

16. William Richmond McNeely was a resident of Iredell County and was 24 years old when he enlisted as a Private in May 1861. He rose through the ranks and was appointed 2nd Lieutenant in August 1863. He was wounded in the fighting at Spotsylvania Court House and rejoined his company in October 1864. He was killed in action at Cedar Creek, Virginia, October 19, 1864. From Hadden, *Bloody Fourth*.

17. Francis M. Morrison was a resident of Iredell County and was 21 years old when he enlisted as a Private in June 1861. He was promoted to Sergeant in the late fall of 1863 and killed in the fighting at Spotsylvania Court House. From Hadden, *Bloody Fourth*.

18. Williams M. Adams was a resident of Iredell County and was 23 years old when he enlisted in June 1861 as a Private. He was promoted to Sergeant in the spring of 1863 and was wounded two months later at the Battle of Chancellorsville. He rejoined his company and was captured by Union troops at the Wilderness, Virginia, on May 8, 1864. He was held a prisoner of war at Point Lookout, Maryland, and later sent to Elmira, New York. He was released from Elmira in June 1865. From Hadden, *Bloody Fourth*.

19. J. T. Owen was a resident of Rowan County but joined the army in Granville County. He was 36 years old when he enlisted as a Private in July 1863. He was killed at the Battle of Spotsylvania Court House. From Hadden, *Bloody Fourth*.

20. See note 5, this chapter. Nat did not list a company.

21. Osborne, "History."

Chapter 16

1. Steele, *Sketches*, p.36.
2. Steele, *Sketches*, p. 37.
3. Captain Samuel Abner Kelly was a resident of Davie County and was 23 when he enlisted. He was wounded at Chancellorsville, May 3, 1863, and again at Spotsylvania Court House in May of 1864. He was wounded and captured at the Battle of Winchester, September 19, 1864, and held a prisoner of war at Fort Delaware, Delaware. He was released in June 1865, after taking the Oath of Allegiance. From Hadden, *Bloody Fourth*.
4. Private George W. Roe was a resident of Beaufort County and enlisted as a substitute in March 1863. He was 16 years of age. He was wounded at the Battle of Chancellorsville. He was wounded again on August 27, 1864, but it is unknown where. Roe died on September 13 and was buried at Winchester, Virginia. From Hadden, *Bloody Fourth*.
5. No information.
6. Eli L. McHargue was a resident of Iredell County and was 29 when he enlisted as a Private in April 1863. He was captured at Fredericksburg, Virginia, May 3, 1863, and held in Washington until he was exchanged later in the month. He was wounded August 24, 1864, and on April 6, 1865, captured near Burkville, Virginia. He was released in June 1865. From Hadden, *Bloody Fourth*.
7. Private George D. Suggs (Manarin and Jordan spell the last name "Snuggs") was a resident of Rowan County and was 25 years old when he enlisted in June 1861. He was captured at the Battle of Sharpsburg on September 17, 1862, and exchanged in November 1862. Suggs was wounded at

the Battle of Chancellorsville, May 3, 1863. He returned to duty in the fall of 1863, and remained with the regiment until the surrender. He was paroled at Appomattox Court House, April 9, 1865. From Manarin and Jordan, *North Carolina Troops*, Vol. 4, p. 112.

8. Captain Marcus Hofflin was a resident of Rowan County and was 27 when he enlisted. He was promoted to Captain in December 1863. From Manarin and Jordan, *North Carolina Troops*, Vol. 4, p. 104.

9. Nat is referring to the incident at Petersburg known as "The Crater." Union soldiers dug a tunnel under the Confederate lines and packed it with over 8,000 pounds of gunpowder. On July 30, 1964, it exploded and killed over 300 Confederate soldiers. Union soldiers then launched an attack at that spot. In the fighting, the Confederates lost over 1,000 men and the Union over 5,000.

10. Steele, *Sketches*, pp. 37–38.

11. Steele, *Sketches*, pp. 38–39.

12. Steele, *Sketches*, p. 39.

13. Giles M. Shives was 22 years old when he enlisted in June 1861. He was paroled at Salisbury, NC, in 1865. From Manarin and Jordan, *North Carolina Troops*, Vol. 9, p. 82.

14. See note 3, this chapter.

15. Thomas M. C. Davidson was a resident of Iredell County and was 21 years old when he enlisted in April 1861. He was captured at the Battle of Winchester, September 19, 1864, and held a prisoner at Fort Delaware, Delaware. He was released in June 1865 after taking the Oath of Allegiance. From Hadden, *Bloody Fourth*.

16. Henry May Warren was a resident of Wilson County and enlisted in April 1861. He was captured at the Battle of Winchester, September 19, 1864, and held a prisoner of war at Fort Delaware, Delaware. He was released in June 1865 after taking the Oath of Allegiance. From Hadden, *Bloody Fourth*.

17. 1st Lieutenant Addison N. Wiseman was a resident of Rowan County and was 24 years old when he enlisted in May 1861. He was wounded at Chancellorsville, re-

joined his company around September in 1863, and was killed at the Third Battle of Winchester, September 19, 1864. From Hadden, *Bloody Fourth*.

18. Steele, *Sketches*, pp. 39–40.

19. Steele, *Sketches*, p. 40.

20. John Alexander Stikeleather was a resident of Iredell County when he enlisted in June 1862. Because soldiers knew where their regiment was by the flag's location, many flag bearers were targets of sharpshooters. If the flag went down in battle, the regiment might falter. A number of the 4th Regiment's flag bearers had been killed or wounded before Stikeleather volunteered to take the flag at Seven Pines and survived carrying it for the rest of the war. He was paroled at Appomattox Court House. From Hadden, *Bloody Fourth*.

21. See note 16, chapter 15.

22. Samuel Moore Barnes was a resident of Iredell County when he enlisted as a Private in February 1862, at age 28. He is listed in the records as serving as a teamster during the war. He was paroled at Appomattox Court House. From Hadden, *Bloody Fourth*.

23. Nat's letter lists J. H. Cohen. The closest match in the records is John W. Coan, Company A, who was captured October 19, 1864. He was held prisoner at Point Lookout, Maryland, and exchanged in February 1865. From Manarin and Jordan, *North Carolina Troops*, Vol. 4, p. 16.

24. No information.

25. Henry C. Miller was a resident of Rowan County when he enlisted as a Private at the age of 20 in June 1861. Miller was promoted to Sergeant in 1863. Miller was captured at Cedar Creek and held prisoner at Point Lookout, Maryland. He was exchanged and paroled at Salisbury on May 12, 1865. From Hadden, *Bloody Fourth*.

26. John W. Gullet was a resident of Rowan County when he enlisted as a Private at age 30 in July 1861. He deserted in the summer of 1863, was caught in August, and later rejoined his company. He was captured at Petersburg, April 3, 1865. He was held prisoner at Hart's Island, New York Harbor, and released in June 1865. From Hadden, *Bloody Fourth*.

27. See note 13, chapter 11.

28. W. R. Moore was a resident of Granville County and was 38 when he enlisted in April 1863. He was captured near Fredericksburg on May 3, 1863. He was later released and rejoined his company in the late fall of 1863. He was present or accounted for through February 7, 1865. From Hadden, *Bloody Fourth*.

29. John C. Turner was a resident of Iredell County and was 23 years old when he enlisted as a Private in June 1861. He was captured during the fighting at Boonsboro, Maryland, in September 1862, and exchanged in November 1862. He was wounded at the Battle of Chancellorsville on May 3, 1863, and again at Cedar Creek. Turner was surrendered at Appomattox Court House. From Hadden, *Bloody Fourth*.

30. Abner S. Mills was a resident of Iredell County and was 19 years old when he enlisted as a Private in June 1861. He was captured at the Battle of Chancellorsville and released the following day. He was captured at Burkeville, Virginia, on April 6, 1865, and released in June 1865. From Hadden, *Bloody Fourth*.

31. See note 18, chapter 11.

32. No G. A. Reid can be found in any record, but this may be an incorrect recording for James A. Reid, also of Company C, a resident of Iredell County, who was 32 when he enlisted in 1861. He was wounded at Seven Pines and again at Chancellorsville. He was paroled at Appomattox Court House. From Hadden, *Bloody Fourth*.

33. No information.

34. No information.

35. No information.

36. Hadden's records list a John B. Lane in Company D, but report no further information after September 1864. Manarin and Jordan report a John Lane in Company G who was captured at Cedar Creek on October 19, 1864, and confined at Point Lookout, Maryland, until he was exchanged in February 1865. From Hadden, *Bloody Fourth*, and Manarin and Jordan, *North Carolina Troops*.

37. Edward Tripp was a resident of Beaufort County and was 18 years old when he enlisted as a Private in Company I in July 1861. He was promoted to Sergeant, then to 1st Sergeant, and was transferred to Company E in October 1863. One month later he was promoted to 2nd Lieutenant. He was wounded in the right thigh and captured at Cedar Creek. He was held prisoner at Point Lookout, Maryland, and later at Fort Delaware, Delaware, from February 1865 until he was released on June 17, 1865. From Hadden, *Bloody Fourth*.

38. No information.

39. John N. Hawkins was a resident of Beaufort County and was 19 years old when he enlisted as a Private in June 1861. He was wounded at Seven Pines and was later captured by Federal forces at Fredericksburg in May 1863. He was exchanged later in that month. He was wounded in the left foot at Cedar Creek (according to Nat's letter) and was with the regiment when they were paroled at Appomattox Court House. From Manarin and Jordan, *North Carolina Troops*, Vol. 4, p. 60.

40. Lewis Latham was a resident of Randolph County and was 22 years of age when he enlisted as a Private in February 1863. He died in a hospital in Virginia on November 6, 1864. The cause of his death was not given. From Hadden, *Bloody Fourth*.

41. No information.

42. No information.

43. Bennett B. Rhodes was a resident of Wilson County and was 28 years old when he enlisted as a Private in June 1861. He sustained right leg wounds at the Battle of Fredericksburg, December 13, 1863. From Hadden, *Bloody Fourth*. No information is available on the type of wound received at Cedar Creek.

44. John B. Woodard was a resident of Wilson County and was 28 years old when he enlisted as a Private in June 1861. He was wounded in the left leg and captured at the Battle of Chancellorsville, May 3, 1863, and later exchanged after being hospitalized in Washington. He was captured at Cedar Creek and held prisoner at Point Lookout, Maryland, until his release in May 1865. From Hadden, *Bloody Fourth*.

45. Asbury Athan was a resident of

Davie County and was 45 years old when he enlisted as a Private in June 1861. The records are varied on Athan. Some indicate he was AWOL in 1862; that he was a prisoner of war after Sharpsburg; that he later deserted; that he was paroled at Appomattox; and that he was mortally wounded in Virginia on May 15, 1864. From Hadden, *Bloody Fourth*. No information is available to confirm Nat's statement that he was wounded in this October 1864 battle.

46. Thomas M. Waller was 18 years old when he enlisted in Wake County in August 1863. No information is available to confirm Nat's statement that he was wounded in this October 1864 battle. He was paroled at Appomattox Court House. From Hadden, *Bloody Fourth*.

47. No information.

48. John W. Stephens was a resident of Beaufort when he enlisted as a Private in June 1861. From Manarin and Jordan, *North Carolina Troops*, Vol. 4, p. 102. No information is available to confirm Nat's statement that he was wounded in this October 1864 battle.

49. No information.

50. Wilburn C. Fraley was 21 years old when he enlisted in May 1861. He was mustered in with the rank of Sergeant and was later promoted to 1st Sergeant. No information is available to confirm Nat's statement that he was wounded in this October 1864 battle. Fraley was paroled at Appomattox Court House. From Hadden, *Bloody Fourth*.

51. Crawford Holtshouser enlisted as a Private in February 1864. No information is available to confirm Nat's statement that he was wounded in this October 1864 battle. He was paroled at Salisbury, NC, in May 1865. From Manarin and Jordan, *North Carolina Troops*, Vol. 4, p. 108.

52. Arnold Friedheim was a resident of Rowan County when he enlisted at age 23 as a Private in June 1861. He was later promoted to Corporal. He was paroled at Appomattox Court House. From Hadden, *Bloody Fourth*.

Chapter 17

1. James H. Sherrill was a resident of Iredell County and was 17 years old when he enlisted in March 1862. He was mustered in as a Sergeant and rose through the ranks. He was promoted to Captain of Company A, 49th Regiment N.C.T., in March 1865. From Manarin and Jordan, *North Carolina Troops*, Vol. 12, pp. 29–30, 116.

2. Captain Henry Alexander Chambers had been a Private in Nat's Company C in the 4th Regiment. He was appointed Captain of Company C, 49th Regiment N.C.T., in December 1862. Chambers sustained a head wound in the fighting at Five Forks, Virginia, on April 1, 1865. He surrendered at Appomattox Court House. From Manarin and Jordan, *North Carolina Troops*, Vol. 12, p. 55.

3. William C. Morrison was a resident of Iredell County and was 42 years old when he enlisted as a Private in February 1862. He was wounded at Drewry's Bluff, Virginia, in May 1864. Morrison was captured at Five Forks, Virginia, on April 1, 1865, held prisoner at Point Lookout, Maryland, and released from there in June 1865. From Manarin and Jordan, *North Carolina Troops*, Vol. 12, p. 77.

4. No information.

5. No information.

6. John Thomas Crawford was a resident of Iredell County and was 25 years old when he enlisted in April 1862. He was mustered in as Sergeant but rose through the ranks to Captain. He was captured at Five Forks, Virginia, on April 1, 1865, and held prisoner at Johnson's Island, Ohio. He was released in June 1865. From Manarin and Jordan, *North Carolina Troops*, Vol. 12, p. 72.

7. Abner Clayton Sharpe was a resident of Iredell County and was 21 years old when he enlisted as a Private in February 1862. He was promoted to 2nd Lieutenant in August 1864. He was captured at Five Forks, Virginia, on April 1, 1865, and held prisoner at Johnson's Island, Ohio. He was released in June 1865. Manarin and Jordan, *North Carolina Troops*, Vol. 12, p. 72.

8. No information.

9. Richard A. Bailey was a resident of Iredell County and was 23 years old when he enlisted in March 1862. He was mustered in as Sergeant. On July 30, 1864, two things happened to him: He was wounded at the Battle of the Crater near Petersburg, Virginia, and he was promoted to 1st Lieutenant. He was captured at Five Forks, Virginia, on April 1, 1865, and held prisoner at Johnson's Island, Ohio. He was released in June 1865. From Manarin and Jordan, *North Carolina Troops*, Vol. 12, p. 72.

10. Charles Fulton Conner was a resident of Catawba County and was 31 years old when he enlisted. He was promoted to Captain in February 1863. He was captured at Five Forks, Virginia, on April 1, 1865, and held prisoner at Johnson's Island, Ohio. He was released in June 1865. From Manarin and Jordan, *North Carolina Troops*, Vol. 12, p. 116.

11. Steele, *Sketches*, p. 47.

12. Steele, *Sketches*, p. 47.

13. Steele, *Sketches*, p. 48.

Chapter 18

1. Osborne, "History," pp. 278–279.

2. Steele, *Sketches*, p. 62.

3. Raymer, private papers.

4. Western North Carolina Railroad.

5. Thomas L. Stevenson died in a hospital in Richmond, Virginia, on July 15, 1862, after sustaining a bullet wound in the chest. From Hadden, *Bloody Fourth*.

6. York Collegiate Institute was one of many educational institutions founded by Brantley York in the mid–19th century. Nat and Mr. Flowers were co-principals there.

7. Raymer, private papers.

8. Brantley York was a well-known Methodist clergyman, educator, lecturer, and author in 19th century North Carolina. Even though he had become completely blind by 1853, he founded a number of schools. Union Institute Academy later became Normal College, then Trinity College. It moved to Durham in 1892, and in 1924 it became Duke University.

9. The Rev. Professor Brantley York's book was *An Illustrative and Constructive Grammar of the English Language* and was published by Warren L. Pomeroy, Raleigh, North Carolina, in 1869.

10. A freshet is a sudden rise in the level of a stream, or a flood, caused by heavy rains.

11. Brantley York, *The Autobiography of Brantley York* (Durham, NC: Seeman Printery, 1910), p. 91.

BIBLIOGRAPHY

Allen, T. Harrell. *Lee's Last Major General: Bryan Grimes of North Carolina*. Mason City, IA: Savas, 1999.

Clark, Walter, ed. *Histories of the Several Regiments and Battalions from North Carolina in the Great War, 1861–'65, Written by Members of the Respective Commands*. Goldsboro, NC: Nash Brothers Book and Job Printers, for the State of North Carolina, 1901. Reprint, Wendell, NC: Broadfoot's Bookmark, 1982.

Gallagher, Gary A., ed. *The Antietam Campaign*. Chapel Hill: University of North Carolina Press, 1999.

_____. *Extracts of Letters of Major-General Bryan Grimes to His Wife, Written While in Active Service in the Army of Northern Virginia. Compiled from Original Manuscript by Pulaski Cowper (1884)*. Reprint, Wilmington, NC: Broadfoot, 1986.

_____. *The Shenandoah Valley Campaign of 1864*. Chapel Hill: University of North Carolina Press, 2006.

Hadden, R. Lee. *The Bloody Fourth: The Roster of the Fourth North Carolina Regiment CSA, 1861–1865*. Unpublished manuscript.

_____. *The 4th Regimental Band*. Unpublished manuscript.

Keever, Homer M. *Iredell—Piedmont County*. Statesville, NC: Brady Printing, 1976.

Lee, Laura Elizabeth. *Forget-Me-Nots of the Civil War, A Romance, Containing Reminiscences and Original Letters of Two Confederate Soldiers*. St. Louis, MO: A. R. Fleming Printing, 1909.

Manarin, Louis H., and Jordan, Weymouth T., Jr., comps. *North Carolina Troops, 1861–1865: A Roster* (Raleigh, NC: Division of Archives and History, Department of Cultural Resources, 1966–).

Mangum, A.W. "Memorial Sketch of William R. Gorman." In S. D. Pool, ed., *Our Living and Our Dead; Devoted to North Carolina— Her Past, Her Present, and Her Future* (Raleigh, NC: North Carolina Branch Southern Historical Society, 1874–), Volume II, March to August, 1875, pp. 20–21.

Miller, Francis Trevelyan, editor-in-chief. *The Photographic History of the Civil War*. New York: Review of Reviews, 1911.

Osborne, Edward Augustus. "The Fourth N. C. Regiment, Col. E. A. Osborne's Sketch of It." *Daily Charlotte Observer* (Charlotte, NC), May 31, 1896.

_____. "History of the Fourth Regiment." In Clark, Walter, ed. *Histories of the Several Regiments and Battalions from North Carolina in the Great War, 1861–'65, Written by Members of the Respective Commands*. Goldsboro, NC: Nash Brothers Book and Job Printers, for the State of North Carolina, 1901. Reprint, Wendell, NC: Broadfoot's Bookmark, 1982.

Pool, S. D., ed. *Our Living and Our Dead; Devoted to North Carolina—Her Past, Her Present, and Her Future.* Raleigh, NC: North Carolina Branch Southern Historical Society, 1874.

Powell, William S., ed. *Dictionary of North Carolina Biography.* Chapel Hill: University of North Carolina Press, 1979– .

Steele, James Columbus. *Sketches of the Civil War Especially of Companies A, C and H, from Iredell County, N.C., and the 4th Regimental Band.* Statesville, NC: Brady Printing, 1921.

Stewart, Bruce H., Jr. *Land Battles of the Civil War, Eastern Theatre.* Jefferson, NC: McFarland, 2002.

Watt, W. N. *Iredell County Soldiers in the Civil War.* Taylorsville, NC: W. N. Watt, 1995.

Wheeler, Richard. *Voices of the Civil War.* New York: Thomas Y. Crowell, 1976.

York, Brantley. *The Autobiography of Brantley York.* Durham, NC: Seeman Printery, 1910.

Newspapers

Carolina Watchman, Salisbury, NC

Iredell Express, Statesville, NC

North Carolina Standard, Raleigh, NC

Raleigh Register, Raleigh, NC

Statesville Landmark, Statesville, NC

INDEX

Manassas Junction 17, 27, 101
Marching 51, 93
Marsh, William T. 22, 40, 42
Martinsburg, VA 85, 88, 135, 136
Marylanders, reaction to invasion 36
Massanutten Mountain 141
Massey, J. 87
Mathis, B. 142
Mayhew, Jack 88
Mayhew, M.B. 87
McClellan, George B. 18, 27, 36, 38, 40
McHargue, Eli 134
McIntosh, A.C. 157
McNeely, Francis M.Y. 22
McNeely, William 129, 142
McRorie, William F. 129
Meade, George G. 132
Measles 25
Mechanicsville [VA], Battle of 35
Merritt family 151
Middletown, VA 138
Miller, H. 142
Millers 48
Milligan, Thos. 21
Mills, A.S. 142
Mine Run Battlefield 127
Mine Run Campaign 107–110
Misenhimer, Alexander 48
Misenhimer, James L. 11
Misenhimer, Sarah 11
Mitchel, J.W. 156
Mocksville, NC 154
Monocracy River 132
Moore, C.A. 107
Moore, W.R. 142
Moose, W.A. 81
Morrison, Francis M. 87, 129
Morrison, William 150
Mortar fire 149–151
Morton's Ford 116, 126
Mortuary warrant application 180–181
Moses Raymer's mill 155
Moss, Edith McClain 22, 161
Mount Crawford, VA 148
Mt. Moriah Masonic Lodge No. 82
Mt. Sidney, VA 141
Music for General Lee 154

Neave, E.B. 80
Neff, Amanda 141
Neff, Dr. 141
Neff, Eliza 141
Neff, Kate 141
New Bern, Battle of 118
New Market, VA 143, 145, 148
New Town, VA 145
Newton, VA 138

Nolly, W.B. 88
North Anna River 131
North Carolina Railroad 22
Norton, Jas. 88

Old Fort, NC 12
Opequon Creek, VA 42
Orange & Alexander Railroad 101
Orange Court House, VA 28, 66, 68, 91, 93, 105, 107, 127
Osborne, Edwin Augustus 18, 19, 32, 42, 115, 130
Owens, J.T. 129
Owens, P.T. 129

Pamlico Riflemen 22
Paralysis 162
Paris, VA 46
Patterson, Robert English 17, 81
Payne's Farm, VA 108
Peace movement 96
Pennsylvania 83, 86, 89
Petersburg, VA 15, 25, 137, 147–151
Pickets 109, 143; duty 52, 58, 61, 64, 77, 91, 98, 112, 116, 126; trading 52, 98
Plank road 66, 68
Plantation (description) 157
Pleasant Hill Masonic Lodge No. 380 168
Pleasant Plains, AK 162
Point Lookout, MD 131
Polk 78
Pony Mountain, VA 103
Pool, Jno. 13
Pool, S.D. 18
Port Hudson, MS 88
Port Republic 141
Port Royal, VA 49
Potomac River 18 35, 38, 39, 40, 85, 88, 90, 132, 137, 138
Power, W.C. 94
Prairie County, AK 11
Pranks 151
Pressly, W.B. 155, 160
Pulaski County, AK 11
Punch (Raymer), Margaret E. 172

Raccoon Ford 97, 125
Railroads, destruction 44, 101, 138
Rain 31, 44, 60, 61, 70, 90, 101, 105, 116
Rainey, William 87
Raleigh, NC 22, 42, 54
Ramseur, Stephen D. 18, 49, 125, 129, 130, 141, 142–143
Ramseur's Brigade 77, 83, 85, 88, 91, 96, 108, 110, 118, 130
Rapidan River 18, 49, 84, 96, 97, 98, 99, 103, 104, 121, 124, 125

212 Index